# ENOUGH

# ENOUGH

## Breaking Free From the World of More

## John Naish

First published in Great Britain in 2008 by
Hodder & Stoughton

An Hachette Livre UK company

1

A CIP catalogue record for this title is
available from the British Library

Hardback ISBN 978 0 340 93590 3
Trade paperback ISBN 978 0 340 93591 0

Typeset in Sabon MT by Hewer Text UK Ltd, Edinburgh

Printed and bound by Mackays of Chatham Ltd, Chatham, Kent

Hodder & Stoughton policy is to use papers that
are natural, renewable and recyclable products
and made from wood grown in sustainable forests.
The logging and manufacturing processes are
expected to conform to the environmental
regulations of the country of origin.

Hodder & Stoughton Ltd
338 Euston Road
London NW1 3BH

www.hodder.co.uk

For the memory of my Mum and Dad

# CONTENTS

*genoeg* Dutch

*kylliksi* Finnish

*suffisant* French

*genug* German

*abbastanza* Italian

*satis* Latin

*nok* Norwegian

*bastantes* Portuguese

*basta* Spanish

# INTRODUCTION

*He who knows he has enough is rich*

Tao Te Ching (c. 260 BC)

If an alien spacecraft were orbiting the blackened husk of Earth in centuries' time, its pilots might be appalled to learn how the human inhabitants had been wired to get such kicks from producing and consuming more and more of everything, that they had ultimately burnt the whole planet out. 'Daft buggers,' our aliens would say, shaking their silvery heads. If those visitors also learnt how we had only got grumpier, sicker and more exhausted as our pursuit of more of everything reached its climax, they would scratch their scalps and ask: 'What were they thinking?' One of the wiser ones might wonder, 'How on Earth did they fail to evolve?'

It would be just as sad if, in another scenario, those intergalactic visitors were our own descendants who had escaped the stricken planet moments before eco-geddon and were now, centuries later, orbiting Earth in a gleaming ship that travelled at light-speeds and could meet every material need that a creature should desire. The pilots would be muttering to each other:

'This heap's nowhere near as quick as the new Mk1192a.'

'And those teleporting pods are just like, *so* last aeon.'

'Can you hear that little buzz in the dashboard whenever we accelerate? It's reeeeeally pissing me off.'

We have some evolving to do. And quickly. We need to develop a sense of *enough*. Or, if you fancy, enoughness. Or even enoughism. We have created a culture that has one over-riding message – we do not yet have all we need to be satisfied. The answer, we are told, is to have, see, be and do even more. Always more. But this is bearing strange fruit: levels of stress, depression and burnout are all rising fast, even though we live amid unprecedented abundance. Our planet doesn't look so happy, either.

We urgently need to stop over-stimulating the powerful ancient instincts that make us never satisfied. Instead we must nurture our capacities to appreciate the unprecedented wonders now at our feet. In the Western world we now effectively have everything we could possibly need. There is no 'more'. We have to learn to live 'post-more'. This isn't about turning the clocks back or having less. It's about realising that we've arrived (hurrah times three). Enough-ness is a path to contentment. It's about personal ecology, about each of us finding our own sustainable balance as individuals. Enoughness is the tipping point, beyond which getting more of anything makes life worse rather than better.

Simple, eh? But the path to enoughness quickly becomes complicated. Blame evolution, the thing that got us here. Our evolutionary wiring led us down from the trees and around the world, through ice ages, famines, plagues and disasters, right into this age of technological and material bounty. And still that old wiring constantly urges us: 'I. Want. More.

Now.' So far, it's been superbly successful. It made us lords of the planet. But it's about to dump us on the cosmic ash-heap, in the box marked: 'Good idea, but . . .'

We have at least now spotted the basic problem. On my ferretings for this book, I've found that you can't enter a meeting of psychologists, economists or politicos without someone warning that half of us wealthy Westerners are certifiably miserable, and that getting richer no longer makes us any happier. These pundits also complain that we're suffocating on our own exhaust pipes. But then they blame the economy. Or the Government. Or 'society' (short-hand for 'the greedy git next door, but not me'). Or they even say it's a sickness. Meanwhile, the world carries on worrying about global warming, grumbling about overwork and complaining of not being happy – while still chasing, making and consuming evermore, in the hope that it will cheer everyone up.

So long as it is always someone else's problem, the cycle will continue until the planet is fit only for cockroaches. Evolution got us into this luxurious crisis – with all the wonderful heating, lighting and high-tech healthcare that comes with it. Now it's down to each of us to start evolving our species out of it (and with any luck we will get to keep all the heating, lighting and other good stuff, too).

It's time to ditch our ancient habits – and all the things that weld us to them. In this book I'm going to explore the many ways in which we keep tripping over our obsolete brain-wiring. We rely on instincts that give old answers to new challenges – in particular the challenge of living amid abundance when our minds are still programmed to fear scarcity and to consume everything that we can. We were built to seek comfort and food, but not designed to find them all the time. We are lumbered with 'wanting' brains. Now, thanks to breakthroughs in neuroscience and medical technology, we can glimpse these ancient responses as they fire up in our heads.

These discoveries, along with advances in evolutionary psychology, show how we have built a culture that drives us to switch on all the wrong instincts – ones that respond to excess by seeking even more, that react to convenience by encouraging us to work harder, that make us hurry more when our leisure time increases, and that even make us eat more whenever we hurry. All of this creates a feedback loop where our needless desires drive our culture's economy more, and our culture's economy in turn drives our needless desires more. We've become like Imelda Marcos and her shoes: the best pair is always the next pair . . . dammit, it's the *only* pair worth having.

As Robert Trivers, an evolutionary biologist at Rutgers University, says, 'We've evolved to be maximising machines. There isn't necessarily a stop mechanism in us that says, "Relax, you've got enough".' But just because our basic brains evolved in the Pleistocene era, between 130,000 and 200,000 years ago, that doesn't condemn us to blundering around the 21$^{st}$ century like Flintstone families. So far we've been able to evolve quite quickly to beat newly emerging problems, because our mental hardware can cleverly reconfigure the bits it came in the box with. There are circuits in our heads that can enable us to take the next essential step, although modern society increasingly sidelines these little lifesavers. These circuits can encourage us to savour, to appreciate and to grow.

We need to revive them, to evolve an 'enough' button in our culture and in our heads, to break the vicious spiral of more, more, more.

Otherwise we're stuck like Spinal Tap's Nigel Tufnel, perpetually stencilling an extra number on our amplifiers: 'You're on ten all the way up. Where do you go from there? Eleven.' Hardly. Our new enoughist responses will tell us when we have obtained the optimum amount of any one thing, to be glad of it, and to stop exhausting our precious, finite personal resources – time, attention and energy – by chasing evermore.

Sustainability is the key – and personal sustainability in particular. All but the most cotton-headed among us now believe that the Earth's ecosystem is in danger. Trouble is, life is so padded with minor preoccupations that it's hard to recognise the threat as monstrous enough to make us do anything more than make gestures at it. 'Yeah, it's scary. Whatever.' Modern technology exacerbates this problem: I'll show later in the book how many of our more-of-everything conveniences work in unexpected ways to short-circuit our ancient drive to improve the world.

Am I downhearted? No. There's hope in the steady flow of surveys reporting how modern life increasingly leaves us miserable, tetchy, fearful and mad. Amid the global warming, we are seeing more personal warming – more stress and depression, more melting of our circuits. That's dismal for individuals. But, hey, it's our one hopeful sign of potential cultural shift. It may push growing numbers of us to embrace enoughism, to balance our personal ecologies in the pursuit of contentment, sanity and sustainability. As individuals, we can try to find balance by seeking only the things that we truly desire, rather than chasing manufactured rainbows. The knock-ons for our planet would grow if we could shift focus from ever-more to enoughness.

I'm perched on my wobbly moral plinth here by dint of having spent 20 years trying to live this idea. At first it was the result of personal quirk, of having grown up quite happily in straitened circumstances. My mum was a widow, a child of the Second World War, and our approach to acquiring things carried a strong air of rationing: 'Is a new xxxx really necessary?' was the family mantra. Throughout my upbringing we had the same three-piece suite, a relic from my late dad's bachelor days, though we refurbished it in the pre-green spirit of make do and mend. (I've still got the sofa – though now it's apparently a '1950s design icon'.) Over the past decade, my sense of having an inner ration-book has become indispensable as the external clamour for more, more, more has multiplied. I've had to put more effort into deciding what is 'enough' for me, to discriminate between new things that might enhance life, and those that will ultimately – despite their glister – detract from the good stuff already in it.

Ultimately I had to start becoming somewhat militant. That's why I no longer own a mobile phone. I did for a while. It seemed a good idea, but then my work colleagues got hold of the number. The little convenience-enhancer turned into a conduit for constant demands. It's the telecoms equivalent of Hemingway's *The Old Man and the Sea* – you set off to catch some tasty sprats, but instead you suddenly find yourself on one end of the line with a massive fish at the other. It feels like a prize, but it drags your little boat way into the middle of the ocean. Still you keep hanging on. And then it turns out that the huge fish is no use anyway. Not wishing to live like Hemingway's harried angler, I didn't replace the mobile when, by accident, it got broken.

We don't have a telly at home either. I do, however, manage to work at the sharp edge of information as a national newspaper journalist and author. Saying 'enough' isn't about self-denial: in our communications-saturated society, if you staunch some of the torrent that jet-hoses us every day, you don't end up with less useful knowledge. The opposite happens (as I explain in the first chapter). Anyway, our house receives a welter of info through broadband, DVDs and radios. How much more does one need? And what's the price of more, in terms of time, space and inner life? We are now so rich with things that every time we get something extra, we have to push something aside to make room, and the swaps are getting ever less rewarding.

Practising enoughness may also help make one's finances more sustainable. If you budget for enough, it will hopefully be easier to work to earn just enough, to liberate life for the nourishing stuff beyond the narrow sphere of getting and spending. Thus the path of enough can lead, paradoxically, to more. Smugly, enoughism gives me time to practise t'ai chi and meditate daily (let's not be afraid of clichés here). Likewise, the missus and I can spend hours trudging through fields and drinking flasks of tea on top of drizzle-misted hills – activities that are clinically proven to boost morale and strengthen relationships, as well as fending off the Grim Reaper.

Simply being, rather than perpetually doing, also fosters the creativity so often demanded by modern career-life. Minds need space to think. Hence the old Zen joke: 'Don't just do something. Sit there.' But in this era of unheralded riches, we often feel convinced that we can't afford to spend valuable time balancing on one leg or sitting, eyes shut, just existing. We gotta be out there, chasing.

Let's not pretend that the answers are all simple. We all like to think we are rational creatures, easily capable of balanced decisions. But human actions tend to show the opposite. Studies of drivers in central London, for example, consistently find them complaining that they can't afford the city's congestion charge. And they moan about the time they lose in traffic jams. They say they understand that they are polluting the air and know they should be using less toxic transport. Then they declare that they intend to keep driving through central London for ever. This doesn't even seem to be short-sighted self-interest at work.

Likewise, we have great difficulty setting our levels of enoughness and keeping anywhere near them. Surveys perpetually find us lamenting that we are overworked and lack free time. Other studies hear us complaining that our homes are full of clutter. Then we put even more hours in at work to buy more stuff that we never seem to enjoy. Blame our ancient instincts for nagging us into believing that new possessions will boost our chance of genetic immortality. Back in our neolithic villages, there were strong evolutionary reasons for this. But now our culture has amplified that nagging into a continual harangue.

No one is immune: I'm writing much of this book at home on a flash, powerful laptop bought in a typical moment of weakness. It consumes so much juice, emits so much heat and is such a gilt-edged invitation to thieves that the hefty great thing never leaves the house. I got suckered. I have also written a big chunk of these chapters while on the move, using a cheap old battery-sipping light-weight that I bought second-hand eight years ago. It does the job just as well.

Nevertheless, there are many enoughist strategies that we can all adopt to dodge and block much of the get-more, have-more, be-more stimulation. First of all, we have to change how we respond to the barrage. I hope that this book will help to arm you for the task – by exposing the many snares that our own Pleistocene-era minds unintentionally lay for us, and explaining how the modern world of consumption hijacks our social brains so that we step right into these traps.

That might sound a little paranoid, but we are girdled by multimillion-pound industries that use an ever-growing array of overt and hidden persuaders to get us to want things, work for things and buy more of them. We don't tend to complain, but if you were physically forced by powerful gangs to spend all your time and energy in the pursuit of things you didn't need, didn't want and ultimately didn't enjoy, you'd feel sorely misused.

Enoughism requires us to defuse the status obsession fostered by constant consumption. As a culture, we need to value different emblems of cool – such as time, space and autonomy – rather than trinkets. There are promising signs, both negative and positive: on the negative side, the world of more, more, more is getting uglier: rather than just 'you are what you eat', the fact that we can now satisfy all of our actual needs means that 'we are what we want'

– and all that branding, bling and blubber is increasingly not pretty.

On the positive side, green is now considered hip (even if it often only involves having a recycling box, glutting on costly ethical goods or spending thousands jetting off to ethical holidays). Moreover, practising enoughism offers plentiful opportunities for mischievous fun – just try surrealist ways of cutting pointless options out of your life (chapter five), or even committing the ultimate twenty-first-century sin of switching all your telecoms off for regular periods. Woo-hoo, can't catch me.

But declaring 'enough' also demands that you challenge your own internal propaganda. Yes, your brain feels immortal; yes, it whispers that (in the poet Walt Whitman's words) you can contain multitudes; yes, your brain says that you can have it all and do everything. These egoistic inklings are all turned up loud and proud by consumer culture's persistent promises of infinite self-realisation. But in fact no, your brain isn't immortal and you can't have it all. Those are just convictions that your head evolved to persuade your body out of bed on damp mornings. We are human and limited, and we have to live within our lives' realistic limits for them to be sustainable and satisfiable. We can hit personal bests in our time, but there will be many other things that we won't ever see, be, own or do. Enoughism requires us to accept that the carrot of infinite promise will always dangle just beyond our noses. Embracing this fact is a path to contentment.

Only contentment? This little c-word sounds like the dull, swotty sibling of capital-H Happiness. But humanity has never before had a chance to enjoy widespread contentment.

We're now at that point, but are intent on overshooting it in quest of that fleeting high called happiness. As the American novelist Edith Wharton said: 'If only we'd stop trying to be happy, we could have a pretty good time.' Our culture wants to make happiness a perpetual bliss, even if we have to carbonise the planet in the process. But achieving mere contentment is itself a heady challenge that demands skilled balancing. It requires the wisdom of enoughism – a wisdom I first heard articulated in the late 1980s at an NHS conference, when an obscure Civil Service economist declared: 'Don't let your desire for perfection ruin your appreciation for that which is just "good".'

This brings us to a conundrum that has challenged sages since civilisation began: how much, exactly, is *enough* – and can we create a way in which to measure that? These are bear-traps of questions, the sort that confounded Jeremy Bentham, the eighteenth-century English philosopher who created Utilitarianism with the aim of bringing the most happiness to the most people. To check whether government policies were boosting people's joy sufficiently, Bentham devised a system for measuring happiness – the 'felicific calculus'. To explain how the calculus should work, he wrote hundreds of pages of guidance filled with odd, clunky terms such as 'fecundity' and 'propinquity'. His system failed miserably. Trying to quantify subjective states such as happiness or enoughness is like trying to grab a cake of soap in the bath. The harder you grasp, the faster it flies into some hair-strewn corner.

But I think that I can prod my finger at where enoughness generally lies: it's the point where the curve falls off – the curve of the satisfaction that you get from getting, having, being or doing, more. Beyond that dip, you are on a perpetual slide of diminishing returns. Your primitive acquisitive instincts tell you to keep going, to put more effort in . . . despite the fact that the paybacks are evidently shrinking. At the point of enoughness you need to stop and enjoy. You need to appreciate the liberation that getting there brings you, rather than slogging ever onwards in the hope that the fun will eventually come back in larger doses.

So this book shamelessly offers no regime, no prescription, no solemn promise to empower you to *Find Your Enough in Seven Days/Six Months/Whenever*. Researching it has taken me on a long trip through the art and science of enoughness, exploring the instinctive mechanisms that make us ignore it, investigating the ways by which we may achieve it, and meeting people who manage to live it. I hope it will help you to reach your own conclusions about where your own enoughnesses lie.

It may be the sparse life of the ascetic, but more likely it will involve balance, thought and the occasional endorphin rush that results from dashing to your favourite shop counter. My favourite stores sell obscure bits for vintage guitars and rusting old Japanese motorbikes. Can I ever get enough of them? Well, umm, hmm. But I have at least liberated enough time, space and energy to enjoy those toys. It's not ambrosia, of course, but it feels satisfying. Thus, I like to think that I practise enoughness. Enough enoughness.

*PS*
*A brief note to my accountant*
Hi Barry. In the interests of global and personal ecology, and in the true spirit of enoughism, I have resisted the

temptation to travel the globe researching this book. All physical visits were conducted within an hour's drive of my home, and all other information and interviews were obtained via the marvels of technology. Hence the extreme lack of travel-expense receipts.

Sorry.

J

# 1 | **ENOUGH** Information

*I have reached an elegant sufficiency and anything*
*additional would be superfluous.*
Edwardian saying, now considered quaint

If the police were to burst in at this point, it might take some explaining. I'm on a low stool in a country cottage overlooking an English village green, wearing a swimming cap pierced with little holes. Sixteen probes and a multi-coloured web of wires protrude from it. No drugs are involved and no animals are being harmed, but the room is crammed with strange artefacts, including framed tissue samples, vintage model aircraft, antique displays of brains and a desk that once belonged to the philosopher Lord Bertrand Russell. Next to it, there's an electronic monkey head that is programmed to laugh loudly whenever anyone in the room so much as giggles. This Gothic scene provides an unlikely venue for trying a high-tech method of smart-bombing our data-stuffed minds with more information.

I'm enjoying the hospitality of Dr David Lewis, a neuro-scientist who has spent the past 20 years developing devices that study how your brain makes decisions. He's enthroned in a black recliner with its own inbuilt lights and remote-control panel. He likes a gadget. His latest project uses some of the latest head-examining technology to crack an increasingly difficult challenge for the marketing men – how to penetrate our modern mind-fug of continual media stimulation, and reach deep into our addled heads to transmit messages that will prod us to purchase more.

Lewis and others in this field are being paid by the planet's leading corporates to pioneer this technique, called neuro-marketing, because of a fast-growing problem: we are starting to drown in our own data, to the point where painstakingly targeted advertising messages roll off our brains – along with lots of important personal stuff, too. Back in the 1970s my local council ordered the town's aquarium to stop keeping dolphins, because the animal welfare experts had protested that Flipper and co's sonar clicks were bouncing back on the poor creatures from all angles in their cramped pools. 'They are being blinded and deafened by a world of their own white noise,' the campaigners said. Now we know how the dolphins felt. Everywhere you look, every time you listen, someone is trying to snag your attention. Your neurones are being pinged by marketing messages, badgered by adverts, stalked by product-placements.

We are bombarded with up to 3,500 sales shots each day, or one every 15 seconds of our waking lives. In 2004, companies worldwide spent more than £200 billion on advertising. In the past decade, the number of British TV advertising spots has jumped from 3,000 to 8,000 and our channels have multiplied from four to 123. Six trillion business e-mails were sent in 2006, and ten million spam e-mails are sent each day. And more new information has been produced within the past 30 years than in the previous 5,000. That's probably enough data to digest for now. Oh, and every week sees more new podcasts, magazines, supplements, cable channels and radio stations. Then there are websites, texts, blogs and those DVDs with extra discs featuring the bits you didn't see first time round. Even the coiffure chain Toni & Guy has begun to install wireless broadband in its salons: you can't get your barnet cut without being plugged in to the infoverse. 'Hello darling, I'm on the hairnet.'

Some of society's most creative minds are attracted by high salaries and glam cachet to help the advertising and marketing industries push products at us. In earlier times, these people might have been great artists or writers. But increasingly the sheer mass of sophisticated information they churn out just leaves us bewildered. Experts at the Henley Centre, the media-forecasting company, fear that we are being deafened by sales chatter. Fewer than one in five conventional ad campaigns now has any significant effect. And this info-glut sets off an instinctive human response that nowadays only worsens the problem: when we are confused by excessive information, we feel compelled to seek more information in order to try to make sense of our confusion.

A survey run by Henley suggests that we are becoming a society of info-hoarders, the new-media equivalents of crazy types living in homes crammed with newspapers. More than 70 per cent of people ticked the survey box saying: 'I can never have too much information.' But more than half also said that they don't have the time or energy to use the information that they already have. One way of trying to cope with this sense of overload is to try to cram in even more information-seeking – by multitasking. The majority of twentysomethings now watch TV while also being online. But how much do they take in? Television advertisers worry that viewers' attention and retention are in freefall: the more information we get, the less we comprehend.

One of the reasons I have ridden over to Dr Lewis's cottage is that he was probably the first to highlight this problem. Back in 1996, he identified a new social sickness and gave it a snappy clinical name: 'information fatigue syndrome'. Lewis had conducted a global study for Reuters of 1,300 businesspeople who were labouring under what today would seem a comparatively minor deluge of data. Two-thirds of his interviewees told him that stress from information overload had damaged their relationships, given them insomnia and made them doubt their decision-making. Many sufferers responded by trying to seek even more information to help them make sense of it all. Lewis, a tidily small bundle of sixtysomething mischief, blamed the syndrome directly on the information revolution. His newly coined illness chimed so well with our times that it rapidly acquired its own mythology. The *Daily Telegraph* promptly interviewed an 'IFS sufferer' about her painful five-year path to recovery. The following year, Edward Welsh even reported in the *Sunday Times* that the syndrome had first been detected in Allied intelligence officers during the Second World War.

Recent studies support Lewis's early findings. Researchers at London University report how the effects of over-communication can be more deranging than cannabis. They claim that if you smoke a joint, four points are temporarily knocked off your IQ. But just being in a situation where you are able to text and e-mail can knock a whole ten IQ points off your brain – similar to the head-fug caused by losing a night's sleep. The study claims that this is because your concentration gets depleted by constantly feeling compelled to stop and check your inbox. This continual background state of distraction means that we lose productivity by checking for messages that are supposed to boost productivity. Likewise, we spoil our social lives by obsessing about text messages instead of paying heed to the people right next to us. The report coined its own snappy word for the compulsion: 'infomania'. To witness how deeply this compulsion runs, you only have to sit in a busy pub and watch how the civilised etiquette of paying polite attention to one's companions gets binned whenever a mobile rings. We are all increasingly infomaniacs, compulsively grabbing every snippet in the hope that one day we'll find the magic bit that makes all the rest make sense.

This paradox typifies many of our troubles in this unprecedented time of abundance. The survival strategies that saw us through millennia of scarcity and threat, when other hominids died away, are scuppering our chance to enjoy the plenty now surrounding us. The roots of infomania lie deep in our evolutionary psychology, which is also the source of our potentially destructive drives for evermore food, work, possessions, choice and happiness. Out there on the savannah lands where our ancestors evolved, you had to pay attention like your life depended on it. Indeed, it did depend on it. You needed to make the best of all the information you had. Novelty – new faces, shapes and concepts – was rare compared with today, and would spark a mental conflict between fear and curiosity. It would take a heady burst of inquisitiveness to stimulate an early human to overcome their fear of extinction to explore potentially rewarding questions such as: 'What happens if

I kick that lizard?' But the people who went ahead and explored often landed the best opportunities to feed and breed. As generations passed, a reward system evolved in primitive human brains to encourage information gathering – and it proved a winner in the great game of evolution.

Clinical tests show that this mechanism is still busy in our brains – it's an opium kick that our bodies give our minds whenever we learn something. A study in 2006 by a neuroscientist at the University of Southern California reported that when we grasp a new concept, the 'click' of comprehension triggers a cascade of brain chemicals that rewards the brain with a shot of natural, heroin-like opioids. Irving Biederman, who conducted the research, says human brains have a cluster of opioid receptors in a brain region associated with acquiring new information. He believes that we have evolved to get high whenever we learn something about our world or grasp tough or witty ideas, because it gives us a head start on our rivals. 'Human beings are designed to be infovores,' he says. 'When you are trying to understand a difficult theorem, it's not fun. But once you get it, you just feel fabulous.'

Until recently, our brains regularly switched off this chemically inspired quest for new ideas. The reward system is automatically over-ridden by more pressing needs for food or safety. On today's comfy sofas we have no predators or famines to threaten our leisure, so infomania can run wild in even the laziest and most risk-averse people, creating a mass desire for scary news, banal texts, celeb gossip and general media trash. As long as it's got novelty we will get a kick from it. We keep seeking new sources for our mini-kicks because the opioid reward diminishes each time a novel experience is repeated. Biederman watched volunteers' brains with a functional magnetic resonance imaging (fMRI) scanner and found that they showed less stimulation each time they saw the same picture. In response to this, the media industry is selling us increasingly quick-fire stimuli that squeeze our 'duh seen that' response ever harder, intensifying our novelty addiction and curtailing our attention spans.

It's against this background of compelled, confused, bored and overfed info-junkies that Dr Lewis has been working with a company called NeuroCo to pioneer the concept of neuromarketing in Britain. In America there are about 90 neuromarketing consultancies. Major corporations that use them include Procter & Gamble, GM, Coca-Cola and Motorola. Whatever is left of your attention span, they're after it. Traditionally, advertising strategies run on the lines of: 'Tell us what you want . . . and we'll tell you that we've got it.' But since our actual needs and common wants have become satiated, those industries have had to work ever harder to lure our desires to their brands. As we hit media saturation, advertisers are turning to neuroscience in the hope that it offers new ways to tap and tickle our sub-conscious machinery. The strategy promises to show companies the effectiveness of their marketing strategies at firing up the 'interest' parts of consumers' brains. It may also help them to hit us with pinpoint-targeted information.

Neuromarketing promises to tell manufacturers which particular stimuli actually lead people to decide to pick one product over its competitors. For despite what our conscious minds like to tell us, the choices we make can have deeply arbitrary grounds. It appears that our subconscious minds make most of the decisions in life and our conscious minds then spend time justifying them: brain-scanning tests show that when a decision forms, the subconscious brain prepares to act up to 500 milliseconds before its owner consciously decides to act. One example of the wacky ways in which our primitive hardware makes 'rational' choices in the twenty-first century comes from a DaimlerChrysler study which discovered that images of sports cars activate the same reward centres of men's brains as alcohol and drugs. Wheee. And brain scanners at the Ludwig-Maximilians University in Munich, Germany have confirmed that our minds light up faster and more positively in response to well-known brands than to less famous ones. Now teams of scientists around the world are trying to work out why some top branding campaigns work better than others at sparking our neurons.

One clue comes from a renowned study by P. Read Montague, a neuroscientist at Baylor University in Texas, who asked volunteers to take the Pepsi/Coca-Cola taste test – drinking both brands of the sugary brown fizz out of unmarked cups. When served blind, their tongues preferred Pepsi. Their brains did too: fMRI scans showed that Pepsi triggered more activity in a region of the brain that signals reward. Then, however, the individuals were shown an image of either a blue or red can and given a random sample of drink. The scanner again watched their brains. Coke's brand colour made the hippocampus and pre-frontal cortex light up, while the Pepsi colour had no effect. This brought real cheer to everyone involved in the Real Thing's ad campaigns, because it indicates that despite the taste, Coke's image is embedded more positively in our heads. The hippocampus is buried in the forebrain and regulates emotion and memory. The pre-frontal cortex is roughly behind our eyes and plays a crucial role in our behaviour, noticing social cues, restraining impulses, directing attention and fostering conscious awareness of feelings. It is believed that by lighting up these areas, you stimulate the brain's sense of self. Zap: Coke's brand has got knitted into your ego.

All this neuro-study means that our brains increasingly face being subverted by scientifically honed advertising. In less than a decade's time, claim neuromarketing's strongest proponents, the technology will enable marketing strategies to illuminate your brain's 'want-it' circuits like a billion-watt Christmas tree. Dr Lewis is less bullish: 'I don't think that we will ever find the "buy" button in people's brains – though [he clears his throat] I may be wrong. But we can certainly tell a lot of interesting stuff about what is attracting people's attention and how they are responding.' Lewis uses a technique called quantified electro-encephalography – hence the rubber skullcap, dotted with holes for electrodes, which his assistant has glued to my scalp. The electrodes are plugged into an EEG machine no bigger than a car radio. It reads the level and type of electrical brainwaves and provides a real-time read-out of how your brain responds to, say, different packets of soap powder. The magic of this kit is that it is portable. You can stick a hat over the skullcap, pop the EEG machine in a bag and go shopping while it records your subconscious responses. 'Effectively, it can read your brain activity,' says Dr Lewis. 'Modern advances mean that the power of the software is increasing exponentially.'

And there it is, spatchcocked on a laptop screen: my brain, beavering away, trying to make sense of the world.

Sadly, it's just a serried bunch of squiggles. My inner life resembles a maladjusted video player. To give Lewis a baseline picture of my brain's different wavelengths, I gaze vacantly into the middle distance while mentally focusing on a meditation mantra I've used for more than a decade. The nine lethargic spider lines on the screen suggest that there is markedly little happening under the skullcap. 'Try blinking,' says Dr Lewis. Several lines leap across each other as I pay attention to the good doctor and do his bidding. Fortunately for my self-respect, the EEG data can be configured to create a variety of more attractive screen displays – my favourite one creates a kind of psychic weather map across a top-sliced section of my skull. Clouds of colour grow, shrink and disperse as different parts of my brain show different activity. The zones at the back of my skull seem to be working overtime. 'Those are the areas to do with vision,' says Lewis.

But what precisely is my vision focusing on? And how am I responding emotionally? It's currently very difficult to interpret the enormous amount of raw information that the technology provides. And even that mass of brainwave frequencies hardly tells the whole story – who knows how all those disparate areas of the mind are interacting? On top of that, we can all have different emotional responses to apparently similar brain-states. Some of us, for example, have had past experiences that make us wary of colours, smells and shapes that other people love. Lewis agrees: he says that using the machine is like standing outside a football ground, trying to interpret the action in the game by listening to the roars of the crowd. But he is confident that the technology can at least tell him when something has attracted its wearer's attention – and by linking this with data from skin sensors and blood-pressure monitors, he can estimate whether the attention is sparking desire or repulsion. Using eye-tracking cameras hidden in a pair of spectacles worn by his shopping subjects, he can also tell exactly what his volunteers are looking at when their brains fire up.

Much of Lewis's current work involves getting consumers to wear his 'neurocaps' under their hats and then walk around shopping centres such as the giant Lakeside mall in Essex, to see how the buyers' brains respond to the centre's layout and the shops' sales strategies. One early discovery is that if you want to open a shop, don't do it next door to a bank. People's buying brains switch off as they walk past a bank. Maybe it reminds them that they still owe for their last spree. Another of Lewis's commercial exercises scanned cinema-goers' minds while they watched film of a car ride through Paris. The audience didn't know that the route was dotted with digitally inserted cinema adverts for a Twentieth Century Fox film. Dr Lewis's team was able to give Fox's marketing chiefs a read-out showing which posters and poster-sites seemed most attractive. He has also worked with car manufacturers and other big corporations, none of which wishes to have its name made public, lest their customers fear that they are getting brain-jacked by Frankenstein science.

Lewis is not alone in building mind-reading machines for the marketeers. Peter Robinson, a Cambridge University professor, is developing an 'emotionally aware' computer that uses a camera to film people's faces, then measures their expressions and infers their emotional state. His machine can already track subtle muscle movements at 24 facial points and then attempt to match them to one of the crucial emotional states that he claims are involved in shopping: sadness, confusion, excitement, surprise and anger. Robinson believes that scanning-cameras could be built into screens in internet cafés, bars and waiting rooms, enabling computers to read our moods and respond with adverts that connect with how we're feeling.

Such developments are merely the beginning, claims Lewis. 'I compare it, in aviation terms, to being ten years on from the Wright Brothers. We're still using flimsy biplanes, but we can advance into building supersonic jets.' And when we reach the jet age of neuromarketing, could we discover the holy grail of sales – an advertising technique guaranteed to capture consumers? No, says Lewis. The reality will be far messier, because our novelty-seeking brains don't work that way: 'Everything that is found to work will get continually used until it is over-used. Buyers will tune out until the next new thing comes along.' The arms race will never end. With the aid of brain-scanners there will be more carefully targeted stimuli, more stealth, gimmickry and sensory bombardment. The marketeers will get evermore efficient at developing new tricks to convince us that we don't already have enough of anything.

Well, good luck to Dr Lewis. I like his style and admire his dedication. But I prefer a diametrically opposed approach to tackling information-overload. It involves fighting – and here's my own new word – *infobesity*, by restricting one's data diet. There are compelling reasons. The glut of information is not only causing stress and confusion; it also makes us do irrational things such as ignore crucial health information. The British Government's latest survey on our food-buying patterns shows that while we are given more information than ever about healthy eating, our consumption of fresh food has fallen. This is partly because we are too busy getting and spending to enjoy the simple pleasures of cooking. But Catherine Collins, of the British Dietetic Association, says that info-overload is often to blame for this food-choice paradox: 'We are so informed that we can't be bothered.' That's a fantastic slogan for the twenty-first century. We are so wired to gather information that often we no longer do anything useful with it. Instead of pausing to sift our intake for relevance and quality, the daily diet of prurient, profound, confusing and conflicting information gets chucked on to a mental ash-heap of things vaguely comprehended. Then we rush to try to make sense of it all by . . . getting more.

Nowhere is this more starkly apparent than in the world of 24-hour rolling news, the high temple of speculation, rumour-chasing, non-stories and trivia, whose arch-priest is a man in a raincoat reporting, 'I can confirm that nothing has happened since I last said that nothing had happened.' You can spend all day watching 'Elvis still dead' bulletins. This continuous story-chasing seriously distorts our view of the world. Our minds fill with exaggerated anxiety as they witness regular re-runs of the day's most shocking images. How many times does one have to see the same detonating car bomb in order to get the idea? The horror is replayed continually, but we learn nothing more. Instead we gain the impression that the world is dangerous and beyond control. We also forget that the definition of news is: something that happened today which was unlikely to happen yesterday and equally unlikely to happen tomorrow. Instead we feel compelled to watch still more news, in order to try to get an even bigger 'bigger picture' of the threat – one that might help us to get a handle on it.

This is exacerbated by the fact that our primitive brains have a rotten sense of geography: if we see footage of a massacre somewhere far off, our minds don't instinctively think, 'Phew, that was thousands of miles away.' They believe that it must have happened close at hand, within the scope of a Neolithic human's wanderings. We feel compelled to learn everything we can about this 'nearby' threat. The continual stimulation causes continual stress. Some psychologists believe the effect is so strong that we should limit our news-watching to only 30 minutes a day – or risk developing anxiety-related depression.

Beyond such immediate impacts, our info-drenched culture may ultimately stop our species evolving further by killing our desire to switch off the screens and do anything purposeful. The danger lies in the increasingly seductive lure of virtual reality, which provides short-cuts that enable our brains to experience exciting biological cues, such as attractive and willing mates, that they have been built to go out to find in the real world. Our thrill-seeking circuits no longer have to leave the sofa to get their kicks. And our subconscious, instinctive brains don't care tuppence that these stimuli only exist as pixels. They don't even care that we consciously know it's cheap fakery. They still get turned on just as much. This explains why people increasingly prefer to watch porn rather than pursue sexual intimacy in a complex human relationship, play virtual video sports rather than practise real-world athletics and watch *Friends* rather than spend time with friends.

'We are already disappearing up our own brainstems,' says Geoffrey Miller, an evolutionary psychologist at the University of New Mexico. He claims that the bulk of human ingenuity is now being poured into creating virtual-life experiences, rather than into industries that make real things such as hydro-electric dams. He even suggests that this is why we have never been contacted by any of the advanced alien civilisations who should – in theory – have evolved on one of the planets orbiting our galaxy's 100 billion stars. Intelligent life out there has never successfully managed to pass the technological stage of inventing virtual reality without becoming completely besotted with it: the aliens would rather go extinct playing Martian versions of PlayStation at home than do the work necessary to colonise the galaxy.

Miller does suggest, though, that Darwinian genetic variation might throw up another possibility – a new line of humans may evolve away from our virtual-reality culture, reject the temptations of cheap screen thrills and use technology to live more productive lives in the real world. 'Those who persist will evolve more self-control, conscientiousness and pragmatism,' says Miller. But he fears that the only people who might build such rigorous societies will be hardline religious zealots – the sort of people with long beards and headgear who abhor leisure, pleasure and liberal ideals. I hope instead that these evolvers will be warm, humane, life-affirming enoughists.

Whatever happens, we have reached a point where our lives are logjammed with junk data. I don't just mean illegal spam, but also the time-robbing, nourishment-free information that we lay on each other every day through e-mails, phone calls and texts. My own trade, journalism, like all the other communications industries, is drowning in this soul-clogging pollution (and very guilty, of course, of producing it). If you work in a cream-cake factory, you get to eat a lot of cream cakes. If you work in high finance, you take lots of money home. I have spent the past 15 years shovelling facts and opinion in various media, so I get a maelstrom of information swirling around my head every day.

Journalists tend to be a greedy bunch, the fattest guys in the cake factory, convinced that if the information that they've got already is good, then more must be better: more background, more gossip, more opinion. But journalists are also employed to use the reverse approach: we edit. Editing banishes irrelevance and pares data until it is whippet-sleek. It's one of my favourite tasks, and some-where in my head I'm humming Mike Batt's novelty 1970s song lyric, 'Womble up de rubbish, and put it in de bin.' If someone scoots along with extra stuff for a story, my habitual response is to ask, 'What will it add?' As we sit deluged by ever-proliferating communications, it's a ques-tion that we all must learn to wield, in order to decide: 'Enough. That's my optimum info-take.'

This is not about being a Luddite. On the contrary, it's about deciding to take the most from new technologies, rather than having our lives taken over by them. Why must we use all our information conduits all of the time? We don't leave all the lights and taps on just because we've got electricity and plumbing fitted. Going on a personal data diet brings positive advantages. Cutting your workplace e-mail usage, for example, can significantly boost your levels of confidence with co-workers. Offices, despite their veneer of sophistication, basically provide spaces where higher primates can interact without breaking into physical conflict. There's still a lot of naked-apey stuff going on though, and new technology often nixes the positive side of this. Rather than sending a colleague an e-mail, walking over to chat with them face to face raises both your levels of bonding hormones, because the friendly human contact stimulates production of dopamine, the attention and pleasure neurotransmitter, along with serotonin, a brain chemical that reduces fear and worry. Research also indicates that getting to smell someone increases your level of trust in them. What tends to keep us stuck to the swivel chair with our fingers on the 'send' button is the initial fear of entering another person's primate desk territory. If you can get over it, your collegiate trust rises. If you can't, then the mutual discomfort is likely to increase.

The data-dieting answer that works for me (though I'm not prescribing it as a panacea) is to consider curtailing your mobile phone use. Seriously. As I've already mentioned, and much to the consternation of colleagues who believe that, as a journalist, I must be super-plugged-in to the whole damn pattern, I don't own a mobile phone. I used to but soon after I first got it, people started ringing me with work-related demands – journalists are devils for finding out phone numbers. It wasn't as if the demands were essential, inspiring or beneficial to society. Most were frivolous, arrived early in the day and ran along the lines of, 'We've got a breaking story about plagues of voles. Can you send us 500 words for a sidebar on how voles damage your house?' (I was a freelance property correspondent at the time.) I'd put on my vole-pundit's hat, trawl the world for wisdom on rodent depredation, mould it into an alarming new threat to homeowners' peace of mind, and file it before deadline. But few of these sidebars ever made the paper. Big stories would break, rolling the news agenda over our fecund voles and squashing them down to an in-brief slot. No room for my wise words. And who couldn't have guessed? So why did I keep getting sent on fool's errands? Becuase suddenly, I was permanently available.

I'm hardly alone. Twice a week I commute by rail to London. The carriage calm is punctured by passengers fending off mobile calls with a battery of blocking excuses, such as 'It's at home/in the office and I can't get hold of it,' as well as blatant buck-passing: 'I think that's Peter Barclay's department. But he's on holiday'; sheer devious-ness: 'I'm just going into a tunnel' [pressing the off-switch]; and bare-faced lies: 'My train's been badly delayed.' Result, raised blood pressure and the wheels of commerce turn not one extra centimetre. Family and social calls are frequently answered with brusque exasperation: 'Well, I can't do anything about that. I'm on the train.'

The fundamental problem is that telecoms can make us victims of convenience. For my editors, it's easy to make instant vole demands if their reporter is only one push of a quick-dial button away. Way too easy. If, however, the editor has to make an effort to track down their writer – a process, say, that subjects them to three per cent of the inconvenience that their request will cause – then they tend to think twice before making it. I should point out that, if there is one freelancing sin far greater than being unavailable (which can be as tantalising as it is annoying to questing editors) it is regularly saying 'no thanks' to story commissions. Do that once too often and they will stop trying to contact you completely. My best solution is to give everyone my e-mail address and warmly invite them to use it. I love e-mail. If an editor genuinely wants something, then they have to write a couple of sentences to ask for it. That's a chunk out of their time budget. Their momentary inconvenience is water in my moat. And there's something ever so slightly leisured about e-mails nowadays, which means that people expect you to respond less quickly than to mobile-phone messages or texts.

Convenience-abuse fosters our growing love-hate relationship with mobiles. Over my years of non-ownership, the insults that friends have heaped upon me have morphed, from slowcoach, to loser, to weirdo, to lucky git and, ultimately, to: 'How the hell do you think you can get away with it?' Surveys such as the Massachusetts Institute of Technology's Lemelson Invention Index consistently finger the mobile phone as our most hated modern tool. The Lemelson Survey says that people dislike mobiles because 'they feel tethered to them or annoyed by others who use them inappropriately' – though of course it's OK for us to ring anyone when it seems convenient. I'm guilty of doing this to my wife, a phone user who successfully practises mobile purdah: unless she's making a call or specifically expecting one, she tries to keep it switched off. It works quite well for her, although when I suddenly decide we need to talk and find that she's off-network, it tends to throw me into the standard mobile mini-tantrum, yelping, 'What the hell's the point of carrying a mobile around if you don't switch the bloody thing on?' at her voicemail. Naturally, this causes strife.

More evidence of mobile misuse comes from research by the chip company, Intel, which found that mobile phones make people far less socially reliable. One in five people admits to being wilfully late because they can reschedule at the last minute via mobile, and three-quarters say that mobile-ownership has made them 'more flexible when meeting friends' (i.e., they are wilfully late, but lie about it). Mobiles are even being blamed for causing mental illness. A Granada University study of hundreds of 18-to-25-year-olds claims that 40 per cent may be addicts, who feel 'deeply upset and sad' at missing calls, and for whom switching off phones 'causes anxiety, irritability, sleep disorders or sleeplessness', and even 'shivering and digestive problems'. Then there is the dependence of workers on personal digital assistants such as BlackBerries, often called CrackBerries for their supposed addictiveness. But is it addiction, or a cycle of social pressure caused by the pursuit of more?

Western life has adopted the mantra of Ken Kesey's coach-touring Merry Pranksters: 'You're either on the bus or off the bus.' Despite its many apparent freedoms, our culture requires rigorous levels of personal conformity. We are told that, in order to pass 'Go', we must be constantly connected, highly competitive and corporately compatible – and must want more goods, more status and more happiness. If you don't agree, then the alternatives can seem very alternative, such as low income, low status or life on a muddy commune.

Mandana Ruane is not convinced. She is the hostess of the Academy Club, a picturesquely distressed little Georgian terrace that is a Soho haunt of London's lit and art crowd. She is a social whizz, up with the goss, a regular at launches and viewings. And she abhors the very idea of owning a mobile. She has decided that she has enough connection. 'Mobiles are at worst quite sinister,' she says in her husky tones. 'They sum up the "Life Is Elsewhere" attitude, where you can always be with a better friend, lover or companion at the end of the line, rather than enjoying where you are. It's demonstrative of insecurity, thinking that there's always something better somewhere else. But you can tell by listening in on people's conversations that there's no way the person on the other end is more interesting,' she laughs. 'Life is fun just in the here and now. And the idea of being always accessible to everyone, 24/7, strikes me as rather whoreish, it's so indiscreet and indiscriminate. I'm already available to people for so much of my waking time that if I want to drop below the radar, I'm happy to know that I can.' Aren't there disadvantages? 'Yes, if you're at a far-flung railway station on a Sunday and the train's cancelled. But there's always a way round it. And it's not worth the sacrifice.'

In America, people who refuse to use all formats to the max are becoming labelled 'tech-no's'. They may be the sharp edge of a growing trend, says Paul Saffo, who works as a Silicon Valley futurist. He predicts that being able to cut loose from the puppet-strings of communication will become a sign of status cool. 'It is going to be very fash-ionable at some point to be disconnected. There will be people who wear their disconnectivity like a badge,' he says. Saffo's belief is backed by the British industrial consul-tancy The Work Foundation, which says that senior managers can often function better without e-mail, because this liberates them from their underlings' persistent sleeve-tugging. One of office technology's early promises was that it would break down hierarchies. But the foundation reports that bosses are reasserting hierarchy by refusing to check their inboxes, because the system creates an unhelpful illusion of accessibility. People start to expect prompt answers, and if you are at the pinnacle of an information-rich organisation, this becomes impossible.

We can all emulate the high-status monkeys by going on a personal data diet. Being selective in your use of telecoms does not necessarily mean avoiding mobiles. Whatever works best for you, works best. Bob Geldof, the charity star and former Boomtown Rat, eschews my favourite conduit: 'I don't have e-mail,' he says. 'It's a great encumbrance.' He only had broadband installed in his home in 2006 because his daughters wanted to do their homework on it. Mobiles are much more his thing, he says, because he can talk and pace around at the same time. Likewise, the Labour minister Estelle Morris says that she ran the Education Department for two years without sending a single e-mail. Tony Blair wasn't much of a one for computers either. And you can even be extremely clever without having a cloak of information wrapped about you: Peter Higgs, the Edinburgh University professor of theoretical physics famed for proposing the existence of a crucial quantum particle called the Higgs boson, admits that he possesses neither e-mail nor telly.

Similarly (though less cleverly), I have never owned a television set. It began as a sin of omission. I didn't think to bring the box along when I left the family home for college, and I got along quite happily there without it. Failure to fret about the news meant that I missed the American invasion of Grenada without suffering any ill effects other than cheerful ignorance (well, it was one of their lesser incursions). Time passed and I got my nose stuck so far into books and social life that television seemed superfluous. Then I went travelling. And on returning to Britain I inhabited a shifting series of low-rent London bedsits. Television would have been one more object to hoik about. Books, guitars, going to gigs and seeing pals seemed more interesting. I was also fearfully aware that a single young man can die a quiet, lonesome death at home in the 'burbs in front of a flickering screen. Suddenly you look up from your can of beer and TV dinner to find that your salad days have wilted in a blur of ad breaks.

Instead, I met a like-minded soul. Kate, my wife, had decided to ditch her set several years before we met. Hers was a straightforward decision to go cold-turkey. 'Sundays used to be spent flopped in front of the box. And that was the weekend gone. It seemed such a waste of life,' she says. It's not that Kate and I grow our own wallpaper or spend evenings knitting muesli. Being boxless is just our way of maintaining some mental greenbelt, some respite from the attention-grabbers that pop up every-where, including our household. Nowadays we have broadband, a tool bought for home-working that also brings an express train of infotainment roaring through our home night and day. How much more on-tap data could one want?

If we want to know what's happening on television, then we turn on the radio or read an online newspaper: they often speak of little else. And that's how we make our enoughist stab at keeping informed rather than deformed. Is it Utopia? Hardly. Books and magazines lie about, swiftly browsed but guiltily unread. We miss films and concerts we vowed to see. I'm still not sure where time goes, even without the telly's help. It does mean that we can grasp the opportunity to cook for each other, to eat and chat together, to nit-pick, bicker and do all the other soulful interactions that daily feed a relationship. Being a little info-lite also helps to reduce our exposure to the endless show-and-tell of things we could have if we were richer, taller, wittier, happier and went shopping more – and had friends who were richer, taller, wittier etc.

Going on a data diet does not necessarily mean junking the telly, but most people will soon be doing that anyway, albeit for different reasons. This is because bundling, the practice of adding more and more functions together in one box, will kill off the plain TV and replace it with a do-it-all, high-definition module that picks up terrestrial, satellite and cable, downloads films and entire television series, surfs the internet, does e-mail, texts and helps with the household accounts. The screen-that-never-sleeps will present a super-sized challenge to enoughism. The temptation will be to try to keep up with its uninterrupted output for fear of suffering ignorance and social isolation.

In the recent past, when television was restricted to, say, four channels, watching telly was a communal experience. People's viewing options were rationed, and thus they could chat in shops and offices the next day about what they had seen, without having to worry that they were either talking nonsense or had never seen the latest programme to have everyone raving. With our entertainment options proliferating, that experience is becoming atomised to the point where communality will soon prove impossible unless you watch absolutely everything all the time. It's a safe bet that many people will try to do just that. Our info-addled brains will again yearn to make sense of the confusion by grabbing as much information as they can get. Our socially competitive brains will want the best and latest gen on everything. Anything less than 24/7 multi-channel consumption will leave open the dread possibility that something more entertaining is being missed.

The only sane alternative to choking on this cornucopia is to create your own enoughist policy. Many of us already try to do this by imposing a quality threshold – namely, the 'I don't watch crap' rule. But quality is such a slippery thing, and the gravitational pull is always downwards. Anyway, what's wrong with slumming it in front of some junk every now and then? Instead we can take a much more pragmatic approach to infotainment by appreciating its true nature and enjoying it for what it is – a pleasurable yet habit-forming, mind-altering and potentially depressing substance that is evermore cheaply abundant. This description may sound rather familiar. It's just like alcohol.

Treating infotainment with the same cautious hedonism that we employ with booze offers a sustainable answer, because we are at least already practised at this approach. Amid all the headlines about binge drinking, the vast majority of us manage to use alcohol to lighten our lives without completely lacerating our livers. And we often do that by imposing personalised practicable rules on ourselves, such as sun-over-the-yardarm, only half a bottle on schoolnights, just at weekends or only with food. Likewise, you can make a life-habit out of data-dieting strategies that are based on identifying which information conduits work best for you and being reasonably disciplined about when to switch them on.

It does require vigilance. Compared with alcohol, the negative impact of infotainment overload is less immediate – there's no fat-tongued hangover, so it's easy to ignore the insidious long-term effects. These primarily involve monopolising time that might otherwise be spent on a range of nourishing activities that not only ensure we remain free of the need to sit incessantly consuming entertainment, but are also proven to promote lasting wellbeing. These include exercise, hobbies, getting out in the weather and enjoying the countryside, being creative, engaging meaningfully with partners, family and friends, being active in one's community, developing one's own inner resources and sense of spirituality . . . and simply sitting around doing absolutely nothing. Despite our brains' primitive tendency to be dumbly magnetised by communications, clinical studies show that a rewarding full life for our higher cortexes isn't sustainable without these other activities. Their lack makes us head for the sofa in fits of chocolate-chomping misery.

Data diets are a kind of carbon-trading for your mind's ecology, but they involve time-trading instead. Here, ironically, new technology may come to the enoughist's aid. According to the flyer for a digital telly channel that recently poked through my letterbox, my 'get-more' media provider can already offer 1,500 films and TV programmes that are constantly available and which 'start and stop when you say so'. Broadband means that we are no longer slaves to the schedules. But can we become masters of the off-button, too? Developing this ability to be cautious consumers may prove crucial for our children, who have never known anything other than a life enveloped in media. Teaching them to handle the stuff carefully is going to be like trying to convince a goldfish about the judicious use of water. But while the kids are getting more infotained than ever, we are also seeing a welter of worry about the effects upon them. Video screens and fast-action children's shows are now being blamed for a whole range of modern conditions, including obesity, premature puberty, autism, attention deficit hyperactivity disorder (ADHD), clinical depression and even increased susceptibility to cancer.

Baroness Susan Greenfield is leading the backlash against infant-tainment. The Oxford professor and brain-chemistry expert has established a parliamentary group to investigate the effect of screen culture on young minds. She is not one for brooking arguments, as I quickly learnt when I met the Baroness in her glass-walled eyrie at the top of London's Royal Institution, of which she's the director. She believes that young human brains are so uniquely adaptable that they may easily get bent out of shape by frenetic virtual stimulation: 'What human beings do better than any other species is to learn. But it also means that whatever happens in the environment will leave its mark on your brain,' she argues. Greenfield and her fellow campaigners fear that we are creating generations of square-eyed youths who are dangerously dumb compared with their book-reading fore-bears. 'When you are reading a book, you read it and digest it. You can find yourself staring at a blank wall, thinking about the story and its implications,' she says. 'On-screen stories can militate against that. Children are likely to go for the most easily available stimulating things, such as speed, noise and so on, rather than digesting the text.'

The result, she fears, will be a nation of gullible Googlers who won't even know how to vote responsibly. 'I'm concerned about the effect of all this on attention spans and on our ability to reflect, to absorb information and use it to create abstract ideas independently. How would you put democracy on a screen?' she asks. 'Such abstract ideas develop quite late in children. On-screen, with search engines, the information is limitless and its apparent truth or falsehood is often hard to discern.' And then there is the great fear that has always haunted techno-sceptics . . . the prospect of computerised mass mind-control. Greenfield says we are on the threshold of a new era of 'invasive technologies', high-tech games that children can play by using direct links between their brains and computers, but which might ultimately end up being misused in wicked sci-fi ways. 'There is already something called the Play Attention helmet, which kids can use to manipulate a screen icon by thinking,' she cautions. 'In future, manufacturers may be able to use similar technology to manipulate what is happening in the mind.'

Not everyone is so worried. Fans of screen culture point out that, historically, new technologies often get scapegoated for society's ills. When for example that diabolic contrivance, the railway train, first appeared in Britain, it was blamed for an epidemic of new lifestyle diseases, including something called 'railway spine'. Steven Johnson, the American author of *Everything Bad Is Good For You: How Popular Culture Is Making Us Smarter*, argues that mass culture is in fact increasingly intellectually demanding. TV programmes have complex narratives, postmodern ambiguity and plot-lines that are far more challenging than the *Terry and June* sitcoms of old. 'Video games are a great teacher of fluid intelligence,' says Johnson. 'The second most popular PC game in the US in 2005 was *Civilization IV*, where you re-create human economic and technological history. Here you have 12-year-olds trying to figure out whether they should go for an agrarian capitalist society or a monarchy.' Indeed, screens may even be partly responsible for the Flynn Effect, discovered in the early 1980s by James Flynn, a professor at Otago University in New Zealand. He found that IQ scores around the world are rising at a rate of about three points a decade. One possible factor is that we have filled our greatly expanded leisure time with cognitively demanding amusements, such as games that force you to think on your feet.

Well, maybe, but who can ever know which side of the argument should hold sway? Perhaps they both contain truths. It is impossible to assess virtual life's precise effect on our children, because liberal ethics bar us from capturing large numbers of babies for use as lab rats, then spending decades subjecting them to the controlled-environment experiments that could provide an accurate scientific picture. In the real world the results of tests of screen-time on children are messed up by crucial variables such as the children's diet, social class, environment, home life and schools.

That leaves the poor old parents stuck in the middle, people such as Sue Eckstein, who is trying to strike a healthily enoughist balance for her kids. Ms Eckstein, an academic administrator, is partial to watching TV costume dramas over a couple of beers on Sunday nights, but tries to avoid the box on weekdays. 'Partly that's down to my work-ethic upbringing,' she says. Imposing her values on her children, 14-year-old Anna, and Sebastian, 11, feels like quite another moral dimension. The telly problem got serious when Sebastian fell out with mainstream education three years ago and went to the best local alternative, a school run under the Steiner approach, which ignores the National Curriculum and instead aims to nurture children through creativity. It strongly opposes letting children see TV for fear that it will fry their attention spans and expose them to insidious adverts. 'Some of the more, shall we say, extreme parents ban telly outright,' says Eckstein. 'But I think a balanced approach is better, so we just restrict it.'

Sebastian is a bright, elfin lad who, despite his precocious knowledge of Bond films, seems happy with the compromise. 'I know that television is quite bad for your brain, but some people at Steiner school seem to think it will *kill* you,' he says. 'One of my friends has hardly seen any in his life. Another can only watch a tiny screen once a week. I only really see two programmes a day, *Neighbours* and *Hollyoaks*. The rest of my life? Uh, I'm doing schoolwork,' he says with mock woe. 'At the weekend I'm allowed to watch *Top Gear*. And I love *Top Gear*.' Sue hopes her regime will forestall any mutinies. 'If you ban TV, it will only be much more attractive and my kids will watch it at friends' all the time. But we've resorted to subterfuge in the past: the television was 'broken' for about a year and they didn't miss it. They didn't seem to notice that we'd simply taken the plug out. Even now, the internet connection "breaks" from time to time.' There's payola, too, in the Eckstein household. 'If you make access to all that lovely electronic stuff hard, you have more opportunities for bribery. Sebastian had to sign a contract saying that if I allowed him to buy some inappropriate games console, then he would do ten minutes of reading to me each evening without any fuss.'

## Know *enough*

### Take a data diet

What's the optimum level of information that you need to thrive? Beyond that crucial point, getting more can just create mind-fug. One way to find your level of enoughness is to go on a radical data diet. You'll be in good company: even Bill Gates takes a think-week away from his computer twice each year.

As a rule of thumb, it's best to treat communications and infotainment warily – as habit-forming substances to be consumed only when they offer the potential to enhance life. It makes sense to treat adverts and marketing as particularly toxic: they are only designed to entertain in order to catch your attention and make you dissatisfied with the life that you already have. If you pare down your communications to the minimum, you can escape from the anxiety cycle that is fostered by excess communications. For example, watching too much news makes you worry . . . so you watch more news.

With a clearer head, you can start to decide what's helpful and what's just a hindrance. Holidays offer a great opportunity to try switching everything off and allowing your own mind to entertain you instead. But going into holiday blackout mode can require rigorous self-discipline. We all tend to tell our work colleagues that we should only be contacted 'in emergency' while on vacation. But around 60 per cent of us check our work e-mails while we are away. Are there really that many emergencies?

### Budget your time

Set daily time budgets for your consumption and stick to them. It's easier to do this nowadays, because you can break free from stations' schedules by accessing on-demand TV programmes and listen-again online radio. So there's no need to sit around waiting for the next interesting thing to come on. Try to download only as much infotainment as meets your rationing limits – and then be happy about the fact that you are deliberately choosing to miss things, because it means that you have a life.

### Rediscover space

Ensure that you start doing enjoyable, productive things to fill the time that your media diet opens up. It is like being a recovering substance addict. You need to keep occupied until you readjust. You can revive your data-addled brain by stimulating the growth of new neural networks, through learning or rediscovering a creative skill such as painting, cooking or playing an instrument. It's helpful to keep in mind the fact that your personal downtime is so incredibly precious that marketing companies and multinationals spend billions of pounds every year trying to take it away from you.

### Go for local news

The thirst for knowledge that can keep us glued to 24-hour global news channels is in fact a manifestation of our ancient human need to know all about the people immediately around us. Rolling news acts as an easy proxy for an activity that we often find increasingly alien: gossiping with our neighbours. But swapping goss with people in our locale can break the cycle that keeps us stuck indoors watching news channels. All that televised catastrophe makes us fearful of the world outside. So we have less to do with our neighbourhood and the people in it, because it feels potentially dangerous.

When local social networks wither, there often follows an

increase in local crime, because there are fewer people on the street who feel confident and connected enough to intervene when they see dodgy behaviour. There's also less chance of people joining in with community action to improve local amenities such as parks. Knowing the faces on your local streets, and being able to stop and chat, extends your sense of home security far beyond your front door. The stories you hear may be far spicier, too.

## E-tiquette

Mass-communications technology has proliferated so rapidly that we haven't had a chance to develop healthy protocols about when and how to use it. Now's the time to change that. To develop sustainable and rewarding relationships, it is always best to communicate in the most brain-friendly ways possible. Human contact fosters warmth and trust; distance and brevity breed contempt. So we should adopt a hierarchy of communications: face-to-face rather than e-mail; e-mail rather than mobile; mobile rather than text.

We should also be extremely wary of becoming e-bores. Is your mail, text or phone call really necessary? If you don't pollute other people with your communications, you can feel justified in ignoring others when they have nothing to offer. For example, why respond to emails if they are only being cc'd to you? Multi cc'ers cause data pollution. If the sender really wants to know your opinion, they will ask you again individually. They probably won't expect many replies, thanks to their subconscious understanding of the hitch-hiker rule: the more cars there are, the easier it is for the drivers to ignore the hitch-hiker.

Likewise, delete unread any e-mail sent with a red exclamation mark (I always do: I'm still alive). If the sender is so devoid of social skills that they think they can barge into the queue for your headspace just by wielding brightly coloured punctuation, then they have nothing useful to communicate.

## Limit interruption

It takes about four minutes to recover from an electronic interruption and regain your train of thought. So if you have 30 e-mails a day and look up 30 times, that's 120 minutes of recovery time. Try setting up your computer system to receive mail every 90 minutes. That way you don't get barraged by those tempting blips. If you're expecting something utterly urgent, you can always over-ride the system and check it yourself.

And remember: communication swallows lives. By the age of 75, most of us will have spent more than twelve and a half years' worth of 24-hour days watching television. Plus a year watching commercials. Surely some of that time could be better spent. There are many things in this info-crowded life that you can happily ignore. For example, the witty weblink you've been sent is bound to be viral marketing – the new junk mail. And do you actually need to read the mailshot that just landed on your doormat? Just green-bin it. If you have really won a million pounds, they'll get back to you.

## Recognise futility

As media formats, channels and programmes continue to prolif-erate, the money spent on producing them shrinks because they all have a smaller slice of audience and advertising revenue. But as the competition hots up, the hype on these 'brilliant, amazing, earth-shattering' programmes only gets greater. If you over-stimulate people's expectations in this way, it creates a hunger that remains unsatisfied. It encourages us to keep seeking the marvellous quality entertainment we've been led to believe exists somewhere out there. We need to recognise channel-flipping for what it is – a time-sucking form of futility-chasing.

Likewise, the sheer physical impossibility of keeping up with electronic media should liberate us from even trying. For example, the latest generation of iPod competitors comes with a storage capacity of 16,000 songs. That's the equivalent of 1,300 albums. If each song lasts 3 mins 30 secs, that's 56,000 minutes – which is 933 hours, which is 38 days of your life without sleep. That's just to listen to them. You have to upload the lot, too.

# 2 | ENOUGH Food (a key to our problem)

*They are as sick that surfeit with too much as*
*they that starve with nothing.*
Shakespeare, *The Merchant of Venice*

**M**artin Yeomans glances around at our fellow lunchers, leans across the table and says confidentially: 'There are some *awfully* big people round here.' A trifle rude perhaps – particularly from such a self-effacing academic – but frankly I am surprised that he is surprised. Yeomans is, after all, one of Britain's leading experts in the psychology of appetite. And we are, after all, sitting in the middle of a vast all-you-can-eat restaurant. I'd arranged this visit to our local Wokmania, one of a fast-growing chain of cheap'n'easy face-crammers, after encountering an old pal and his new girlfriend in a pub. I was keen to catch up with Andy and get to know his partner, but they seemed reluctant to talk. It turned out that they were almost physically incapable of speech. The pair were gullet-full, having chomped through Wokmania's £11.90 Chinese-based buffet for the maximum allowed time of two hours. 'It was the free ice-cream machine at the end,' Andy gasped sweatily, 'I went back eight times.' This I had to see.

All-you-can-eat deals are the latest American-inspired food phenomenon to proliferate on Britain's high streets.

A Thai restaurant in my neighbourhood advertises its lunch deal as 'Eat all you can' – not 'like', or 'want', but *can*. You don't need to say 'supersize me' – you can jolly well supersize yourself. As the comedian Alexei Sayle recently wrote, 'Many novelists struggle to find a metaphor that typifies their age. For Saint-Exupery it was the aeroplane; for J.G. Ballard it is the M40 Westway; for me it is the all-you-can-eat buffet.' Wokmania has taken the philosophy to heart: the eight-strong Chinese chain (with its Indian and Italian counterparts, Spicemania and Pizzamania) doesn't do anything else: just push through the plush glass doors, load up at the hot-food counter and start chowing. While you graze, you can gaze at one of the wall-mounted widescreens playing continuous music videos.

I'd persuaded Yeomans to catch the bus down from nearby Sussex University to discuss the havoc our calorie-crammed world is wreaking on our brains and bellies. What better meeting-place, I thought, than Brighton's biggest buffet. But Yeomans is a little nervous: 'It's difficult to talk about this while I can see that guy sitting behind you,' he says. My head swivels in a most unsubtle manner. Staring back at me is an obese man in a red T-shirt, sitting before a towering plate of food. He's pouring a large glass of cola into his face. It's only Tuesday lunchtime, but the place is crowded. On Saturday nights the action is belly to belly. Yeomans is not surprised at the restaurant's popularity. According to his theories, the bumper buffet should offer an earthly paradise for our ancient instincts.

Our appetite is always going to tell us that food is fearfully scarce, and historically it's been right, he says: 'First World War British soldiers were on average only 5 feet 5 inches tall, for example. They had grown up being malnour-ished. Fifty per cent of their parents' income had gone on food, and the families still did not get enough to nourish them.' Yeomans is formulating a theory that says food was the reason we evolved our super-sized social brains in the first place. 'It's a very difficult job to perform, finding food, particularly for hominids. So our ancestors had to be very bright,' he says.

What was bright back then might not look so clever now. Yeomans explains that humans are born with hardly any pre-set taste preferences. But we don't remain blank slates for long: our appetites are rapidly moulded by the flavours around us. Nowadays that can mean trouble because our taste-tastic culture radically amplifies our inbuilt urge to consume food whenever it appears before us. 'Experiments show that babies' only clear taste preference is for sweet tastes,' he says. 'The rest is learnt. And we are very adaptable. Every time you get a new taste experience, your appetite goes up. You will quickly get to enjoy tastes that You didn't originally like. Even rats won't do that. If you consume something that affects your brain positively, you're going to start liking it. This is why initially repulsive, bitter tastes such as alcohol become attractive. You quickly learn that high-fat food is positive because it's got lots of energy. So the easiest way to get food to entice the human brain is to pack in energy and provide a wide spectrum of tastes. The food industry now does both of these things, but it didn't start doing this intentionally – it's just discovered over time what's most popular. So in the modern world, you are surrounded by things that spark off your hunger associations – the lunch bells are ringing all the time.'

We wander to the buffet bar for some starters. I seldom eat more than a sandwich at lunchtimes. I'm also a vegetarian, and the vast majority of the dishes are chicken or beef. Nevertheless, this glutinous array of hot, sweet-smelling savouries tugs at my taste centres. Suddenly I'm hungry. I'm exceedingly hungry. My hands want to pile far more on to my plate than I'd planned. Yeomans is thinking aloud as we move along the dishes. 'Chips? Vegetable samosas? It's not exactly all Chinese, but it's all very energy-dense, using cheaply available ingredients.' He takes a few bites and nods. 'Not bad. I'm quite surprised. I wouldn't bring my kids here, though. There is no definition of what constitutes a healthy portion of food.'

Yeomans's experiments indicate that, without pre-set portions, we have no natural idea of when to stop eating. 'Our appetite system is there to tell us that we are desperately short of food. We spend our lives living in anticipation of hunger and eating to stave it off,' he says. 'We've done tests with volunteers eating pasta where we've repeatedly switched their plates and replenished them, so that they lose track of how much they're eating. In fact, it's a bit like this buffet. One chap happily polished off two kilograms of pasta at one sitting.'

Given the purpose of our lunch, we're both on our best eating behaviour and restricting ourselves to one plate of starters, one plateful of main course dishes . . . and that's it, even though there's always the sore temptation to stuff ourselves into bloated stupefaction. So we rejoin the food queue for our second and final trip: I stick to just plain rice and vegetable dishes – I've another interview to do in the afternoon, so need some wits about me. Yeomans adds the sweet-and-sour calamari to his other main courses. 'I can't believe this won't be rubbery,' he says. The guy shovelling meat on to his plate just ahead of us is the most mountainous hominid I have ever encountered. He's got the word 'Security' on the back of his jacket. Yeomans catches my wide-eyed gaze.

Safely back at our table, he asks, 'But what's wrong, in terms of evolutionary reproduction, in being obese? Obesity doesn't stop people from having children. There has never before been any evolutionary pressure against it. In most primitive societies, the only person who can afford to be overweight is the squire or the chief – the most wealthy and powerful person in their group.'

Well indeed. Time was when you had to be regal, or papal at least, to munch yourself into an early grave. For example, King Henry I died of a surfeit of lampreys, his favourite dish, near Rouen in France in 1135. It's an odd fish, the lamprey – unlike others, the eel-like parasite has no scales, jaws, gill covers or bony skeleton. It sounds like an easy eat, but its flesh is fatty, hard to digest and a perilous bingeing choice for an ailing monarch such as Henry. By tradition, the city of Gloucester still presents the reigning monarch with a rich lamprey pie on important royal occasions – most recently the Queen's jubilee. As a favour-currying gift, it must rank alongside offering new American presidents an open-topped limo ride through Dallas.

A century and a half after Henry's demise, it was a surfeit of proper eels that finished off Pope Martin IV. The French pontiff's insatiable appetite for Lake Bolsena eels, marinated in local white wine and then roasted, earned him and his surfeit a place in Purgatory in Dante's epic

53

poem, *The Divine Comedy*. More recently, an unwise excess of fish almost did for King George VI during the First World War battle of Jutland. Documents released from the Public Record Office reveal that poor George was taken ill after a 'surfeit of soused herring' during the famous sea battle, though thankfully he still managed to man his gun turret.

But as the twentieth century progressed and food became cheaper, the regal sport of binge-eating became steadily democratised, to the point where it wrote off the white-trash king of rock'n'roll, Elvis Presley. The 25-stone Elvis ate himself to death by midnight-snacking on a pair of 42,000-calorie baguettes containing a jar of strawberry jam, a jar of peanut butter and a pound of crisp-fried bacon. The baguettes were followed by up to five hamburgers and five fried peanut butter and mashed banana sandwiches – at which point Presley suffered, in a coroner's words, 'a terminal event on the commode'.

Now we're all at it. A quarter of European, North American and Australian adults are obese and another third are overweight. The majority of Westerners will, it is predicted, be overweight or obese in the next 20 years. There are already more obese people in the world than starving ones. Western culture has become like the four world-weary, middle-aged men in the 1973 movie *La Grande Bouffe*, who gather at a villa one weekend and chew themselves to death in a frenzy of excess. So that's us, chomping our way into an epidemic of fatalities from diabetes, high blood pressure, heart disease, stroke, asthma, osteoarthritis, gall-bladder disease and cancer – millions of people condemned to trun-cated, waddling existences merely through eating more than

54

they need. It's death by appetite, and it feels like the sort of sharp punitive slap that might be delivered by a disgruntled deity with a mean line in poetic justice.

Step forward the Old Testament God who, as the Book of Numbers explains, got into a right biblical fury over the Israelites' nagging food demands. His chosen people had just absconded *en masse* from bondage in Egypt and were holed up, under a kind of holy witness protection programme, somewhere in the desert near Mount Sinai. Jehovah was generously providing daily bread from heaven. But the Israelites were bored with their manna-only diet. It was fine . . . for a while. But it tasted like nothing and stuck to the roofs of their mouths. So they started chivvying Moses. 'If He can do bread, then He could do meat,' they said. 'Go on. Ask Him.' God heard his messenger's lamentations, then decreed: 'The Lord will give you meat and you shall eat. You shall eat not one day, not two, not even five days or ten or twenty, but a whole month, until it comes out of your nostrils and becomes loathsome for you.' And down came the quails. Falling from the sky in thousands. In millions. The Israelites' desire for meat was met with so much precipitated protein that it drove them mad with gluttony. Then they contracted a hideous surfeit-related disease, from which the greediest died agonising deaths.

Be careful what you wish for. From the earliest days of civilisation, our hungry ancestors indulged in impossible dreams of enjoying exactly the sort of conditions we have today – a life of continuous, conspicuous, affordable plenty. Their famine-struck fantasies obsessed about one marvellous abundance above all: food – great flowing piles of it, fresh, filling and forever at hand. Ancient Greek mythology brought us the miraculous Cornucopia, the horn of the goat that suckled Zeus, which broke off and filled itself with whatever comestibles its owner desired. Medieval peasants tantalised each other by swapping protein-packed stories of the mythical land of Cockaigne, where turkeys flew ready-roasted, pies walked into your mouth, rivers ran with wine and inhabitants lay muttering, 'Uhhh, I'm full.' The early twentieth century offered another version, in 'Big Rock Candy Mountain', the American hobo anthem: 'There's a lake of stew / And of whiskey too / And you can paddle all around it in a big canoe.'

But although our forebears' daydreams drew ravening pictures of abundance, they were also savvy enough to view this prospect with caution. The medieval European folktale of the little porridge pot tells how a starving family is given a magic pot by a mysterious visitor and told that it would fill with porridge whenever they gave the secret command. The pot would stop only when given a second secret command word. One day the daughter went out, leaving her mother behind with the pot. When the mother got hungry she commanded the pot to start producing. She ate her porridge, but then realised that the pot was still pouring. She tried to stop it, but had forgotten her password. The old woman and the entire village began to drown beneath a sticky tsunami that flooded all the houses until finally it reached a hovel that the daughter was visiting. On the little girl's command, the pot stopped, but not until the whole village was so swamped that the survivors had to eat their way out through the goo. It's a parable for our times: we must learn to say 'stop' to our magic pot.

The problem lies deep in our nature. Knowing when to

start, but not when to stop, is one of humankind's defining characteristics – even though we are loath to acknowledge it. The very name we choose to call ourselves betrays how deeply in denial we are. Around 250 years ago, a flower-collecting Swedish physician called Carolus Linnaeus sparked a debate over what scientific Latin title we should choose to describe ourselves. Linnaeus had devised the species-labelling system of taxonomy that we still use today, in which all the world's plants, animals, fungi and bacteria can be logically named and grouped according to their place in the world and their defining characteristics. But what about us? What could be our most notable trait? High-minded scientists argued that we should describe ourselves as *homo rationalus* (rational man); others of a more puckish disposition suggested *homo ludens* (playful man), while some with a practical bent posited *homo fabricans* (tool-using man). But Linnaeus settled on *homo sapiens* – 'wise or thinking man'. What an impressively warm, reflective, even metrosexual name. No wonder we've been happy to stick with it.

But really. Our species hardly evolved by pondering wise thoughts. What characterises us most is our capacity to want, to desire, to covet, to yearn for and generally lust after. We want to know what lies over the hill, we want to see it, and then to possess it, along with everything that lies above and below the ground . . . and, after that, we want to know what lies over the next hill. This explains why it only took us less than 60,000 years to colonise most of planet Earth. And that's why we should really call ourselves *homo expetens* – or 'wanting man'. The basic desire-driven architecture of our brains evolved during the late Pleistocene era, between 130,000 and 200,000 years ago. Our instincts were moulded by the voracious behaviour of small groups of hard-pressed hunter-gatherers who gradually turned into early farmers, fretfully watching as their crops failed with appalling frequency. Life was extremely tough. As recently as 1321, one in five English people is thought to have died of famine. More than 150 famines were recorded before 1620, and cannibalism was reported in England in 1563.

The covetous basic instincts of *homo expetens* ensured that some of our forebears made it through all the ice ages and the long lean years. In rare times of plenty, our ancestors gorged themselves to bulk up for the thin days ahead. They never evolved to say, 'Enough food.' If they had, we might very well not be here. But the instincts that were vital to surviving the next famine are now making it hard for us to leap the next evolutionary hurdle. For if you offer a voracious omnivore the chance to create its ideal environment, it will leap head-first into an all-you-can-eat world of sugar and fat – and wallow there until the food pokes out of its nostrils. It's porn on a plate. Instead we should be fostering an enough-food culture that's designed to defuse our deeply imprinted munching mechanisms.

We should now know enough about our ingestive instincts to treat them with extreme caution. In the 1990s scientists discovered why eating is such a compelling pleasure: when we scoff something sweet or fatty, the brain rewards itself with heroin-like chemicals called endogenous opioids. This means that snacks such as sweet biscuits act on the same pleasure centres that respond to addictive drugs. More recent studies show that the mere thought of yummy ice cream can set off the same pleasure centres in healthy people as photos of crack pipes do for free-basing addicts. We also get a druggy kick from physically stuffing our stomachs, according to an experiment that electronically stimulated the vagus nerves in overweight people. The vagus is a phone-line from our bellies to our heads that tells the primitive lower brain when our guts are brim-full. When it was artificially activated, junkie-type highs were seen in the volunteers' minds.

So we like food. A lot. And our brains don't let us forget it – thanks again to our ancestors. The secret of hunter-gathering is being able to find all the edibles faster than the next guy. The best practitioners survived to pass on their genes, so we have inherited gastrophile minds that constantly ruminate about where we've eaten, what we've eaten, how it tasted and how we might get it again. Then our reward centres badger us to repeat the experience. All this makes it extremely hard for many of us to diet. Studies show that it takes four months of complete abstinence for us to start losing our cravings for forbidden fattening foods.

There's also a physical obstacle to weight-loss: once we've put on fat, the podge tends to stay put because our bodies have learnt to act like calorie-hoarding hamster cheeks. The human frame contains around ten times more fat-storing cells in relation to its body mass than most animals (polar bears are similarly fat-rich). Our famine-resistant frames have strong mechanisms to stop weight loss, but weak systems for preventing weight gain. If you manage to lose 10 per cent of your weight, your body starts to think there's an emergency. So it burns less fuel by slowing your metabolism and dropping your temperature. This plateau effect kicks in after around eight weeks of dieting. So the weight-loss stops, morale slumps, and the cravings remain.

Dieting also makes our metabolisms rebound badly. An analysis of 31 long-term clinical studies found that diets don't work in the long run. Within five years about two-thirds of dieters put back the weight they lost – and more. It concluded that most of them would have been better off not dieting at all. Their weight would be pretty much the same and their bodies would not have suffered wear and tear from yo-yoing. This backfire effect is worst among teenagers: people who start habitually dieting young tend to be significantly heavier after five years than teens who never dieted. The young starvers tend to skip breakfast, then binge-eat later in the day, just as their primitive brains would prime them to do. Thus they set the pattern for a lifetime. All these physical responses are a fantastic survival strategy for the Pleistocene age, but a cruel trick in the twenty-first century.

It's not the meanest trick of all, though. Mother Nature seems to have designed us to operate as perpetual dissatisfaction machines. A study in the *Journal of Neuroscience* says that mammal brains appear to be built with fewer mechanisms for feeling pleasure than they do for suffering pangs of desire. The Michigan University experiments report that our sensations of wanting and liking are run by two separate 'hedonic hotspots' – circuits buried deep in the brain. The circuit for wanting appears to have around 30 per cent more influence on our behaviour than the circuit for liking. This means that our hard-wiring may condemn us to want to keep spinning that hamster wheel for ever, no matter how much physical pleasure we get. People whose 'want' circuits run way ahead of their 'like' circuits may suffer a wide range of addiction-type problems. But that's not only a problem for the badly wired. We have created an environment that persistently fires up everybody's want circuits with the tantalising prospect of more – and especially of more food.

This is where we throw Pavlov's dog on to our heap of difficulties. Our desire-heavy reward systems aren't only automatic. They can be intensified by conditioning. Pavlov famously rang a bell every time his dog ate its meal. After a while, the dog would salivate whenever a bell rang, creating a breakthrough for behavioural psychology (and a sticky doormat). Our want-food instincts have likewise been conditioned into permanent salivation by a perpetual peal of ads and marketing. Normal people's brains fill with reward chemicals at the mere sight of it all. And this visually stimulated pleasure response is stronger than the one we get from eating food itself, claims Dr Nora Volkow, the director of the US National Institute of Drug Abuse. This is why junk-food marketing has such a strong hold on people, she says: 'It is an old mechanism by which nature ensures that we actually consume food when food is available. We never know when food is going to be available. Well, now we do because we have convenience stores. But when we were evolving we didn't, and when there was food accessible you had to eat it. Unfortunately, we really have created a system where we are flooded with information about food.'

It's like continually dining out with the infamous Père Gourier, a wealthy eighteenth-century French landowner with a gargantuan appetite who murdered people for fun by persuading them to feast with him on vast, rich dishes until they died from over-indulgence. Each of *le Diable Gourmand's* victims was taken to gorge every evening at the best restaurants in Paris. The *maîtres d'hôtel* knew perfectly well what Père Gourier was up go, but legally they could do nothing to stop him. He would even boast of his exploits. When a waiter enquired after a recent dining companion, Gourier replied: 'I buried him this morning. He was nothing. I got him in less than two months.' Gourier's kill rate averaged one victim a year over an eight-year reign of dinner-table terror. The success of his homicidal tactics highlights another of our central problems with food: our bodies simply don't know when to stop eating. We have instead to rely on external cues, such as how much the other people at our table are putting into their faces. So in our consume-more society, it is all too easy to get swept along with the crowd. Even without the wiles of an evil French epicure to lead us on, we tend to increase or decrease our food intake by more than a fifth to copy what our fellow diners eat, says Professor Brian Wansink, who directs Cornell University's Food and Brand Lab.

Wansink neatly exposed our food-cue problem through his own bit of saucy subterfuge – a trick called the bottomless-soup-bowl experiment. He and his team crafted a bowl that could secretly be replenished through a tube attached to its base and which, like the magical porridge pot, could never be drained. He used it to discover what sort of stimuli would make people cease eating: visual cues or a sensation of fullness. While people using normal soup bowls ate about nine ounces, those spooning from the bottomless bowls consumed on average around 15 ounces. Some ate more than 32 ounces and didn't stop until told that the 20-minute experiment had ended. When asked to estimate how many calories they had consumed, the bottomless soup-bowlers were convinced that they had eaten the same as people with ordinary soup bowls – on average about 113 calories fewer than they actually had. Other studies have shown that we make more than 200 food decisions a day, many of them determined by rough estimates based on misleading visual clues from the world around us. Bigger plates, larger spoons, deeper packets – as well as food-crazed companions – all make us eat more.

*Le Diable Gourmand's* homicidal hospitality continued unabated until he met his match in dining-guest number nine, a man named Ameline, who was said to have hollow legs – and who was also the second assistant to the government's public executioner. For two years the pair fought their pitched battle with knife, fork and tablespoon across the finest tablecloths of Paris. Ameline, knowing that Gourier could not be prosecuted for the deaths, had probably decided to beat him at his own game. He would disappear for two or three days at a time under cover of 'travelling on public duties', when in fact he was purging his body with castor oil and other laxatives. He never seemed to put on a pound. In frustration, Père Gourier began to feed him the richest and heaviest dishes known to Gallic cuisine, food that even the diabolic diner had difficulty digesting. The end came one night in the Cadran Bleu, the most expensive restaurant in the city. Ameline was scoffing his 15th sirloin steak when Gourier, struggling one steak behind, turned pale, gasped and slumped forwards into his plate, dead.

Dead, but not gone. Modern life is suffused with the ghost of Gourier, prodding our ancient inclinations to eat evermore with a devil's brew of *amuse-bouches* that manifest themselves as ads, marketing, convenience, packaging, junk, cookery shows, sweets, snacks, all-you-can-eats and – in the latest Gourier guise – luxury 'finest' foods (which marketing people call the 'treat sector') that are just the same old superfats and supersugars squeezed into posh frocks. But all is not lost. There are ways in which we can exorcise many of these instinct-tickling incubi – through practising enoughism.

Conventional commercial diet plans are fantastically successful in one respect – they keep selling chart-topping books. But if a single recipe-based diet plan really worked in a sustainable way, there would be no need for any more new books. Modern plans offer quick-fix, short-term solutions: the gimmicky cabbage-only, no-carbs types of regime that promise rapid results so that dieters can get back to 'normal' life – the life that put the weight on in the first place. But food-reducing diets founder on one basic problem: they encourage people to fixate about food.

This only exacerbates what our bodies are already doing to us. When our calorie intakes drop significantly, our famine-panicked circuits send our minds chemical alerts telling them to concentrate on one essential task: go and find food, no matter what the cost. Lab tests by Uppsala University scientists show that falling food consumption fires up the brain's mesolimbic dopamine system, one of our most important circuits for reward-related motivation.

Again, it's an area stimulated by heroin and cocaine, as well as physical pleasure. It can drive us to seek sex, drugs and – in times of hunger – sausage rolls. So rather than obsessing about food all the time, we need to try focusing our minds on anything but.

Enoughism doesn't offer a food-focused strategy. Nor does it make promises in the tradition of: 'This will halve your bodyweight in nanoseconds.' It involves picking up a few scientifically based long-term life habits that help to block, counter or evade the flood of food stimuli that surrounds us. Enoughism involves enjoying a long-term healthy relationship with one's appetite. There are no faddy regimes, no celebrities, no daily plans and no banned foods.

It was Wally, a former Second World War Lancaster bomber crewman, who alerted me to the idea that habits can determine how you eat. Wally and I worked together in a dreadful old paper factory, making those little rolls that go in cash tills to produce the receipts. This was my first full-time job and, most probably, Wally's last. He was thin and wiry, sharp as a tack and maniacally sprightly – and far beyond the horizons of retirement age. As well as enlivening our dull days with his tales of nights in enemy skies at 20,000 feet, Wally had another party trick – he could tell the time just by his stomach. His hours turned on a wheel of strictly set mealtimes. The regime had been instilled in him during his RAF days and he had stuck with it ever since. 'I never feel hungry unless it's 15 minutes before a meal,' he'd boast.

I was whippety thin, too, in those factory days. But when I hit my late twenties, it became sadly apparent that I'd inherited my father's genetic disposition for being pot-bellied (as well as being short, dammit) in the full bloom of adulthood. How demoralising. And how dangerous.

Dad had collapsed on a railway station platform at the age of 54, the victim of a massive and unexpected heart attack. He was pronounced dead on arrival at a nearby London hospital. Dad worked on national newspapers. He commuted from Brighton to London. He was overweight. And he smoked. The warnings were clear. Determined never to repeat his mistakes, I have ended up working as a journalist on national newspapers. Oops. And I commute from Brighton to London. I have at least given up the smoking and cut my commuting days.

The weight remains a trial. My body will always, at best, be in a perpetual state of pre-porcine preparedness, ready to bulk out at a moment's notice. And, in all likelihood, my ticker won't be able to take it. Like many of us, I'm a walking metabolic time bomb. But I stave off the weight, not through a dreary succession of yo-yo diets, but with a Wally-like regime of set habits that has the side-effect of bolstering an enoughist approach to life. I always have a light breakfast to start the day (for the past couple of years it's been a chopped frozen banana, nuts and another fruit dropped into a blender); lunch is at 1.30 p.m. and dinner is around 8 p.m. Ploddingly predictable. My stomach now knows precisely when to pang, which enables me to say: 'Get behind me, snacking.' The mechanism behind this is explained, along with nine other strategies, below.

## Eat *enough*

### Let savouring be your saviour

Savouring is at the heart of the art of enoughness. Where food is concerned, it offers a proven way to lower your calorie intake and make you feel replete for longer. Trouble is, savouring contradicts the way our culture encourages us to live. We often feel we don't have time to pause to taste our food. Instead it ricochets past our larynxes. Twenty years ago, we spent on average 33 minutes over our evening meals, chewing and chatting with loved ones. Now that time has shrunk to a breathless 14 minutes and 27 seconds. Meals get bolted as we refuel ourselves mindlessly over desks, at railway stations, in front of the telly, while reading, texting or talking on the phone. A survey in 2006 found that fewer than 20 per cent of Britons regularly give their plates their full attention.

But eating while harried or preoccupied does us no good. Our natural response to stress is good old fight or flight, rather than fill-your-face. The body sends blood to our muscles so that we're ready for action, rather than to the stomach in preparation for digestion. It's hardly a recipe for satisfaction. A Japanese study of 4,700 volunteers found that fast eaters weigh on average 7 kilos more than slow chewers. The researchers believe that eating too fast generates excessive insulin and may increase one's risk of diabetes. Being preoccupied or stressed while eating also makes us overeat, particularly if we're trying to stick to a diet, according to the journal *Appetite*. Your mind fails to experience the full spectrum of pleasure that it can obtain from consuming food. The 'I've eaten loads, thank you' message fails to get sent from brain to body, and snacky pangs soon return. The effect is particularly strong with children who eat in front of the telly.

The idea that calm eating might cut calories was first suggested more than 30 years ago. It had become considered little more than a folk-tale, but in 2006 Kathleen Melanson, a professor of nutrition at Rhode Island University, tested it scientifically. She asked 30 women students to make two visits to her lab. Each time they were given a large plate of pasta and told to eat as much as they wanted. When they were told to eat quickly, they consumed 646 calories in nine minutes, but when they were encouraged to pause between bites and chew each mouthful 15 to 20 times, they ate just 579 calories in 29 minutes. When the women ate mindfully, they also said they enjoyed their food more, felt fuller at the end of the meal and still felt fuller an hour afterwards.

'Satiety signals clearly need time to develop,' Melanson says. Other research indicates that it takes 20 minutes for your brain to realise that your stomach is full, so taking time to chew enables your mind to keep up with your golloping. Having more chance to glug water with meals may also help. The volunteers in Melanson's trial were given jugs and glasses with their meal, and when eating slowly they had considerably more time to drink it – and to notice that they were getting thirsty, too. The water might have enhanced their sense of fullness. As well as lifting your water glass, Melanson advises: 'Put down the fork between bites and take time to have a conversation and linger over the meal.'

It can be a meditational experience, dedicating leisured concentration to the textures, tastes and contrasts of what you are eating. A houmous salad sandwich becomes a small adventure – slowly sensing the crunch of the crust, the squadge

68

of the bread, the high-toned tang of houmous slicing against the cucumber's sharpness. And what does garlic actually taste like, apart from, uh, garlicky?

## Dine only in small restaurants
Aside from the ambience, the intimacy and the fact that you're likely to be fed by people who care about their business, there's another good reason to dine in small eateries rather than cavernous chains – you may well consume less. Studies on children indicate that we are primed to stuff ourselves when in crowded environments.

The research found that children eat more, faster and for longer when they are in larger groups. They also spend less time socialising. Why? The sense of urgency and unsociability is interesting – it seems that humans may have a primitive group-feasting response. Imagine: the hunters have at last scored a kill and the spoils are being shared among the ravening tribe – so your survival circuits tell you to pitch in for all you can eat before everyone else hogs it. There's no time for pleasantries. The researchers conclude that the sight and sound of many other humans eating seems to over-ride the brain's normal signals of satiety. It's small wonder that fast-food chains are so keen to encourage children's parties. And there's little doubt that the effect works on grown-ups, too.

## Avoid high-variety meals
Variety is one of the great promises of today's food culture. After all, you wouldn't want to get *bored* while nourishing your-self. The food options on supermarket shelves have increased exponentially in past decades, particularly where fat-rich, sugary, high-novelty, low-nutrition items are concerned. And

while it is true that a spectrum of healthy foods is good for the body, when they are packed into the same meal it often causes over-consumption.

Studies of human eating show that our appetite is partially governed by a mechanism called sensory-specific satiety (SSS). Our bodies get to feel fuller quicker if they are eating only one food. You know how it is, you've had a plate-load of meat and potatoes, and think you would burst if you had just one more fork-full . . . but then there's pudding, and you can happily sink a bowlful of that. Somehow you've magically developed a second stomach. It is not only the taste of food that influences SSS. Variety in colour and shape also persuades us to eat more than we intended. People consume more sandwiches when offered three different fillings and more pasta when it comes in a variety of shapes.

These mechanisms were crucial in our hunter-gatherer days, when a pick'n'mix approach was essential for satisfying the full spectrum of our nutritional needs. Now we must act to prevent this urge causing death by novelty. You could take this non-variety thing too far, of course, and end up like the notorious vanished aristocrat, Lord Lucan, who ate lamb chops for lunch every day of his adult life (fried in winter, grilled in summer). But cooking simple, wholesome meals, packing a modest lunch, or putting only two foods on your buffet plate all offer easy ways to control this instinct to over-consume.

**Keep good company**
We've all had those 'Oh, well then I won't have the pudding either' moments in restaurants with pals. (As well as the ones that go: 'Well, if you're having afters, I'll have a gâteau as well.') Self-discipline can require two people, as Gourier knew so well.

Our willpower and sense of portion proportion are determined largely by the appetites of the people we eat with. So it's best to share table space with abstemious types, whenever possible.

## Make mealtimes sacred

Regular mealtimes, as old Wally had learnt, can help to train your brain out of its environmentally boosted tendency to think about food all day. Such self-discipline also involves making enoughist decisions about the amount of work, information, stuff and hurry you take on, because you have to build three sacred spaces into the day for breakfast, lunch and dinner. These should be dedicated solely to eating thoughtfully and slowly – and ideally in good company.

The social aspect may be particularly beneficial for adolescents. Those who regularly eat with their families have healthier weight levels. Research suggests that the mindful ritual of shared meals may help to ease the angst of fast-paced teenage life and reduce the urge for teens to take refuge in comfort calories.

Fixed mealtimes have other cultural benefits. A comparison by Nottingham University nutritionists of the way that English and French people consume food confirms that the stereo-types tend to be true. The French traditionally cook from basic ingredients, eat at set times in convivial groups and seldom snack. Common English habits involve microwaving meals, eating hurriedly alone and grazing all day. This may well explain the significantly different obesity levels between the two nations.

Now even the French way is under attack from the world of more-more. France's government is having to confront a sudden jump in youth obesity caused by the appearance of fast-food chains and convenience foods. Health warnings are being put on junk food, although this attempt to counter consumerism may well prove merely Canute-like. Western calorie culture continues to spread ever onwards, bringing the ghost of Gourier back to his homeland. If our neighbours lose their cultural safeguards, they will have to learn as individuals to say 'suffisant'.

## Get more daylight

Seasonal affective disorder (the neatly named SAD) is the extreme end of a phenomenon that affects us all in winter, or when we spend our daylight hours indoors in front of computers. When our lives are short of natural sunlight, our bodies prepare for a season of bleak foraging by going into hibernation-lite mode. Levels of the feelgood neurotransmitter serotonin drop, hunger levels rise and activity rates fall. Most people with SAD report that they crave carbohydrates, eat more and gain weight. American doctors call this phenomenon 'blizzard bloat'. Getting into the open air to shine up your brain's light-sensitive pineal gland with a dose of full sunlight is the answer – though it will require you to cut the time you spend in artificially illuminated offices, at least by stepping outside at lunchtimes to enjoy your food.

## Sleep tight, sleep light

Tiredness, wakeful nights and poor-quality sleep knock our appetite hormones out of kilter. A Chicago University study that cut 12 young men's nightly sleep down to just four hours found that their levels of ghrelin, a hormone that increases appetite, rose by 28 per cent after only two days. At the same time, their levels of leptin, a hormone which tells the brain that the belly is full, dropped by 18 per cent. The men also said that the sleeplessness made them crave high-carb foods.

Another study, which compared the sleeping patterns and hormone levels of 1,024 people, found that those who slept an average five hours or less a night had 15 per cent more ghrelin than people who slept for eight hours, and 15 per cent less leptin. These hormonal changes may be the result of another old survival instinct. Most animals skip sleep only if they need more time to find food.

It doesn't take much additional shut-eye to repair the damage. Research in the *Archives of Internal Medicine* shows that getting an extra 20 minutes of sleep is linked to being slimmer. But that will again mean making enoughist life decisions about working fewer hours or watching less TV. There's another practical reason why less sleep equals more fat: red-eyed drowsies are far less likely to cook for themselves. They're too tired to bother, and instead stodge out on fast food.

## Change your kitchen

Is your kitchen too cosy? Low lighting encourages us to overeat, because it makes us too relaxed. Making the kitchen the hub of the house can also cause problems because one of the main stimulants to overeating is the sight and smell of food. The more time you spend in the kitchen – socialising or working at the kitchen table – the more likely you are to overeat. If you can't bear to decamp from the kitchen, you can at least Wendy-House the utensils. It's a simple but highly effective ruse. Restaurant studies show that we consume significantly more when given big portions. Just swapping your kitchenware for smaller crockery and cutlery can fool your brain into believing that you are eating more than you are.

## Eat in quiet little places

Humans' nervous systems are wired to respond to loud noise with a faster heartbeat and higher blood pressure so they are physically prepared to flee from danger. But in clangingly loud trendy restaurants, decibel-battered diners respond by eating faster (thus eating more) and drinking more alcohol. Restaurateurs love this because it speeds their tables' turnaround time.

## The magic glasses trick

If you want to improve your balance between calorie-laden booze and healthy hydration, take a look at your glassware. When imbibing healthy liquids such as water or fruit juice, pour it into short, wide tumblers. And when drinking alcohol, use tall, narrow glasses. It's an optical illusion: a Cornell University analysis of drinking habits in the *British Medical Journal* found that people pour more liquid into tumblers, thinking that tall glasses hold more. But it's not true.

# 3 | ENOUGH Stuff

*There are only two tragedies in life: one is not getting what one wants, and the other is getting it.*
Oscar Wilde

Like it or not, a gleaming red Ferrari is a guaranteed ooh-gosh sight. A pair parked together is a feast for any fan of road-sculpture. So are three, and maybe even ten. But somewhere along the line, the expensive aura starts to evaporate. When you get to twenty, ranked like taxis opposite rows of Aston Martins, with just as many Rolls-Royces and Bentleys stacked behind them, the cars lose their costly cachet. I'm in a high-security storage block somewhere in West London, looking at all these icons of success sitting forlornly in rows of rarely used metal. They hardly ever see the road. But they don't get to gather dust either – because the staff in this giant lock-up are paid to polish them every week. Workers also run the engines once a fortnight so that they don't seize up, and roll the cars back and forth to prevent their tyres (at around £1,000 a set) developing flat-spots.

Here is the answer to the vexed question of what to do next after you've achieved that lifelong dream of joining the Ferrari league, of owning a rocket-fast motor that makes schoolboys point and supermodels squeal. Obviously you

75

could try driving the thing as regular transport. Hmm, well it's a tippy-toe experience, frying the clutch as you judder round town in first gear, keeping a wary eye on your paint-work amid all the careless drivers in their cheaper machines. Out on the open road, if you can find any open road, your driver's licence quivers in the shadow of speed-cameras and radar traps. And if you fancy parking up for a spot of shopping, your shiny machine is a magnet for youths wield-ing keys, coins and Stanley knives. Better just hide it away. And pay to leave it there. The fear that afflicts people who own supercars translates into profit for luxury vehicle stor-age companies. Colin McCoy, the boss of the storage depot, shrugs at the dog-in-a-manger display outside his tiny office: 'I don't know why some people have them,' he says. 'One bloke with a £100,000 Ferrari just turns up, takes the car round the block and comes back. Others just sit in them, smell the leather and listen to the stereo.'

Cars that you don't drive are just one high-end example of all the other items that we strive for, work for, yearn for and earn for. We crave them almost as much as we crave food. Our more-more world stokes the appetite with the bait of ever better, bigger, faster, more *expensive* icons of limitless enjoyment. Shame that they steal your life and duff the ecology. Shame, too, that if we finally get to own them, we inevitably discover that they don't meet their promise of a better life. Inevitably? Psychologists call this process 'hedonic adaptation'. At first, you get a whacking great bang out of becoming that rare and impressive thing: a *Ferrari* owner (or a Rolls owner, or a Range Rover owner or GTi owner, etc). Wow. But after a while, the wings and halo that come with this newly elevated status start fading.

Mr or Mrs Flash-Car then begins to feel just like their plain old yearning self once again. One answer is simply to purchase another esteem-revving status symbol. Why not splash out on a speedboat? (They might constitute the perfect consumerist totem: most hobby sailors get two days' unadulterated pleasure out of a luxury boat: the day they buy it and the day they sell it. The rest is mooring fees.) But most of us nowadays have every material thing that we need to support an enjoyable and rewarding life, so why the continued yearning for more stuff?

We have long been warned about acquisitiveness. Epicurus, the ancient Greek philosopher, cautioned that while pleasure is the basis of contentment, extravagance is unlikely to bring us joy. But one of the things that makes us humans unusual is our desire to acquire. Jackdaws might nick shiny objects and octopuses make gardens, but we are in a league entirely of our own. Collecting is an age-old human habit: prehistoric fossils have been found hoarded as prize possessions in Roman villas in Britain. Emperor Hadrian collected Greek marbles and Egyptian antiquities. Our forebears thought they knew the reason for our materialist instincts. You will find the brain's 'organ of acquisitiveness' featured on those porcelain phrenology heads you see in antique shops. A certain Dr Vimont, writing in the *Phrenology Journal* in 1850, pinpointed the brain's shopping centre at the 'anterior inferior angle of the parietal bone'. It was also known as the 'organ of covetousness'. Dr Vimont wrote: 'The primitive faculty manifested by the organ appears to be the sense of property, of which the desire to acquire is the active form.' This was utter balls, of course. But recently, experts have tried to offer more evidence-based explanations.

Karl Polanyi, the late economic historian and anthropologist, tried to persuade everyone that today's mania for material goods is more learnt than instinctive. He claimed that while every society is designed to meet its members' basic needs, only modern capitalist countries concentrate intensely on material greed. We don't have to be like this, he claimed, arguing that pre-capitalist societies ascribed highest worth to family, clan, religion, honour and tradition, rather than shiny objects. In Polanyi's eyes, the most basic human instinct is the need to relate to others and to feel part of a community. We are social animals above all, he insisted, and consumerism is just a social trick played by a small wealthy élite to boost its own power. Maybe, but then again, Polanyi's sympathies lay with traditional old leftie ideas. He led a radical student movement in his native Hungary and lectured for the Workers' Education Association in England. Perhaps Polanyi's romantically optimistic view of innate human nobility is a bit too Pollyanna. After all, it was far easier to take pride in family, clan, religion, honour and tradition in the days when there weren't any sexy sportscars and speedboats to tickle your materialist palate.

His claims run smack in the face of evidence that the child psychologist Bruno Bettelheim gathered while living on Israeli kibbutzes, which themselves are the fruit of old socialist sharing ideals. Bettelheim found that the kibbutz kids were anything but born communists. They started life with a strong instinct for owning personal property that could only be unlearnt through persistent parental reprogramming. In his book, *Children of the Dream*, Bettelheim said that the kibbutzism's lack of private possessions actually damaged their ability to have personal relationships: 'Nowhere more than in the kibbutz did I realise the degree to which private property, in the deep layers of the mind, relates to private emotions. If one is absent, the other tends to be absent as well.' Take my knick-knacks, take my soul? I'd like to believe that I'm suspicious of material possessiveness, but then again, if someone walked off with my motorbikes, books, guitars and record collection, my anorakish sense of self would, to be frank, feel mortally dented.

The scientific evidence seems to support Bettelheim. One significant clue lies scattered throughout the artefacts that archaeologists unearth at Neolithic cave sites. It's hand-axes. Millions of them. Far more than any sensible tool-wielding hominid would ever need. But these aren't just neatly napped rocks – they are the stone-age prototypes of Gucci shoes and Rolex watches. Our Neolithic forebears became highly skilled at crafting lumps of flint into handy tools, but it appears that the implements were not prized only as practical objects for slashing foes or slicing bison. Anthropologists now believe that they served another crucial role – as show-off exemplars of design technology, jagged precursors of Philippe Starck lemon-squeezers and Sabatier knives.

Honing your tool-crafting skills could turn you into a sexy stone-age axe hero, claims the evolutionary psychologist Geoffrey Miller (who warned us in chapter one about the perils of virtual living): 'The tools were made in a way that would show off the symmetry, the perfection of the surface, the quality of the craftsmanship,' he says. 'They clearly were made for aesthetic reasons. In some archaeological digs they have found tens of thousands of these things. It was runaway competition, as if high fashion was popping up in caves.' Miller believes that art in general evolved as a sexual ploy, because it shows off the dexterity, creativity, imagination and intelligence of the maker.

Nowadays, though, that instinct has been craftily subverted: we are encouraged to believe that we can acquire chunks of mate-pulling mojo by waving a credit card at impressively branded mass-produced items. It's a crying shame that the mojo seems to wear off so quickly. But that's what keeps our wasteful system whirring around – there's always an improved, more impressive modern hand-axe substitute waiting to drop off the production line as soon as you've paid for yours. This also helps to explain our culture's current obsession with having everything fashionable and new, rather than items that are sustainably constructed to last for donkey's years.

Still more enticing to your poor old neolithic brain is the fact that all the newer, even better products always seem to be owned by beautiful people. There's Liz Hurley in perfumed ecstasies over a new cosmetics range, there's Daniel Craig manfully tapping on a product-placed laptop and cellphone combo while pretending to be James Bond. Our minds tend to over-identify with celebrities because we evolved in small tribal groups. In neolithic times, if you knew someone, then they knew you, too. If you didn't attack each other, you were probably friends. Our minds still work this way – and give us the false idea that the celebs we hear so much about are somehow our acquaintances.

Humans are also born imitators: this talent underlies much of our species' success, as it enabled us to adapt to changing environments far quicker than our competitors could via biological evolution alone. What gets us far ahead of other primates is our attention to detail. A chimp can watch another chimp poking a stick into an ant-hill and then mimic the basic idea, but only humans can replicate a clever technique exactly. As a result, we need to choose with great care who we copy. There's little point aping the dopiest member of your group, except for comedy value. So we have evolved to emulate the habits, idiosyncrasies and clothes of the most successful people we see, in the hope that imitation will elevate us to their rank. This helps to explain why many of us feel compelled to keep up materially with celebs, the mythical alphas in our global village.

There's a dark side to the celeb effect, too. We so want to be part of our tribe's top clique that we're perpetually anxious about being snubbed by it. Feeling left out makes us so mad that our intelligence goes awol. This was shown by a series of tests that involved making students feel sorely excluded (what fun psychologists have). Roy Baumeister, a psychologist at Case Western Reserve University, invited undergrads to meet a group of impressive strangers and then asked them to name two of the group that they would like to work with on a project. But next the students were told that, sorry, the strangers didn't rate them. The rebuffed students' IQs plummeted by about a quarter for several hours. Their aggressiveness went up. Baumeister says his tests reveal that tribal rejection interferes with our self-control: 'It strikes a blow that seems to interfere with our ability for complex reasoning,' he says. 'You may do stupid things.' Thus our perpetual exclusion from the celeb clique makes us more likely to dumbly, impulsively buy stuff – just because it's endorsed by the people we so desperately want to love us.

All this has led us to create a world where we have so many gadgets, novelties and general ephemera around us that our ability to relate to it all gets swamped. We just call it 'stuff'. The lower-priced stuff often promises to solve some of our lives' little niggles, though often these items only temporarily sate a nagging need to purchase *some*thing. A while back, my friend Kay suggested that we get a Sunday afternoon coffee. But first, if I didn't mind, we'd go via the high street because she had some little errands to run. We went into five shops, ranging from schminky boutiques to labyrinthine department stores. Five times Kay fished an item from her bag and told one of the staff, 'I bought this yesterday but I realised that I don't want it. Would you take it back, please?' Each time, the assistant smiled, took the lipstick, blouse, bra or whatever, and gave her a credit note. Kay was happy. She could use the note in future to buy something else that she might subsequently not want. 'Must have been a mad Saturday's shopping you had there,' I said to her. Oh no, she replied, she does this all the time. Kay would call herself a keen shopper, wise to the ways and wiles of modern consumer life. But such behaviour struck me as odd.

The following week, I needed to buy a pair of black work shoes from a chain store. I asked the assistant if many people returned the footwear that they'd bought in a froth on Saturdays. 'God yes,' he said. 'We get about 20 women coming in every Monday. Some of them are regular returners. We call them shoe-limics.' Why do it? Blame our old friend, the pleasure-hormone dopamine, for sparking a daring emotional surge of what-the-hell-let's-buy-it. Brain scans performed by researchers at Emory University show how the dopamine neurotransmitter gets released in waves as shoppers first see a product and then ponder buying it. But dopamine is all about the hunt here, not the trophy. It is only the anticipation, rather than the buying itself, that squirts dopamine around our skulls. And the effect is only fleeting. Once you've sealed the deal, the chemical high flattens out within minutes, often leaving a sense of regret that shop-owners call 'buyer's remorse'.

At least the shoe-limics return their unwanted buys. A survey of 1,000 Britons shows how frequently we regret cluttering our lives with more purchases, frittering more than £9 billion away on gadgets that rarely, if ever, get used. Top of the list are sandwich toasters. OK, so they ain't Ferraris, but, mmm-mmm, those toasted sandwiches, eh? Around 15 million of us have bought kitchen scales that only saw daylight once or twice. Ditto coffee machines, foot spas and electric knives. These products have one thing in common, the seductive promise that owning them will transport us to a world of leisured sophistication where there's time to weigh ingredients for delicious meals, make proper coffee and loaf about sipping it in fluffy gowns.

You can watch this phenomenon on eBay. Check out the windsurfers, motorcycles, home-spa kits, guitars – pick any lifestyle toy and you'll find pristine examples crowding the auction pages, each with a vendor lamenting: 'It's a lovely [bike, surfboard, guitar, home spa, sandwich-toaster, stuff-thing] but I just don't have time to use it.' You can almost hear the seller's bemused sigh. They bought the object in a lather of anticipation, hauled it home, got it out of the box and discovered to their dismay that, uh-oh, it didn't come with its own extra packet of lifestyle time in which to enjoy it. Much of that precious time has been used working to acquire it. And filling out an eBay listing to re-sell it.

So maybe we buy something else, hoping that will do the trick instead – whatever that trick is: perhaps it will transform you into a gourmet cook, free-spirit, sexual icon or surfer dude. In our world of plenty, there is no limit to what you can purchase, so long as your credit stays good. But if your credit isn't good, then perhaps you're suffering from an illness. Dr Lorrin Koran of Stanford University School of Medicine claims that one in 20 American adults now suffers from 'buying addiction', which causes them adverse consequences – most notably (*quelle surprise*) debt. The disorder even has its own proper-sounding medical name, oniomania, derived from the ancient Greek *onios*: for sale. Koran says that 'shopping addicts' buy things they don't need, don't use or can't afford. They lose interest in their purchases, have trouble paying for them and then get into rows with their spouses.

For his report in the *American Journal of Psychiatry*, Koran asked more than 1,200 adults about their shopping habits and found that more than one in 20 met his criteria for compulsive buying. Men and women are equally prone, says Koran, who cautions: 'People who have the problem should seek treatment.' Interestingly though, the people identified as disordered shoppers generally tend to make less money than those who keep their shopping 'under control'. So the logic runs like this: if you can afford to splash out on a few more things than you need, you're in rude health – but if you can't afford your extravagances, you're a sick oniomaniac. That reveals much about our culture. There are parallels with Soviet Russian Communism, where the regime was so convinced of its perfection that it felt that the only reason people would dissent politically was because they had a psychiatric illness and had to be 'looked after'. In consumer-world, there's only one type of insanity involved in wasteful, pointless binge buying – it's when your credit can't fund it.

That's not the only new shopping sickness that psychologists have identified. There is also compulsive acquisition disorder (CAD), which describes people who continually buy and store until their homes are so crammed that the windows bulge. CAD can even kill. In one case, police officers answered a worried husband's missing-person call to find every room of his home stuffed floor-to-ceiling with clothes, dishes and boxes. Police chief Terry Davenport, of Shelton, Washington, says that after a ten-hour search his officers found the man's wife, 62-year-old Marie Rose, smothered under a pile of clutter. Her husband thinks she was searching for the phone. Psychiatric researchers claim that this kind of compulsive hoarding may affect up to two million people in the United States. One study of college students found that anxiety can make people more likely to hoard. This points us to an evolutionary explanation: getting gripped by the urge to stockpile provisions in times of threat would obviously

85

have helped our ancestors' chances of survival. This residual instinct can also help to explain how sales campaigns may work *en masse* by collectively preying on our deepest insecurities – you smell funny, you're not good enough, no one likes you.

We may also blame our acquisitiveness on a much wider crisis of confidence. It is all, perhaps, about trying to buy purpose in a deity-free cosmos. Easter eggs and Christmas presents aside, secular life has little use for religious co-branding. Generally we in the West believe that the old super-powerful God is dead and no one watches over our everyday dramas or hears our inner thoughts. So our only shot left at attaining any kind of immortality is to achieve acclaim in this material life, in the shape of the things we own and wear. It's a form of existential dummy-sucking. And what, indeed, would millions of people do with their time and sense of purpose if there wasn't shopping, and time spent earning for shopping?

This question leads us to a fascinating idea that explains how shopping is far more than mere 'retail therapy' – that it is in fact a way of buttressing our shaky mental universe. In a paper called 'Why Do People Need Self-esteem?' the American psychologist Thomas Pyszcynski developed an idea called terror-management theory. Retail-supported self-esteem is, he argues, 'a shield designed to control the potential for terror that results from awareness of the horrifying possibility that we humans are merely transient animals groping to survive in a meaningless universe, destined only to die and decay'. To block out this vision of life as an interminable Samuel Beckett script, we have created a society which proffers clothes that transform us mortals into fashion gods, and kitchen utensils that elevate us to the status of domestic gods and goddesses. Pyszcynski rubs it in by adding that we may actually have no more significance in the universe than 'any individual potato, pineapple or porcupine', Except, well, have you ever seen a potato, porcupine or pineapple damaging our ecosystem with its retail forays?

So here we are, a species that is uniquely wired, compelled, hormonally drugged and scared into wanting things. And we're surrounded by stuff. Perhaps we should just resign ourselves to riding a spiral of consumption until the day we get buried alive beneath it all. Hell no, argues Aleksandr Solzhenitsyn, the Nobel prize-winning writer and former Soviet dissident. He reckons that the only way we can revive our sense of human purpose is by *not* shopping – by reining back our jackdaw urges.

Despite his objections to the old Soviet regime, Solzhenitsyn has an equally baleful view of Western life. He argues that now we have ditched our old religious and moral frameworks, we have lost our sense of community and of life's higher meaning. Our thirst for personal possessions and pleasures is nearly all that remains, leaving us as little more than a bunch of atomised, alienated consumers. Solzhenitsyn's remedy is self-restraint – a term that is guaranteed to provoke lemon-sucking faces down at the mega-mall. The old dissenter argues that in response to humankind's ever-advancing technology and all the marvels it brings, we must learn a new skill – the art of self-abnegation: 'Today [self-restraint] appears to us as something wholly unacceptable, constraining, even repulsive,' he says. 'Our ancestors lived with far greater external constraints and had far fewer opportunities. The paramount importance of self-restraint has only now arisen in its pressing entirety before mankind.'

So how do we hold ourselves back? Solzhenitsyn suggests that we cultivate a sense of unselfish spirituality, where we politely decline our unprecedented opportunity to use up the planet's resources all at once: 'There can be only one true progress; the sum total of the spiritual progresses of individuals. Self-limitation is the fundamental and wisest step of a man who has obtained freedom. It is also the surest path towards its attainment.'

Now that's the sort of sentence that should come with its own fanfare. And why shouldn't we claim a spiritual aspect to practising restraint in the face of more, more and more? If the journey to enlightenment does lie (as the major religious traditions claim) in learning to see beyond one's grasping-monkey ego, then opting out of the consumer stampede must be part of the ticket-price. On top of that, we now have an ecological imperative to evolve from the angry-toddler level of crying, 'Me more, me more, me more,' into a species that can say, 'Us, and for everyone. Now and for later.' Enoughism asks us to shift from self-esteem to us-esteem. Learning to see beyond ourselves also offers a way of viewing the Earth's bounty in a sustainable way: accepting that it's not ours, but it belongs to the universe, and so do we. We're not lords of the Earth, we are stewards, at best. So we need to lose the illusion that we truly 'own' the stuff we possess and consume – that's a legal construct rather than a cosmic freehold.

These ideas usually get trashed as doe-eyed hippy nonsense, but they are going to look increasingly pragmatic as we face up to the alternative – a blasted world with little to offer our future generations. Even more self-interestedly, you and I look fated to live as vulnerable elderly people among the eco-blighted young-uns. They may have every right to see us as the careless old bastards who squandered their birthrights for a handful of baubles. It's not a prospect to relish.

More immediately, there is another spiritual problem with pursuing ever-more – it is viciously toxic to our inter-personal environment. Take, as just one example, the school run. Twenty metres down the road from my house is the gateway to a busy little primary school. For decades our narrow old one-way street enjoyed a gently cheerful ecology; kids and parents strolled, ran and played their way to the entrance. But now they stick well away from the kerb and up against the walls. Because about six years ago, the first dirty great 4x4 showed up. Maybe the mother who bought it felt compelled by seeing paparazzi snaps of A-list owners driving massive off-roaders (which is why carmakers give them free to their favourite celebs). Maybe she wanted to bounce over the traffic-calming bumps faster. Maybe she felt vulnerable in a normal-sized car. Perhaps her fragile personality needed bolstering with a giant metal super-ego. Down our little road the great thing came, inching its flanks between obstacles, lest it got marred on parked cars, lampposts, parents or schoolkids. Absurd, unecological and dangerous. Rationally, we might expect everyone to shun the dreadful 4x4 and ostracise its owner. But each new term sees more mums driving more-by-mores.

It's the same story outside schools across the land. That first 4x4 poisoned the emotional ecology. It crashed through the collective sense of relative prosperity, raised the bar of ostentation and spread renewed fear of not-good-enoughness. The other mums' initial indignation quickly subsided as their competitive instincts began to persuade them that the ugly great psychic-space invader was, in fact, rather attractive. Four-wheel-drives may also elevate you psychologically as well as physically and financially, because the driving position puts you up above the people in normal cars – so it's like occupying the chief monkey's throne on the top of a rock. A physical sense of fear comes into play, too: our news-saturated world feels beset with danger, so when our early-warning systems see a looming metal mammoth, they pin that trepidation right on to it. This isn't helped by the plain physical fact that your best bet of surviving a collision with a 4x4 is to be encased in one as well. Steadily the idea of ownership becomes so compelling to mums anxious for their offspring that the environmental, personal and aesthetic costs don't count at all.

The logical result of such status races is that all the insecure people end up back on square one, except that in this case, square one now contains more oversized cars, more carbon and less of a future for the schoolchildren. The emotional armistice will hold until someone's mum shows up in an armoured personnel carrier. Look out for that Humvee, kids. The parable of the toxic 4x4 naturally applies to all the other unnecessary mores that somehow become must-haves. Unless we try to transcend our egos, we are fated to get locked in to evermore ridiculous consumer races.

Meanwhile, we're stuck trying to cope with the messy

reality of all the stuff we are so persuasively encouraged to acquire. Back in the early 1990s, while my old acquaintance Bebe was failing at her stage career, she got herself employed by a chaotic pair of wealthy Manhattanites to organise their apartment and file or bin all the clutter that they couldn't bear to deal with. We all laughed at the crazy New Yorkers and likened her job to that of the hefty woman in N. F. Simpson's absurdist film, *One Way Pendulum*, who was paid to eat up a family's leftover food. But since then, the need to organise one's ever-proliferating possessions has spawned a mini-industry – one that even sells us stuff to help us cope with the stuff we have already bought. There are dozens of 'declutter your life' books on the market, as well as a growing pile of CD-ROMS and DVDs. You can also purge yourself vicariously by watching television shows such as *Life Laundry* and *Declutter Your Life*. In the States, people are turning to support groups such as the 12-step programme Clutterers Anonymous.

We can no longer even safely offer stuff as gifts. A *Spectator* magazine reader recently wrote to the magazine's etiquette columnist asking how he could politely tell relatives, friends and well-wishers that he didn't want any presents for his sixtieth birthday. 'My material wants are perfectly well supplied. Our house is full and I have no time for novelty gifts,' he complained. He's hardly alone: a survey by Abbey Banking says that the average Briton receives more than £35 worth of unwanted offerings every year – a national total of £1.3bn wasted on pointless gestures. A third of us feel obliged to keep the things. Of those who don't keep the gifts, equal numbers either give them to charity, sell them or pass them on. In the week following Christmas, thousands of unwanted offerings follow the surfboards and foot spas on to eBay. At Christmas 2005, the site added a special section for redundant presents. Smellies top the list of unwanteds, closely followed by novelty-themed gifts, sweets and chocolates. Does this dismay the eager gift-givers? Not really. A quarter of us admit to having given loved ones presents that we knew they would never use. And if you can't flog the pointless little something that you've been given, you could always lump it on to someone else by practising the dark art of 're-gifting'. The term was originally coined in the 1990s sitcom *Seinfeld*, but has now become a proper grown-up verb with its own dictionary definition.

But if you can't re-gift, what are your other options? The obvious response is to stick the stuff someplace. But where? Our lofts, closets and garages are already chocker. The answer, increasingly, is to pay for more space to stash it all. Last year, the wife and I found ourselves in the absurd situation of paying £75 a month to rent a boxroom-sized lock-up facility in a converted factory to store things from our pre-marital attics that we would probably never need. As well as the old furniture, books, mementoes and photo albums, there was sufficient bedding to tackle a minor humanitarian crisis. Why do this? Well partly because our self-justifying egotistical brains tell us that the problem looks like this . . .

*"I don't have enough space. You have too much stuff. He is a hoarder."*

Our rented room is only one of 900 lining the facility's clanging corridors. Almost all of them are taken. The company that profited from hosting our unwanteds, Yellow Box, is expanding rapidly across Britain. Its winning formula offers householder-friendly storage, rather than the traditional industrial-scale units. Since it launched in 1998, it has opened 39 massive facilities. Another 19 are being built. The entire UK self-storage industry made £310 million in 2005 and is growing by up to 40 per cent each year. Buy shares in it. The average Briton now accumulates more than a ton of unwanted possessions and a quarter of us have been forced to stop using a room in our homes because of the amount of stuff crammed into it. Adrian Lee, Yellow Box's operations director, says the missus and I are typical customers: 'As people have become more wealthy, they've gained many more material possessions. But they also want to de-clutter and have nice homes with clear wooden floors. They are surprised by how much they have amassed.' The high season is spring, when people decide to purge their home of items whose allure or novelty won't last another season. Or they're moving house and realise that many of their possessions would best be consigned in perpetuity to a dark, distant place.

Lee says his company was inspired by the United States storage boom, which shows us the way we are headed. American self-storage space occupies three times the area of Manhattan Island. There are more than 40,000 depots and the industry makes more money than the nation's movie theatres or its music business. And you don't have to be rich to own too much – a third of American units are rented by people earning less than £15,000 a year. Most

renters also have storage space in garages, attics or base-
ments – just not enough.

Such grab-and-stash behaviour is apparently 'essential'
to the health of the world's economy. Joseph Quinlan,
the chief stock market strategist for the Bank of America
Corp, has declared that our ability to squirrel things away
in storage units is a 'critical prop to global growth'
because people will only keep buying as long as they have
somewhere to hoard their purchases. 'If US consumers
run out of storage space,' he said, 'the global economy
is doomed.' Tony DeMauro, a former psychotherapist,
sees a solid future for this consumer quirk, too. He spent
a decade shrinking heads until he spotted this lucrative
trend, jettisoned his couch and started his own American
storage business. 'We learn to pursue material goods as
a way to happiness,' he says. 'If we lose our stuff – even
if it's an old blender – many of us believe we are somehow
diminished.'

Even when we do bring ourselves to part with our
unwanted buys, we often end up performing other illogical
and damaging acts. Leyton Road dump, in Hove, has for
decades been the place where our neighbourhood ditches
its unwanted domestic stuff, big items that the binmen
won't touch. As kids, my brother and I would dodge into
a side-entrance and hassle the dump-men into scavenging
old pram wheels for our home-built soapbox-karts. We
lived on a sharp-cornered hill, so we'd always be pranging
tyres, rims, spokes and shins. Kids can't go cadging old
wheels at Leyton Road nowadays: the refuse-disposal centre
operates on a completely different scale. Government
figures show that in Britain on average we each throw away

our own body weight in rubbish every seven weeks. Municipal dumps have had to professionalise to handle the endless convoy of cars loaded with domestic detritus.

Except that it's not all rubbish. No way, says Peter Beck, the manager of the barn-like YMCA store at the corner of the junkyard. He and his crew intercept household dumpers launching potentially valuable items into the silos. In the three years since the shop opened, he's seen a steady rise in the quality of people's rejects. There's so much good stuff that the store makes more than £1,200 a week selling rescued throwaways to canny members of the public. 'Unbelievable what people chuck out,' says Beck, a tidy fiftysomething man who, in his blue overalls, could pass as a 1950s iron-monger. 'We get those Ikea flat-pack furniture kits – wardrobes, cupboards, tables, and they've never even been assembled. Brand-new in the packaging.'

The nearest Ikea store to Hove is a 100-mile round trip away in south London. Once you get there, it takes a couple of hours to traipse around the place. The products on sale cost money (of course), which takes chunks of time to earn (of course). Even if you just want to throw your newly bought flat-pack furniture away unassembled, you have to schlep across town to queue up at the dump. All this unwanted stuff requires precious raw materials to make (again, of course) and produces greenhouse clouds in the making (ditto). Its disposal only adds to the ecological load. I'm reminded of how those little tin Martians in the instant-potato Smash TV adverts used to laugh themselves witless at the way Earthlings mashed their spuds. They'd have to be hospitalised with mirth if they witnessed this particular bit of human logic.

Flat-pack furniture is merely one example. 'We get loads of those George Foreman fat-busting griddles, usually only used once,' says Beck. Sandwich toasters? 'Yeah, tons. And ordinary toasters, too. They haven't been out of their boxes. We had someone come in with a brand new washer/dryer, still in the protective cladding.' Beyond the shop's tat-strewn entrance, past the plantation of cast-out cheeseplants and palms, are treasures indeed. A tangle of bicycles leans along one side of the long wooden barrack-room. You might expect rusting junkheaps, but they're remarkably good – and some are immaculate. 'This one needed a tweak to the steering, that one needed the gears adjusting. Both jobs took us ten minutes. But the people who'd bought them, they couldn't be bothered,' says Beck. Next to the bikes are piled a dozen bags of golf clubs. The top-class brands sell fast. The rest of it – all fine for amateurs – sits unwanted. 'First thing Monday morning, the dealers turn up,' says Beck. 'They come rushing in looking for antiques and other high-value stuff. They want discounts, too. But we don't give 'em. We get so much good furniture that we send it by van to three shops we have on local high streets. All the electrical stuff we rescue gets taken away, tested for safety and sold elsewhere, too.'

The Leyton store is a rare initiative. Beck can't understand why there isn't one at every municipal dump. Neither can I. His shop does not recycle – it re-sells. This apparently minor difference is crucial. Although dropping our jilted purchases into green boxes and recycling skips makes us feel virtuous, it requires gargantuan amounts of power, water and pollution to take them away, crush them into recyclable shapes and turn them into other short-term durables. The vast majority of the resources sucked away cannot be replaced. All this makes the idea of 'green consumerism' seem a serious contradiction in terms – rather like 'military intelligence'.

Even the establishment has quietly noticed this: in 2007 the government-funded Economic and Social Research Council produced a small report which warned that the UK's recycling drive risks being undermined by the sheer quantity of waste being generated. If our household throw-aways continue to rise by three per cent a year, the cost to the economy will be £3.2 billion and the amount of harmful methane emissions will double by 2020. But mainstream politicians don't dare to encourage us to do the smart thing – to think twice and thrice about buying anything in the first place – lest it hinder our continual economic expansion. So instead, we try to bury our unwanteds out of sight: last year, nearly 2 million tonnes of British rubbish was shipped right across the world to Chinese landfills. Ten years previously, the throw-boat-to-China total was only 12,000 tonnes. Environmentalists predict that the rapidly expanding Chinese economy won't even be able to cope with its own waste by 2020. So what will we do with it then? Perhaps we could dump it where the polar ice-caps used to be.

The YMCA shop is testament to the fact that much of our waste is still perfectly useful without even having to be recycled – it's just been stigmatised by the fact that its owner no longer covets it. As I leave the shop, past a skip piled with computer monitors (there's no market for them, even at a tenner a time), one of the refuse-men puts his head into the doorway. 'Want a box of books I found?

They're really clean,' he asks. 'No way,' laughs Beck. 'I only want the dirty ones.'

Visiting Beck shamed me into resolving to stop our own wasteful domestic habit. After a bout of marital negotiations, a joint policy consensus emerged: we knew we didn't want to pay to store our old stuff any longer, not least because it was kicking a ragged hole in the monthly budget. We did not, however, want to dispose of it in any potentially planet-trashing manner. In fact, we wanted to try to do some good with it, not just because we fancy being canonised as carbon-friendly saints, but because we needed to assuage the nagging qualm that we were actually *chucking good stuff away*.

Charity shops seemed the obvious answer. The piles of as-new textiles seemed a good place to start. Easy, eh? Lump them into black binliners, drop them at the nearest store and Bob's your conflict-resolving uncle. But it doesn't feel like that when you're being chased away by the tough old birds who volunteer to run them. The cancer ladies didn't want our bedsheets. The dementia ladies didn't want them either. I didn't dare try the heart-attack ladies. Many of these local organisations have been given quite enough unwanted textiles for the time being. And they object to being used as a cheap dumping service by people seeking to offload on them as a conscience-cleansing convenience.

Many donations are simply unsellable: Help the Aged shops have to pay councils more than £300,000 a year to dispose of unwanted goods. The Children's Society spends around the same sum. Our increasingly disposable attitude to clothing is one of the main problems, explains Paul Tate, the Children Society's merchandise manager: 'We are losing sales because new clothes can be bought at unbelievably cheap prices. Then people who have bought these clothes give them to us a season later and nobody wants to buy what was a low-quality item to begin with.'

Scattergun charity was clearly not going to work. We needed to be more targeted, to find someone who really needed our cast-outs. Anna, my obsessively green-minded newspaper colleague, recommended Freecycle, an internet dating agency for swapping unloved possessions. The system was launched in mid-2003 as an automated e-mail list by Deron Beal, an environmentalist from Arizona. Now it's a global network, with more than three and a half million members in 4,000 local clusters. Freecyclers use Yahoo! usergroups, moderated by volunteers, to post offers and wants, and everything changes hands for free. In Britain, there are more than 400 groups, each with an average of around 200 members. Brighton, being hippy Brighton, has more than 9,000 swappers. Joining the group unleashed a thrice-daily torrent of gifts and needs into my inbox.

All of human life is there: Steve's offering a collection of newspaper articles reporting the death of Princess Diana. 'Mint' wants to give away a wedding dress, size 8, made in Italy: 'Would like it to go asap, please,' she says. Other gifters' offers include 'Large tagine pot, flip-flops and a part-used scented candle,' as well as poker dice, a toilet seat and a 'Navy blue bean bag, medium-sized. Bit on the tired side.' All of these got snapped up, as did a 'large bag of coat-hangers' and 'various Buddhist items'. I was humming easy-peasy lemon-squeezy as I posted separate offers for three different items: Panasonic microwave oven, hardly used;

bedlinen sets for single bed: clean, as-new and some still in packaging, and a pair of garden-recliner cushions.

The response was instant and eager. Ten people rushed to baggsy the garden-recliner cushions. Some of them larded their requests with sad tales of hard-recliner woe. But no one said they wanted the microwave. Nor did anyone desire the bedlinen. For days they sat there while happy throngs of Freecyclers collected tagines, beanbags and part-used candles from each other. Perhaps the linen and microwave just weren't lifestyle enough. Perhaps I shouldn't have mentioned that the linen had a floral pattern. But I'd felt compelled to be honest. Finally, Clara got in touch and requested the sheets and cases. She was renting rooms for students in the summer, and thought they might come in handy. I don't think she wanted them that much, though. It took eight days, and several reminders, for her to collect them. That was after she e-mailed me an incorrect home phone number that belonged to a remarkably short-tempered pensioner. The microwave only went after a fortnight's continued offering. Jo, who picked it up, said she had a barn that she sometimes rents to artist friends, and she thought that they might like to heat up drinks and soups.

Around the same time, a frustrated Myfanwy let out a wrenching *cri du coeur* on the swap-site: 'Does no one want my monitor?' she asked. 'I've posted it twice on Freecycle; the YMCA don't want it and the recyclers charge for it to be taken. Am I right in thinking it's impossible to get rid of a non-flatscreen computer monitor these days, except at the tip?' The conundrum put Myfanwy into a philosophical mood: 'Times have changed, eh?' she sighed. 'It seems to me that ten years ago Freecycle wouldn't have worked because people wouldn't have given stuff away for nothing. Now it's on the brink of not working again because everyone's overwhelmed by the sheer bulk of their belongings, and if they want something new they can usually go out and buy it – which is not necessarily the ideal we might have thought it was a decade ago.' Poor Myfanwy.

There remained one other avenue that I wanted to pursue. We piled our little Peugeot with excess furniture and set out on the road to Emmaus. It's a short trip, about three miles from our home, to a rambling old Victorian manor house that was bequeathed to an order of nuns in the early 1900s. When the nuns' numbers dwindled to nothing in the 1990s, the order donated it to Emmaus, a charity that had been launched in 1949 by Father Henri-Antoine Groues, a Catholic priest who had been in the French Resistance during the Second World War. After France's liberation, he began to campaign for the rights of thousands of people rendered homeless by fighting. He founded a youth hostel, which he named Emmaus after the biblical Palestinian town. Then he realised that housing people was not enough – he had to help them to find renewed purpose: 'A bed, and a reason to get out of it' became his motto. In post-war France there was no readily available work for Groues' guests, until they began to perform one of the most menial tasks around – collecting scrap and rubbish from houses and building it into something saleable. What was menial then has become green now. This recycling mission, along with Emmaus's collectivist ethos (members are called 'companions') has seen the charity grow to 310 groups in 50 countries.

I'd been looking forward to seeing the old convent. It's on one of the earliest inhabited sites in our city, and the manor-house's history sounded noble and glam. But in fact entering the place felt like joining a giant bring-and-buy sale. First we ventured to the drop-off depot and gingerly asked one of the companions what sort of items they accepted. 'Oh, anything,' he said, shrugging '. . . except televisions.' It's slightly odd, feeling profoundly grateful for being told that you can donate something (there is probably a long German word to describe it). Perhaps it's something we should try to get quickly used to.

Once we had divested the car of tables, chairs, cabinets, clothes and towels, we wandered to the 'second-hand superstore'. No expense has been spent decorating the place, and each cavernous old room opened out into another vista of thematically organised rejects. Rounding one corner, I came across a vaguely familiar figure, a friend of a friend with her children in tow. She was tugging at a recalcitrant drawer-knob. 'We're looking for a bedside cabinet,' she said brightly. 'What are you here for?' I suddenly felt very short of words: 'Oh, we're, ah, just dropping off. Stuff,' I replied, deftly introducing an unwarranted social awkwardness into the proceedings. We looked at each other until the conversational void began to stretch beyond endurance, and I said, 'Well. I'd better leave you to it. Good luck.' If there's a middle-class etiquette for bumping into someone in a charity store who's browsing for exactly the sort of thing you've just donated, then I plainly don't know it. Again, it's something we should try to get used to, and quickly.

**Have** *enough*

**Don't buy that thing (until you ask these nine questions)**

Do I need it? Do I truly, really *need* it, rather than just want it?

Has my desire for this thing been implanted by marketing techniques?

Do I want it because I want to be fitter, cleverer, more leisured or just cooler? If so, will the consumer item really work that miracle?

Is there any other way that I could achieve my goal without accruing more stuff?

How many more hours will I have to work to pay for it? What else could I do with the working time that would bring more fulfilment than the consumer item?

Is there anything I already own that I could substitute for it?

Do I really want to dust, dry-clean, pay to have it serviced, or otherwise maintain it?

If I'm replacing something that I have already got, what's really wrong with the old one?

If I really do need this thing, is there any way I could obtain it on a free-site, or borrow it from a friend, neighbour or relative?

**Make it yourself**
Our inherited instincts ensure that we will always feel the urge to own things that make us proud. But it's only part of the story. Until very recently, many of the objects we owned were made by our own hands – often just little things, but they all stood

testament to our skills. Our relationship with these things existed on a different plane from the one we have with anonymous shop-bought items whose manufacture we don't understand and whose purchase often brings only temporary joy. Our creative bent has largely been subsumed by consumer society, with its message that anything that ain't by this year's designer is irretrievably naff. But you can reclaim your creativity by dedicating time to perfecting any craft that takes your fancy – making clothes, art, even highly complex stuff such as musical instruments. This provides somewhere to put your possessive urge that is rewarding, engaging, meditative, productive and sustainable. It will also give you that lasting hedonic thrill of true proprietorship that motivated our make-and-mend ancestors.

## Be more materialistic

We're all agreed that sustainable resources and energy are Good Things. But what about sustainable possessions? The idea of choosing items for their durability has largely fallen off the purchasing agenda since the 1960s – because we have been seduced by the words 'new', 'more' and 'fashion'. But buying stuff that doesn't last is toxic to our personal ecology. It makes us work more, worry more and want more. We actually need to be more materialistic – in the sense that we care for our material things, rather than just using and discarding them. We need to rediscover the delights of (blush) sentimental material relationships. The 1950s suit I got second-hand more than a decade ago still looks good, long after the new-bought suits I subsequently purchased went shiny-kneed. Likewise our old Peugeot hatchback, which is now a dented jalopy that makes me feel embarrassed in hotel car parks, will prove a reasonably eco-friendly option so long as we keep it for its whole lifetime. The huge energy costs of building and recycling large lumps of mobile metal mean that getting a new eco-car every few years just constitutes another wasteful way to punch holes in the sky.

### Give credit the slip

Usury – lending money and charging interest on it – was condemned for centuries in Europe, thanks to decrees by the likes of Moses, Jesus, Mohammed and Aristotle. The Old Testament put money-lenders in the same sinning bin as 'the shedder of blood, the defiler of his neighbour's wife, the oppressor of the poor, the spoiler by violence and the violator of the pledge'. It condemned them to excruciating deaths. Tell that to the bank manager. On the other hand, usury has always been with us, and consumer credit is hardly a recent innovation: eighteenth-century life in Britain and America was characterised by monthly payments, loan-sharking and bailiffs. But most people back then used credit to buy things that they truly needed. Nowadays, 'easy' credit is mainly for buying things that we merely want, and want now. Credit is no longer a temporary reprieve for the poor, but self-inflicted slavery for wealthy moderns. We have to keep working to service the eternal bill. Credit also swaps the slow pleasure of anticipation for the brief thrill of acquisition. Practising enoughness means taking on only essential credit such as mortgages, borrowing as little as possible, and paying it off as quickly as practicable.

### Don't touch that plastic

'It's shocking how much easier people find buying things with a credit card,' says Drazen Prelec, a psychologist at the Massachusetts Institute of Technology who studies buying decisions in the brain. His tests show that we are willing to spend twice as much for the same thing if we are paying for it with a credit card. There are two possible explanations for this, he says. One is that when you are paying with a card you simply don't feel the sting of payment. The other possibility is that credit cards create a physical craving, so that when you see and touch the plastic it is rather like smelling cookies baking when you're hungry. You act to satisfy that craving.

## Use global neighbours

We often feel compelled to buy status-boosting goods because our tribal instincts make us measure ourselves materially against our peers, to see if we are doing OK in life. In the developed world, this massively distorts our idea of what we need just to be averagely OK. Wealthy Londoners, for example, no longer feel very rich, because they do not mix with less affluent people any more. We need to look wider, to the global neighbourhood that technology and travel have brought to our doorsteps. About half of humanity lives on less than £1 a day. More than 852 million people do not get enough to eat, around 1.6 billion have no electricity and a third of the world's people have never made a phone call. Meanwhile, a fifth of the Earth's people buy nearly 90 per cent of all the consumer goods. That's us, the stressed guys in the wealthy neighbourhood.

## Frugal cool

Today's society makes constant consumption feel normal and natural, but history shows that our drive for evermore things is a fad. In eighteenth-century Europe, frugal living was considered the cool lifestyle choice: outside royal courts, luxury goods were often spurned, thanks to the practice of 'worldly asceticism', a Calvinist idea that offered the hope of heavenly salvation through diligent use of God's gifts (aka planet Earth). Puritans and Quakers promoted the 'Christianity writ plain' ideal, where it was considered good to produce, but bad to consume more than necessity required. Those who lived luxuriously were criticised for squandering resources that might support their society. We can thank eighteenth-century society, and Josiah Wedgwood in particular, for inventing many of today's marketing tactics. He stimulated demand for his crockery by selling it as high-priced 'prestige' gear that the riff-raff couldn't afford. He also revamped his designs regularly, thus inventing instant obsolescence and the fear of being 'so last year'. Wedgwood also popularised the celebrity-endorsement ad campaign, by publicly exhibiting special ranges that famous customers such as Empress Caroline of Russia were buying.

### Look cheap

Jennifer Argo, an assistant professor of marketing at Alberta University's School of Business, realised that whenever she went shopping with a friend, she changed her shopping habits, choosing brand names instead of no-name foods and buying expensive tops in clothes stores. Was she the only one, she wondered, who splurged extravagantly in the presence of another person? Did her relationship with the person matter, or might it also work with strangers? Argo employed mystery shoppers to stand by a rack of batteries, and found that the mere presence of her stooges made the battery buyers pick the most expensive brand. If no one was there, they'd choose cheaply. The result was consistent over three separate studies involving hundreds of shoppers. 'We will spend more money to maintain our self-image in front of others,' she says. The answer, according to a separate piece of research, may be to go shopping with your relatives: it reports that we buy fewer things when visiting stores under the eagle eyes of family members.

### Avoid special offers

Chainstores love to make you feel that you're getting a deal, because this makes you buy more than you need. When you see low-priced special-offer goods on the shelves, your rational brain tends to go soppy with gratitude at the shop's generosity. That surge of positive emotion makes you want to return the favour by splashing out on unnecessary items. It's called the 'spill-over effect'.

### Toys cost the Earth

Gadgets seem such harmless fun novelties that they somehow seem to hold an ecological 'Get out of jail free' card. But our love of new toys with ever-proliferating functions is swallowing huge amounts of energy, as well as our precious time. The amount of resources used by consumer electronics is set to double by the year 2010, says the Energy Saving Trust. Moves to make appliances more energy-efficient are merely a fig-leaf, because we keep buying more and more of them. And they are getting more powerful: plasma screens, for example, can use up to four times as much energy as a normal television. Sony's PlayStation 3 consumes the same amount of power as an average PC and nearly three times more than the original Xbox game system.

## Beware the web

Watch out for websites that let you try consumer gadgets inter-actively online before buying. When psychologists asked 170 undergraduates to learn about a digital camera, either via an interactive website or through a site with simple text and still pictures, the ones who sampled the camera interactively were convinced that it had better features and functions than it truly offered. The vivid mental images that interactivity stimulates can shift your vulnerable imagination into overdrive, to the point where it fabricates false favourable impressions that get mixed up with bona fide memories. In psychological terms, this is called creating 'false positives'. Reading the dull old brochure will prove far less enticing.

## Gifted ideas

In this possession-saturated age, we must start to declare: enough gifts. For adults, material pressies have mostly lost their sentimental meaning and become mere commodities. That doesn't mean an end to joyful giving. Heartfelt, precious presents just don't tend to come from shops any more. Instead they may be things you have made or cooked especially, or personal commitments such as promising to do someone a real favour, or go on a course or trip together. There's the increasingly popular ethical route, too – donating cash on a recipient's behalf to a whole range of schemes, from fuel-efficient stoves in El Salvador to tuberculosis inoculations in North Korea. Be on personal-crusade alert though: such gifts work best if the recipient is emotionally signed up to the cause. Someone recently gifted us a one-year adoption certificate for a local waterfowl. We were grateful and touched. But while I'm a bit of a bunny-hugging veggie, my wife's love of web-footers primarily involves plum sauce and pancakes.

# 4 | ENOUGH Work

*It is not the man who has too little, but the man who craves more, that is poor.*

Seneca, *Epistulae Morales*

When news broke that Charles Martell's tiny cheese-making company was to have one of its obscure dairy products featured conspicuously in the plot of a Wallace & Gromit film, *The Curse of the Were-Rabbit*, the pundits predicted that he would leap into lactic overdrive, invest heavily in more workers and machinery and cash in on the publicity created by a global hit movie. After all, major brands spend millions every year buying that kind of cinematic product-placement – and when the dairy-loving Wallace & Gromit had featured Wensleydale cheese in a previous movie, its makers' turnover had quadrupled. But Martell, 61, developed no such plans for his unique speciality cheese, Stinking Bishop, or his cottage-industry company.

Even before the film came out in 2006, Wallace & Gromit fans had latched on to the cheese, and orders increased five-fold. 'I'm just a little old cheesemaker on a farm keeping my head down and out of trouble,' Martell says mischievously. 'There are two girls and me working in the dairy and we make 120 of the 3lb Stinking Bishops a day. It's absolutely nothing in the grand scheme of things. We're a small farm. And I don't want to be any bigger,' he explains in his leisured, chatty way. He even turned down a distribution offer from a leading supermarket chain. 'I said, "No way." We wouldn't be able to produce enough, for one thing. Also, selling it somewhere like that isn't the sort of thing I'd want to do.'

More than a year after the film came out, demand remained so high that he could still fill only 20 per cent of his weekly orders. 'I don't like the idea of letting customers down, but I would rather plod on knowing that it's all sold at the end of the day,' he says. Integrity counts more than growth in Martell's world, the heart of which is his small rural farm in Gloucestershire. 'We are very happy here. We can't expand. We're limited for space. If we get another person making the cheese, where will we park their car? I'm quite happy with what I've got at the moment. I can only wear one suit at a time, or drive one car. And I certainly don't want fame,' he says.

There's a touch of the Harrison Fords about Martell, with his trim build and neat grey beard, but he drives an old Land Rover and spends his spare time writing an internet guide to rare apples. He bought Laurel Farm at Dymock, 15 miles north of Gloucester, unseen at an auction in 1972 when it was derelict. But it wasn't profits or conventional hard work that he sought – he had a passion to pursue. He'd dropped out of university and wanted to fulfil his childhood dream of saving an ancient British strain of docile, dun-coloured cattle called Old Gloucesters from extinction. Martell's fascination with the square-shanked breed had begun when his grandmother gave him a book of traditional cattle. 'There were pictures of these mysterious dark cows in it and I think I was attracted to them even then; it was the first stirrings of my yearning to farm,' he says.

When he bought Laurel Farm, he intended to keep Old Gloucester cattle and make cheese. But he arrived to find that the main herd of Old Gloucesters had just been sold and dispersed. 'At that time there were only 68 of them left in the world. I visited all the people who had bought the cows and suggested that we start a breed society. I was the first secretary and I have been president twice,' says Martell, who learnt the basics of cheesemaking from a 1930s local-council leaflet. Stinking Bishop incorporates his other great enthusiasm – the local orchards. It is named after a pear that Martell uses to make cider, which the cheese bathes in to acquire a fruity rind. The pear is named after an old local character who grew it – a Mr Bishop, whose grim personal hygiene had become legend. Martell was savvy enough to copyright the name.

He says he is now perfectly happy with the income he gets from the farm. 'I'm not well off,' he says. 'But if I need money, I'll earn it. Otherwise we live quite happily with what we've got. It's not a frugal life, but money is like sweet pudding to me – and I do have a sweet tooth. Having a second serving can really spoil it.' Thanks to Martell's conservation efforts, numbers of the mahogany-coloured cows have risen in Britain to 500-plus. The herds are bound to continue expanding, too, thanks to middle-class Britain's rediscovery of locally sourced regional food. I doubt, however, if you will catch Martell trying to profit from this additional growth opportunity.

Plenty of entrepreneurs would mock Martell for naively failing to surf his wave of fortune. That's his big chance of wealth, curdled and gone – and along with it an exciting life of business growth, power-breakfasts, marketing drives, bank meetings, fretful investors, tax consultants, human resource issues and myriad other tasks to take him from his cows, cheese and orchards. It's a rare Briton who turns down the prospect of an overscheduled life if it promises the gilded prospect of 'making it'. Britons toil for longer at work than any other nation in the European Union – 42 hours a week on average. This includes putting in millions of days of unpaid overtime and, even though we are at the bottom of the European league for holiday entitlement, we also forgo billions of pounds' worth of paid holiday leave.

And then we die. People who work 41 hours or more a week are significantly more likely to have high blood pressure than those who toil for less. A survey presented to the European Parliament in Brussels predicts that the stress of our over-scheduled lives means that 60 per cent of middle-aged adults will have high blood pressure by 2027. The Japanese have a word for cardiac death from chronic overwork: *Kiroshi*. In English there's a new word for a type of zombified living death through slog: *presenteeism*. This is where people spend hours at their desks not achieving anything because they are too tired, stressed, under-stimulated, distracted or depressed to be productive. It's worse than useless: a fifth of the carbon we produce through work is created by commuting. If we are not going to be productive the least we might do is stay at home.

But although our ever-expanding work hours may sound like indentured slavery, even many of society's richest people now think it's cool to be over-stretched. A study by the Institute for Social and Economic Research concludes that: 'Busyness, and not leisure, is now the badge of honour.' Hang on there. In the mid-1970s, many cultural commentators were busy warning of a completely different threat to our Western way of life: this fifth horseman of the Apocalypse was called unlimited leisure. We were about to run smack into a brave new world of high-powered computers, factory automation and affordable labour-saving home appliances that would do all the work. But what, the experts asked, could we do with all the time that these technologies would liberate for us? What would become of our sense of identity if we did not spend most of our waking hours in productive work? What would happen to our sense of purpose if all our basic needs were easily met? Would there be enough diversions to fill our days without us sinking into lassitude, depression and spiritual barrenness? I remember watching the family TV as a child as the experts predicted mass misery by the swimming pool. The same future-gazers were also forecasting the advent of the paperless office. But today at work we are still busily killing trees, as well as ourselves. So what happened?

Meet George (just George – they don't use surnames). He's a bespectacled interior designer, a gentle character who speaks with dry, considered humour. But boy is he elusive. It took me more than a month of phone calls and visits to pin him down for an interview. Every time I thought I'd buttonholed him, he said he'd love to talk, but that unfortunately he was busy, frantic or had something crucial scheduled in the next five minutes. I began to suspect that George didn't relish the prospect of discussing his life with a nosy, persistent scribbler. But when I finally caught him at a point when he felt he could talk, he proved eminently co-operative. What a forehead-slapper: George wasn't evading me – he just truly believes that his life is flowing over the brim with work. Which is why he has openly admitted that he has a 'work problem'.

Every Thursday, George convenes a weekly meeting of Workaholics Anonymous in a side-room of St Columba's Church in Knightsbridge, on the corner of a narrowing street behind Harrods, at the pushy, pushy heart of West London. The church building is no modest affair, with its tall arched entrance and a white stone tower that soars to cathedral heights. But inside the hall, where the late rush-hour traffic is muffled to a rumble, the WA members attempt to ameliorate each other's runaway industriousness, to find some way to limit their continual, compulsive, endless endeavouring after . . . well, endeavouring after what?

Rather than having to confront the prospect of limitless leisure, we have seen instead the rise of 'workaholism' as the label for a new and rapidly spreading neurosis. Workaholics Anonymous was launched in 1983 in New York by a corporate financial planner and a schoolteacher who considered themselves 'hopeless' work addicts. Eight years ago, the organisation opened its first branch in England. Since then, hundreds of Britons have joined, to the point where WA had to start a second London group – the one at St Columba's. George explains what he sees as the roots of WA's growth: 'People want more of everything. People are no longer satisfied in the way that they used to be satisfied. You have to work harder, so that things don't feel like they are getting worse. That can lead to people overworking. People want the things that they possess to be high quality, better quality than you can usually get nowadays, so you have to work harder to pay for that.'

George joined WA two years ago on the recommendation of a friend, because he had developed 'some symptoms', he says. 'For example, I would always underestimate how long a work project would take, which is typical of one of the problems people at WA have. That difficulty becomes progressively worse and suddenly you're working all the time. I'm a perfectionist, and a lot of people who come to WA are really very good at their jobs. A few of the editors of the top newspapers in Britain and America have been members. But people come from all walks – surgeons, painters and decorators, all of that.'

WA offers a 12-step recovery process based on the Alcoholics Anonymous programme, asking its members to put their faith in a higher power, to seek its support, to ask forgiveness of the people they've betrayed and to treat every day as a new day on the path of recovery. But George wonders whether complete recovery is possible in our culture. 'At our meetings, we've discussed how you can get yourself out of this seemingly hopeless state of affairs where you may either burn out or just keep working. How do we go about "not working"? You can't really go on the wagon in the same way that you can with, say, drink or drugs. And when you're working incredibly hard, people applaud you.

The answer is about managing your relationship with work, but society is against us. In America now, for example, the economy basically requires you to work two jobs if you want to keep buying all the wonderful things it offers. I'm sure that this will start happening here.'

The problem, claims George, is so deeply stitched into our society that even people who acknowledge their workaholism subsequently go into denial. 'Many of us seem to think that we have the whole thing under control and that it's not really a problem. Even people who come here regularly say this. In response we ask, "Why are you still coming here?"' George has a lengthy list of questions for people to ask themselves if they fear that they have a workaholic problem. These include: 'Do you work more than 40 hours a week? Do you turn your hobbies into money-making ventures? Do you take work with you on holiday? Is your work the thing that you want to talk about a lot? Do you take on extra work because you are concerned that it won't otherwise get done? Do you work or read during meals? Do you believe that more money will solve the other problems in your life?'

I like to consider myself reasonably balanced work-wise, so I felt ruffled at having to tell George how several of those questions had me ticking the 'yes' box. 'Oh, a great deal of people in the western world are going to be answering "yes" to those,' he responded eagerly. Hmm. Does this mean that all of a sudden millions of people, myself included, are starting to develop a clinically identifiable psychiatric illness called workaholism? George seems convinced of this. But perhaps something a little different is happening. Maybe we're not actually witnessing the birth of a whole new ism – we are instead responding *en masse* to a broad cultural urge towards overwork that makes many of us feel increasingly conflicted, tired and unhappy, and where people at the extreme breakdown end of this spectrum get labelled as addicted 'workaholics'.

The psychiatric profession is certainly happy to promote this novel diagnosis, along with all the other apparent want-more addictions that our society is throwing up – to sex, love, shopping, texting, spread-betting, the internet, credit cards and steroids, to name just a compulsive few. Dr Neil Brener, a private psychiatrist who runs weekly clinics in the financial heart of London, says the number of 'workaholic' patients he sees is growing considerably. 'The City loves these people. It is designed to make money and it wants people to work hard. It's a macho world and the real top macho person is the one who is last to switch the lights off at night,' says Brener, who is the director of the Priory Hospital, north London, part of a chain of privately owned psychiatric units. Seldom does a week go by without a new job-obsessive patient coming in, he says: 'Very few of these patients come in and say, "I'm a workaholic," but after a few sessions they admit to it. I don't think they do anything with the money they have earned. That's not the point of workaholism.'

So, if it's not for the money or the fun, why do people work too hard? 'These patients' real thing is about avoidance of the rest of their lives, about avoiding control over those lives,' Brener argues. 'Many of them are avoiding relationships or their own feelings. These patients tend to come from emotionally repressed environments. They work harder and harder and harder, but then they come to me when something goes wrong in their lives, for example they have a bereavement, and things start to fall apart for them.'

Such extreme examples of overworking offer us a distorting mirror – a caricature of mainstream society that helps us to understand how our long-hours culture is creating evermore work partly to help us avoid the truly problematic stuff of modern existence. Just like pointless, endless shopping for evermore stuff, it's another form of escapist, existential dummy-sucking. Confronted by the alarming prospect of leisure – of unprecedented amounts of time, space and opportunity to grow as people and to face the big-question stuff about the meaning and purpose of our lives – we suddenly remember that, woah, we still have loads to do back at the office. We drown out the big questions by marching behind the brass band of infinite ambition. It's a march that apparently need never end: today's idea of success increasingly involves attaining unprecedented levels of wealth, power and celebrity.

But it hasn't always been so demanding: ancient classical civilisation developed the belief that success lay in mere modest fulfilment; from working to discover and develop your talents, then using them to benefit others as well as yourself. So long as we moderns think that we haven't achieved enough in our careers – and hey pal, the sky's the limit – we can remain convinced that we're not yet free to explore many of life's other possibilities.

The world of work, perversely, thus offers us liberation of a sort. Our new office gadgets have proved remarkably useful for producing more documents, more demands, more analyses, more product niches, more reports, more data, to keep us preoccupied. In the animal world, this type of avoidance tactic is called displacement activity. When my two cats come to the brink of a fur-flying scrap with each other, they often get stuck ping-ponging between conflicted feelings of fear and aggression. So they evade the dilemma by indulging busily in a little comfort activity such as grooming. Similarly, the industrious frenzy of modern work seems to offer many of us an emotional escape-hatch.

This sort of avoidance strategy helps to explain why divorce lawyers are at their busiest in the weeks following the summer holiday season. Work successfully keeps many spouses apart for the majority of the year, so when they suddenly have to spend a significant period of shared time together within the pressure-cooker atmosphere of 'must have maximum holiday fun', powerful pent-up emotional forces burst free – all too often with catastrophic results.

One seemingly innocuous answer to the overwork problem is to pursue 'work-life balance'. It's a sweet idea, but you may have noticed how in practice it doesn't actually work for most people. In America, large corporations have discovered one important reason why: as individuals, we have an extremely tipsy sense of balance. Given the appropriate support, American corporate execs prefer their work-life balance to favour office over home. Their organisations have discovered that managers do indeed want to enjoy simpler and easier personal lives – they want to ensure that family events such as daughters' weddings are professionally organised, they want to keep their cars spick, span and regularly serviced, to enjoy good home-style food and to watch all the best films and TV programmes.

And what could be better for them than having it all sorted out by the office? Many top American managers can now spend longer at work while personal life-support facilitators tackle their potentially messy and time-consuming domestic arrangements. If the execs want to catch a TV show or film, then sure, there are homely lounges at work where they can relax in front of the box. There are cosy little dining-rooms, too. It might sound rather artificial and remote, compared with the deeper, more intense relationships we might expect to foster in our lives, but US research shows that high-flyers get a real kick out of this new arrangement. The fact is, if you ask your secretary at work for a cup of coffee, you get a cup of coffee, pronto, and the way you like it. If you ask your teenager at home for a cup of coffee, you are likely to be told where to stick it.

Of course we don't openly admit that we may find work life easier and far more amenable to control than our domestic existences. It's taboo, and we camouflage it behind litanies of complaint about long-hours regimes, while the hours just keep getting longer. Then we spend less time at home, and home life starts to feel more fraught and less fun, and so we avoid it more . . . which is why one German psychologist claims that modern life is even swirling us down a vicious relationship cycle where we work too much because we don't have enough sex – and then we don't have sex because we're working too much. Ragnar Beer, of Göttingen University, says his survey of 32,000 men and women reveals that the less sex you have, the more work you seek. He says that people who are sexually deprived often need outlets for their frustrations – such as more time in the office. Beer's team found that a third of interviewees who have sex once a week take on extra work to compensate for not having sex quite as often as they would like. The problem is that the work increasingly consumes time and energy that could be employed for sexual purposes, to the point where couples no longer make love at all. So they work more.

All this social weirdness about employment leaves many of us in a quandary. Call me a creep, but I quite like the work that I do. I find it rewarding, most of the time. When it's enjoyable it is really enjoyable. And when it's not, well, we all need somewhere to stick our sense of being a miserable misfit. The odd spot of career success plumps the ego and helps to maintain a sense of purpose. I've also found some true lasting friendships through work. And then there's the money. So it's a fulfilling component of the rest of my life – as long as I can have a 'rest of life' without work choking my personal ecology.

That's the enoughist challenge: to be able to enjoy within reason many of our society's creature comforts and conveniences, to have honest labour, but also to have space and time to feel content, manageably harassed but fulfilled – and without having to drop out. How do you manage this self-sustainability in a world of evermore work, where the message so often is: 'You're either on the long-hours bus, or you're off the bus completely'? Is it possible, in the corporate world, to sideshift rather than downshift, to practise *enough* ambition without getting deleted from the system?

We might look to the Netherlands for inspiration. Dutch employees spend the fewest hours at work in northern

Europe – nearly four hours a week less than we do. One reason is that their idea of what's industrially cool and clever is markedly different from ours. A pan-European study found that British managers reckon that putting in a lifetime of extra hours proves that you are a dedicated – and thus highly effective – employee. The Dutch, meanwhile, tend to think that if you can't get all your work done in the normal hours allotted, then there must be something wrong with either you or your job. If we were all to go Dutch, it might enable us to experience non-work life more. But to anyone who has been steadily nudged and levered into life as a British long-hours drone, that possibility can sound wasteful and self-indulgent, even perverse.

Around a decade ago I was researching a newspaper feature on track days – a burgeoning British mini-industry where Joe and Jane Public pay to scorch their own sportscars and motorbikes around motor racing circuits. I asked the PR man at Brands Hatch what kind of people went on them. 'Oh, mildly affluent types,' he replied. 'The same sort you see playing golf on weekdays – they've got the resources to take an occasional day off and they're committed enough to their hobby to make time for it.' Sitting in our drab editorial office, I felt a barb of envy. But really, what was stopping me from doing the same thing?

Three years earlier, I had made the break into Fleet Street, working half-weeks in the precarious world of free-lance sub-editing, where a careless fact-check, dodgy headline or an ill-fitting face could spell expulsion from this professional pantheon. I had other part-time work, including editing a healthcare management journal that I had launched as a full-time editor two years previously, when the NHS was just beginning to restructure itself in imitation of the corporate world. To prepare for the launch, I'd bought a pile of bestselling management gospels by a new host of media stars – including American gurus such as Tom Peters and Warren Bennis. This was wham-pow stuff, ideal for repackaging as inspirational advice for health service administrators eager to kick ass in the newly business-oriented NHS.

It wasn't my choice of bedtime reading, but there was one exception – Charles Handy's *The Age of Unreason*. Handy was British and offered a subversively different slant on the world of work. It carried the seeds of enoughness. He proposed that work should not be all about work, but instead be a portfolio of different types of activity – some good old paid-for employment, some charity work, some learning work and some fun life stuff. It chimed with what I thought I desired. And it seemed to make more sense than all the other hero-management books combined. There was only one way to find out if it worked – to try it.

So I poked a cautious leg out of the bed of traditional work-life, by going part-time on the health-management mag. Then, by clinging to colleagues' coat-tails, I got freelance work on newspapers, found other journalistic scraps, worked voluntarily for some comparatively harmless pressure groups and started with a friend to meddle with an obscure new thing called the internet. After a rough start, money began to flow. The mischievous joy of making cash off my own wits steadily eclipsed the 2 a.m. trauma of waking frighted by the nightly panic: How Am I Going To Pay The Mortgage? Then one day, soon after I'd researched the Brands Hatch feature, along came the devil's emissary, in the suave guise of my manager at *The Times*. He had a tempting proposition. In time-honoured news-paper management fashion, he collared me by the photo-copier and muttered that I was to be offered a full-time job, the grail of many a Fleet Street journeyman. Within my grasp was one of those rare, (fairly) lucrative and much-envied prizes in journo life – a pension-and-perks staff post on a national quality paper. That's your career sorted for life (if you can cling on to the door-frame hard enough for long enough). Well blimey. What do you say?

'No thanks,' I replied. Worse, I didn't even think about it. Or have the social grace to look agonised. I heard the echo of Charles Handy's promise and felt the pull of life as a bloke who could decide he'd done enough work that week to skive off on a hobby-jaunt, who could choose the work he did – and even give some labour free for soul-rewarding causes. 'That sounds like a lot of paperwork,' I heard my mouth telling the managing editor. 'Why don't we keep things informal and see how we get on?' Word got round. Colleagues saw me as that perennial pariah in the Bateman cartoon: 'The Man Who . . .' But there are worse ways to blight your career life. I'd had my own mini-Martell moment: enough ambition.

And what does practising enough ambition forsake, anyway? For most of us, beyond a certain level of rank, the demands only become greater and the rewards less worthwhile. My own industry's conditions have changed dramatically in the past few years, and I fear yours have, too. In macho sectors such as newspapers, the cliché used to be 'work hard, play hard'. But now many of us don't get to play at all. We don't even break from the screen for lunch. In the media, we're too busy filling infotainment niches: paper, online, webcasts, podcasts, extra supplements and special reports. One might ask what this all adds to the world in terms of happiness, knowledge and wisdom, but that would be missing the point. Everyone else is doing it, so we have to do it as well . . . unless we take the decision to slip quietly through the side door marked *enough*. In today's work arena, and whether we like it or not, less is less, more is less, and only enough is more. This is the new law of diminishing returns.

For although conspicuous wealth is the great gleaming aspiration that dangles before us, it makes little difference to the morale of those who have got it. The American psychologist Ed Diener reports that even people on the Forbes 100 Rich List (each with more than $125 million lining their pockets) feel only slightly better about their lives than the average citizen. His research also found that people whose incomes have increased over a ten-year period are no more satisfied than those whose salaries stayed the same. Even lottery winners do not get a sustained boost from their sudden riches: a year after their windfalls they tend to return to their previous self-reported satisfaction levels.

Being filthy rich can also increase your risk of intractable psychological troubles. The financially featherbedded tend to have unusually high levels of narcissism, an obsession with litigation and a backwash of emotional neglect from parents who left them to be raised by nannies. Part of the difficulty lies in the fact that super-rich people don't tend to believe that their emotional problems are caused by their heads, says a report in the *Journal of the American Academy of Psychoanalysis*. 'These patients frequently show a strong sense of entitlement and a denial of any psychological problem,' it warns. 'They feel entitled to the "very best", which includes the "best doctor". If their psychological problems cannot be magically erased, they will switch psychiatrists until they find the "right one".'

Rich people also tend to blame the outside world for their angst. So they use their wealth to buy possessions and services that they think will make them feel good. This doesn't make them that different from the rest of us, except that they have the money to fund every one of their neurotically driven desires. But when that doesn't work, they buy more. And when that still doesn't work, they buy even more.

So, as the age-old saying goes, money doesn't make you happy – and not even on a national level: the London School of Economics' World Happiness Survey rates Bangladesh as the most contented nation on the planet, while Britain ranks 32nd and America 46th. Before we all burn our possessions and set sail for blissful penury, though, we should note that it is not poverty that fosters satisfaction. The worst-off nation in the survey was the former Soviet Union, where people are generally neither rich nor satisfied. The report highlights the fact that increased earnings can bring contentment – but only up to a certain point – and that's the point of enoughness. The link between more money and more happiness still works in poor countries, because a small increase in a very low income can mean a considerable improvement in quality of life.

Where is the magic enoughness point? A swathe of recent research indicates that the amount of money required for a life of contentment levels off sharply above the median income of all persons within any specific country. Wherever you live, as long as you are half-way up your national earnings ladder, it seems you are likely to get as much satisfaction from your income as most people ever will. Beyond that, you are flogging an increasingly dead horse. Earning significantly more than average merely ensures that your dinner parties are peopled by whining malcontents, say the economists Daniel Hamermesh and Jungmin Lee. They report that moaning rises with income. They questioned people across the globe and found that the higher a person's salary, the more they complained of suffering from 'time squeeze'. The pair say that the problem runs like this: when people have more money, they tend to think that they could do more things with their time, so they feel that their time becomes more valuable and they increasingly resent the fact that they can't create more of it. That thrumming resentment infects the rest of their psyches.

There's also the money-trap paradox. People expect wealth to bring them something that economists call 'positional goods' – things that keep them ahead of the neighbours. A brand-new consumer durable is infinitely more precious if the guy next door doesn't have one yet. Adam Smith spotted this back in 1776, when he wrote in *The Wealth of Nations*, 'With the greater part of rich people, the chief enjoyment of riches consists in the parade of riches, which in their eye is never so complete as when they appear to possess those decisive marks of opulence which nobody can possess but themselves.' And around 25 years earlier, Samuel Johnson had declared that we reckon how rich we are 'not by the calls of nature, but by the plenty of others'.

This age-old phenomenon exists because we have evolved to be such fearful snobs. A brain-scan study by the National Institute of Mental Health discovered that when people are made to feel socially inferior, two regions buried deep in the brain become more active: the insula and the ventral striatum. The insula is involved with the gut-sinking sensation you get when someone makes you look just *that* big. The ventral striatum is linked to motivation and reward. To stave off the physically dread sensation of feeling second-rate, we feel compelled to work hard to barricade ourselves behind superior social achievements.

It's easy to see how that mechanism would have kept our ancestors competitively stretching for the next rung of social evolution ('Oh my gods, darling, look: the Proto-Joneses have entered the Bronze Age'), but in our wealthy twenty-first century world it has got us locked into a Pyrrhic battle – because the folks next door can also just about afford all the latest status symbols too. The result is an epidemic of over-privilege. Everyone's got everything, so how do we compete next? One common response is to buy it all, just to keep up with the Joneses, and then purchase every incremental upgrade to get a whisker ahead. But it doesn't work. No one truly feels better off: over the past 20 years, the number of westerners who describe themselves as 'rich' has stayed at between 1 and 2 per cent. The rest of us just feel knackered from perpetually trying to run up a down escalator.

The research points to a straightforward solution: you'll

find the secret of work-life contentment if you stay on or slightly above the median-earning level of your country (currently around £355 a week in the UK) and avoid competing socially in materialistic terms. Hey, that was easy. Next, let's solve the Middle East crisis. But it's not so simple, not least because our psychic scales are so heavily weighted towards working ever harder. We are programmed by millennia of ambitious instincts. Plus we live in a culture that repeatedly promises us that we can have it all if we strive for it. Add to that the sophisticated materialistic marketing that constantly subverts our subconscious. And then our egos tell us that we are the clever exceptions to every rule, the above-average ones who can beat the crowds to all life's golden prizes and truly enjoy them, too. It's all pushily positive stuff.

How on earth can we shore up our more rational, balanced, enoughist wishes against this rampaging mob of lower-brain drives? To explore this question, I thought I would badger the original source of my enough-work inspiration, Charles Handy – not simply because I fancied meeting one of my old gurus (often it's the worst thing one can ever do), but because he appears to have become an advanced practitioner in the art of median-temperature success. If you Google any list of the world's most influential business pundits, he'll be on it. And that means serious earning power on the world corporate-speaking circuit – easily enough to make you a millionaire inside 12 months. But Handy doesn't do that. At the start of every year, he and his wife, Elizabeth, calculate how much money is required to fund their simple lifestyle and then schedule their working life to meet that need.

A brief internet search unearthed their telephone number. Elizabeth answered with clipped efficiency and promptly declared: 'Charles doesn't write forewords for other people's books, if that's what you're after.' Mrs Handy sounded rather formidable. However, after some persistent ingratiation on my part, she suggested that if I sent them an e-mail, I might well get asked round to their house. Some e-mails you jauntily fire off, others get nudged into this cruelly capricious world with the gentlest, most persuasive caress of the 'enter' button. The effort spent composing a honeyed begging letter paid off: I got my access-Handy pass, an invite to lunch in Putney, south-west London.

It's an imposing detached Victorian house fronted by a gravel driveway. But the Handys' place is round the side, in one of the garden flats. A small, balding man in a casual pullover answers the door. As far as gurus go, Handy fails the entrance exam for saffron-robed charisma. He looks more like a catalogue ad for senior contentment. Theirs is a lovely home, but you wouldn't call it capacious. 'We used to live next door in a far more impressive flat with a kitchen that made people say "Wow" when they walked in,' explains Elizabeth. 'We sold that to our daughter. This one is more modest, but it suits our needs better.' Charles laughs and adds, 'I rather miss that kitchen, but she is right, of course.'

It quickly becomes clear that Elizabeth, a professional photographer, isn't fierce at all. And she does a good fish-cake. But she has to play gatekeeper in order to make one of their hobbies practicable: playing host to a regular pilgrims' progress of potentially interesting visitors. I'd just missed their previous guest, a young South Korean student who had launched a political magazine. Our conversation quickly reveals that Handy has indeed pioneered a resolutely enoughist path: 'A few years ago we decided we didn't need to maximise our income; we wanted to maximise our life,' he says. 'We had to figure out a way to do that. At the start of each year, we work out how much or how little money we need to get through – I add 20 per cent to that because I worry – and then we plan out how much we need to work to earn it. We're not living in sackcloth; we make sure there's enough for wine and books and those things that we value, but it's remarkable how little you need.'

As we sit at lunch overlooking the garden, Handy recalls an interview he had just given to an American journalist for *Time* magazine. 'I only do ten paid speaking engagements a year, but she asked me if I could do more. Yes, I said, I could probably do 50. So why didn't I do that, she wanted to know. I replied, well, what would I do with the extra money? She said, in all seriousness, "You could *collect* things." Collect things,' he laughs. 'To me, that would not be getting money for a good use.' Handy, a former oil executive, left Shell in 1972 to teach at the London Business School before throwing it in for a third career as a business philosopher, writing guides to new workplace thinking such as *The Empty Raincoat*. For him, capitalism is a system – the best that we've come up with so far – but one that ultimately brings us only to a stepping-off point for exploring the things that really reward us as humans.

His inspiration stems from studying ancient Greek and Roman philosophy as an undergraduate: 'Aristotle first introduced me to the idea of "enough" through his concept of the golden mean. Aristotle says that virtue is not the polar opposite of evil, but lies in the middle ground between two extremes or vices – too much and too little. He thought that wealth was not necessarily good or bad, as long as it was viewed as the means to something greater. The sin lay in exceeding the mean.'

Handy no doubt inherited his ecclesiastically inclined terminology from his father, an Anglican priest. His vicarage upbringing may be the spiritual source of his unfashionable frugality, too. Certainly, he believes that life would be far easier if we all followed Aristotle's lead: 'Until we can define what "enough" is for us in terms of money we will never be truly free – free to define our real purpose in life,' he says, waving his fork. 'Instead, we'll be volunteer slaves to our employer or profession.' For Handy, pursuing this idea meant rethinking what employment and money meant to him. 'Settling for enough does mean that we have to do away with the other uses of money – it no longer works as a symbol of success or a way of defining ourselves, or as an excuse or compensation for not getting on with our real life. The motive of not working so hard is not to lie on the beach, but to have the opportunity to discover other aspects of yourself.'

In practical terms, he believes we all need to do something that's anathema to many British workers – say bye-bye to the full-time employer and their shaky pledge of secure employment. 'If you work full-time for someone, then that's all your hours gone, used up and sold in advance. You have nothing to bargain with your employer, except to ask for more money for the same amount of time – and often people simply want to get that money as a symbol of their self-worth rather than anything beneficial in itself. You can't use it really to enhance your life, you'll just get fatter on it, rather than growing in other ways such as spiritually. When you work as an independent, you can make a different cost-benefit calculation: more money might not be better if it used up too much time, or if it meant doing something that you disliked, that was in the wrong place, or was even conceivably immoral.

'Determining our own sense of enough gives us the power to say "no" to speaking invitations that we don't find inspiring or where we don't think much of the people who are inviting us,' says Handy with evident glee. 'It's threatening for some people and it takes a little courage at first, but saying "no" is very exciting. It gives you a wonderful sense of control. You appreciate the very old theological principle – that if you don't know what enough is, you're not free. We can use the time this liberates to do other things, or we can barter our work for something else – such as first-class air tickets abroad and a stay in an excellent hotel, in exchange for doing a talk for an organisation abroad. We often request that, as part of the package, we are introduced over dinner to four or five of the most interesting people in the area, so that our lives are hopefully enriched in that way.'

Fish-cakes, salad and fruit consumed, along with a leisurely glass of white, Elizabeth brings the guestbook for me to sign – a tactic for declaring, 'Enough visit.' The pair are heading off to catch an exhibition of Holbein paintings. No doubt they'll be mistaken by some of their fellow gallery-goers for a retired couple trying to fill their time. Handy is, after all, in his seventies. But practising enough work has also enabled him to extend his career-span to match his longevity without either risking burnout or seeing his money-earning turn into drudgery. It's something that we will all have to consider as our potentially productive years grow ever longer. 'Retirement equals death, if you ask me,' he says, putting on his overcoat. 'You've got to carry on doing some kind of work, whether it's paid work or pro-bono work. Otherwise you just lose interest and that's the end of you.'

## Work *enough*

### Look abroad

Where is the world of work headed? For a siren warning, we should look to our American counterparts, who make Britons look like the laid-back Dutch by comparison. To afford their ever-larger houses and cars, Americans have to work significantly longer than Europeans. After five years of service at a company, a US worker typically gets 13 days of paid leave a year, compared with between four and six weeks in Europe. Globalisation is spreading this trend. In Britain, employers now get more than £1.2 billion worth of their employees' work free because staff do not take all their holiday entitlement. If we do not actively swim against this more-work tide, we will be dragged along with it.

### Sideshift

Twenty-five years ago, college students sought peace, love and world revolution. Today's starry-eyed young idealists tell researchers that they want to 'develop their work-life balance'. But it is increasingly hard to maintain a sanely sustainable workload amid our frenetic world of work. Fast-moving companies tend to have rapid turnovers of staff, and this often means that we keep getting promoted into taking on evermore responsibilities. That is fine if your ambitions focus solely on working hard, but bang goes your chance to enjoy the full spectrum of life's other potentials.

Telling your employers that you are not ambitious is a form of corporate thought-crime, so the answer is to quietly sideshift, to try to stay at the level of responsibility and workload that suits your competence best. Sideshifting is primarily a state of mind that resists the seductive call of promotion, in the interest of preserving your personal ecology. Practical strategies include doggedly trying to stay below the boss's radar and aiming always to work for happy managers who are likely to stick in their own jobs for as long as possible. With luck there will always be more driven (or foolhardy) souls willing to whizz past you in the corporate hierarchy.

But whatever happens, you should always keep one hand on the ripcord, ready to bale out when the job's demands outweigh the rewards. Too often, people only take the exit once they've burnt out and are hardly fit for a new job, career change or freelancing. Being ripcord-ready requires an honest talk with your ego. If we all had an internal dashboard, everybody's speedo needle would be stuck at 29mph in a 30mph zone. Whether you're Gordon Brown or the bloke pushing a broom down the street, we are all nagged by an inner voice which says that we're underachieving, that if we just put our shoulder to it more, we could make the breakthrough that resolved our lives. That's why 80 per cent of us told a study by the Hay Group management consultants that we fear we lack the commitment to get where we should be in life. But it's a delusion, a crustacean-like psychic defence against reality. 'You could rule your world,' our psyches tell us, 'if only you worked harder.'

## Slack smartly

Anyone who'd peeped into Archimedes' bathroom just before his Eureka moment might have thought that the old Greek's tub-time would produce only pruney fingers. But would Archimedes have discovered the principle of displacement if he'd dashed in and out of a shower? Psychologists have begun to understand how we can do our best thinking when we're not concentrating on work at all. If you've ever had a great thought pop into your head while peeling the spuds, you've experienced a phenomenon that Dutch investigators confirmed in the journal *Science*: the unconscious mind is great at solving complex problems when the conscious mind is either busy elsewhere or not taxed at all. In this era of knowledge-work, it would make good sense for companies to encourage their staff to build some slack into their days. Until they do, you may have to sneak in regular periods of mental relaxation, in order to do some proper thinking for them.

## Use stealth

Beware: practising *enough* work can mark you out for bullying and sabotage. Stealth is the answer. Some of the worst enforcers of overwork culture are colleagues who suffer from it most. They seem motivated by a corporate form of Stockholm Syndrome, where hostages come to collude with their kidnappers (the most famous example is the heiress Pattie Hearst, who in 1974 was caught robbing a bank to fund the anarchist Symbionese Liberation Army, which had snatched her two months earlier). Corporate Stockholmers believe their overwork habits are driven by irresistible external forces – so if an enoughist colleague is clocking fewer hours than them, they can't be pulling their weight. Corporate Stockholmers have to believe this, or their internal logic would implode and they might have to consider getting a life.

Instead they will attempt to stop you having yours, often by sending you barrages of unnecessary work-creating demands and out-of-hours communications. You may wish to confront Stockholmers directly, but that's like painting a target on your forehead. A more fruitful tactic is to make yourself an unrewarding and elusive quarry. If you're getting out-of-hours e-mails and calls, never answer them instantly. Wait until a time that you know will be immensely inconvenient to the Stockholmer. Then respond in the most co-operative-sounding manner, but only by leaving them with a question, the sort of question that makes more work for them. They are already working to capacity, so if you persistently, cheerfully, constructively and supportively keep increasing their load, they'll eventually feel so heartsunk and stressed that they will start hassling someone else instead.

### Value your earning hours

Estimate how many years you have left in your life, by subtract-ing them from the average Western expectancies of 80 for men and 82 for women. And turn that into hours. Now you can say to yourself, 'I have only xx number of hours left before I'm dead. How do I want to use this finite time most valuably? Do I want to use it earning more money than perhaps I need, in order to spend it on more things than perhaps I need? What else could I do with those hours?

The answer will not necessarily require a massive life-shift. But the question is worth revisiting regularly. It may be particularly useful in helping you decide how many weekly working hours are sufficient for your desires. The American campaigning organisation Take Back Your Time considers 40 hours to be enough. It points out that in 1940, the 40-hour working week became enshrined in US law, though since then the average American's working week has steadily grown. Still, 40 hours a week sounds pretty steep to me. I'd sooner go for 35 max.

There is a long and proud history of refusing to work beyond the rewards that you personally set yourself. In the early part of the industrial revolution, when people were encouraged to formalise their working weeks around daily shifts, the phenomenon of 'St Monday' was widespread, as many people chose to earn only as much as they needed to pay for basic food, clothing and shelter. Why go to work on Monday mornings if you don't need to? That balancing act was thwarted when consumerism successfully persuaded people that what they really wanted was not more time, but more material goods than they already had.

### Watch the body-clock

The phrase 'don't work harder, work smarter' has become an empty cliché in a society that wants us to work *both* harder *and* smarter. But you can optimise your chances of getting more done in less time by learning what habits suit your body and mind best. Hopefully, you won't use this tactic to get more work done, but will instead liberate life-hours by having to spend less of them earning money. It seems that we are born with pre-sets that affect our capacity for working at different times of day. An experiment at the London Science Museum found that our genes play a role in determining whether we are 'larks' or 'owls' – people who are at their best in the morning or evening. Researchers took swabs from visitors' cheeks and found that those who identified strongly with larkishness or owlishness tended to have one of two variations in their body-clock genes. As a rule, women are more lark-like than men, although nobody yet knows why.

I must possess the 'owl' variation. I write best in the afternoon and evening. So, before lunch, I stick to non-writing stuff whenever possible – admin, phone calls and research. It took me years to learn to do this. In my early freelancing days, I'd sit in front of the screen in a morning fug, trying desperately to squeeze thoughts into words, words into sentences, and sentences into something sensible, and failing. But I was desperate to get going, so I'd fight on while becoming increasingly despondent. Then I'd start to question whether I was cut out for this stuff and head off for a mini crisis in the pub or under the duvet. By early evening I would have become sufficiently panicked to start trying again. Suddenly it would start to flow.

### Share the load

Working part-time is better for your own ecology, as it liberates space to tend your mind, life and body. It also spreads the available work around to other workers in your community, rather than making you hoard it as a time-starved, exhausted salary earner. It's often more efficient for employers, too, as they are buying only the hours in which you are genuinely interested in working, rather than also funding your tired-time, bored-time and waiting-to-go-home time.

## Keep leisure cheap

Leisure should be about doing things you love, rather than spending money trying to impress. In fact, the more money you spend on leisure, the less time you spend enjoying it. The past decade has seen designer brands invade humble hobby-spheres such as hiking, as well as inflating the prices of premium sports equipment. 'All the gear, but no idea' is an unkind put-down, but there's more than a hint of truth in it. A study in the *Journal of Labor Economics* has shown that when men spend more on recreational goods, they also spend more time at work.

Every 1 per cent increase in the price of the goods they buy translates into the loss of one day's leisure per year. This may be because they feel they have to work harder to pay off the higher prices. Or perhaps they are trying to get fit vicariously by splashing out on expensive goods rather than sweating. This sort of behaviour explains a 2003 NOP poll finding that a quarter of home-fitness equipment that British people buy is used only once. A tenth is never unwrapped.

## Escape on microbreaks

Are we having fun yet? The past two decades have witnessed an epidemic of vacation inflation. Our more-more culture has transformed holidays from simple family-car affairs to competitive global expeditions of the 'what, you haven't been whitewater rafting with Sumatran orang-utans?' variety. The pressure of working life has leaked into the weeks that traditionally acted as an easygoing safety-valve. Dammit, we must have a fantastic holiday, because we've toiled so hard and we deserve one, even if it means big plans, big packing, jabs, pet-sitters, house-sitters, pre-dawn departures, terror-alerts, cancellations, terror-searches, travel-sickness, more terror-searches, jetlag and pressure-induced family implosions. A recent study found that 1.7 million Brits now have to take time off work to recover from their holiday trips. We could just give up on holidays and stay at work, like many of our American counterparts. But we need to take breaks – stress-free breaks – for our health's sake. Men who don't holiday are a third more likely to die from a heart attack.

That's why the wife and I recently found ourselves wandering around near the world's ragged end, trying to navigate the pitch-black lane that leads from an ancient village pub to a wooden B&B on the edge of a crumbling clifftop. In fact we were only 40 minutes' drive from home, still in overcrowded south-east England, but at a beauty spot called Birling Gap. We were enjoying a microbreak, leaving our home hassles in another psychic universe. If you've not heard of microbreaks, that's because I invented the term to describe our regular modest rapid-fire holiday escapades – a regime inspired by the panic that accompanies our annual trophy-holiday abroad.

It's a return to the simple ease of my childhood: while most other families jetted off to the Costas, my mum would make the best of our cash-strapped situation by driving us 53 miles to Folkestone for a week in a genteelly dilapidating hotel. I loved it. When you're a kid, you can have happy holidays anywhere, because so long as you *know* you're on holiday, then you're on holiday. It's a state of mind. Why shouldn't that approach work in adulthood, too? It's useful to remember that modern transport has distorted our natural sense of distance. A 45-minute whizz by car or train would have taken us the best part of a day's travelling 200 years ago – just as flying abroad does nowadays.

*Here are my five rules of micro-breaks:*

★ No more than 60 minutes' journey away

★ Two nights' max (Sunday nights are dirt-cheap, and you can commute from your hotel room on Monday morning)

★ Take only aircraft-locker-sized luggage

★ Location? The odder the better

★ But never, ever, on a bank holiday.

## 5 | **ENOUGH** Options

*Life is a progress from want to want, not from
enjoyment to enjoyment.*
Samuel Johnson, 1776

I needed to buy a digital camera. One that was simply
good at taking good snaps, maybe occasionally for
publication. The state of the art meant six megapixels of
resolution – enough for poster-sized blow-ups – a decent
lens and a bunch of look-ma-no-hands features. Being the
cautious type, I fancied a reputable brand. So I went on
the net, spent 15 minutes skimming product reviews on
good sites, wrote down the names of three top recommen-
dations and headed for my nearest big friendly camera
store. There in the cabinet was one of the cameras on my
list. And it was on special offer. Oh joy. I prodded a finger
at it and asked an assistant, 'Can I have one of those?' He
looked perturbed. 'Do you want to try it first?' he said. It
didn't quite sound like a question. 'Do I need to?' I replied.
'There's nothing wrong with it?' This made him look a bit
insulted and I started to feel bad. 'No, no. But you should
try it,' he said encouragingly. 'Compare it with the others.'

I looked across at the others: shelves of similarly sized
six-meg cameras stretched along the wall, offering an array
of fractionally different sales propositions and prices, with

each manufacturer selling a range of models based around the same basic box. Myriad options to choose from, each nudging your budget. I faced the prospect of spending hours weighing X against Y, always trying to take Z and possibly H into account at the same time. But when I had finished, I would still have only the same two certainties that I had entered the store with: first, as soon as I carried my new camera out of the shop, it would be worth half what I paid for it; and second, my marvellous gadget would almost instantly be superseded by a newer model.

But something in the human soul whispers that you can beat these traps by making the *right* choice, the *clever* choice, the *wise* choice. In the end, I compromised with the salesman. He seemed a sincere enthusiast. So I let him pluck my chosen camera from the cabinet, demonstrate how it took excellent pics of my fellow shoppers on 'auto' . . . and when he started to wade into the special features, I interrupted to ask whether I needed to buy a carry-case and a memory card as well (nothing fancy, mind).

Why do we think that new options still offer us anything new? Perhaps it is because they offer another opportunity for existential dummy-sucking, to avoid facing the fact that our real choices in this culture are far more limited than we would like to imagine. In photography, for example, science and marketing are now catapulting us beyond the point on the curve where new technological advances can make any real difference to the amateur snapper's experience. In the 1870s, if you wanted to take a few photos on your holiday trip, you would need your own horse and cart to haul along a camera the size of a microwave oven, as well as a light-proof tent where you could carefully emulsify the glass plates that would slowly capture your images. It tended to detract from the spontaneity. Small wonder all the shots back then looked so stiltedly formal, rather than, 'Here's one of Junior stamping on his sister's sand-palace.'

The advent of film in convenient portable rolls in the early 1880s was a huge step forward. Then, in 1888, Kodak brought photography to the masses, with a camera that came pre-loaded with 100 shots' worth of film. It was reasonably light, portable and you could hold it in your hand while taking pics. It was priced at $25, with the liberating slogan, 'You press the button – we do the rest.' Welcome to the family snap. But still it was hardly convenient. After exposure, the whole camera had to go back to the factory for prints to be made and new film inserted, a process that cost a princely ten bucks. In 1900, Kodak came up with another shutter-bugging first, the one-dollar Box Brownie camera. Suddenly, everyone was having family-album moments. After that, in the late 1930s technology brought us colour print film (yes, Kodak again). We then had to wait until the early 1990s for the first digital cameras to appear, though initially the cost restricted them to professional use. Since then the technology has become bountifully cheap and easily accessible.

Thanks to high tech, the days of agonising about the 'right' camera should be over for the vast majority of us. The shiny silver boxes on offer are all fit for purpose and produce good downloadable shots at the press of a button. Instead of getting torn by tiny differences and paying big for them, we should be spending the time, energy and enthusiasm on getting into joyous photogenic situations to immortalise, share and reminisce over. Similar technological advances should have kicked the quandaries out of the majority of our gadgets. But instead, we are faced with infinitely more options, niche items and lifestyle-specific concepts than ever. In response we eagerly buy – but don't use – the extras. Nearly 60 per cent of adults employ only half of their new devices' functions, says one study, which says this is because only one in six of us bothers to read the manual. But perhaps this is pragmatism rather than sloth: another survey found that almost two-thirds of mobile-phone owners use only four of the features – calls, text messages, alarm clock and camera. The rest is techno-flannel. More than a third of us don't even know if our mobile takes pictures.

There should, in theory, be a natural limit to all this consumer complexity: one study of mobile-phone-buying decisions, in the *Journal of Product and Brand Management*, found that offering evermore options failed to increase the ultimate level of customer satisfaction. The report cautioned that three options per model is perfectly adequate, while anything over seven causes anxiety and can be counter-productive. The Germans have a phrase for it: '*die Qual der Wahl*' – the torture of choice. Psychologists say that while customers may initially be attracted to a panoply of options, many end up so confused by all the alternatives that they give up in despair.

In an oft-quoted experiment, two university professors, Mark Lepper and Sheena Iyengar, set up a pair of tables in a supermarket, one with 24 jars of jam and the other with six, and offered discount coupons to anyone who stopped to sample the jams. Of the people who stopped at the 24-jam table, only 3 per cent went on to buy jam, while 30 per cent of the people who stopped at the six-jam table did. In similar vein, Swiss consumer researchers Thomas Rudolph and Marcus Schweizer say that customer confusion may cause retail slumps. They claim that their studies show how, even when choosing toilet paper, people fear making mistakes and dislike trying to decide what is right for them. But hold on, this is toilet paper. What exactly do customers expect to do with it? Meanwhile, and despite all these psychologists' warnings, the shops just keep piling on more options.

There's a solid practical reason for this: our society has pretty much invented everything necessary for a comfortable life. But marginal options, even if they aren't ultimately satisfying, can be used to lever us into buying more things. In the early industrial age, it was comparatively easy to invent something that fulfilled a genuine unmet need. Patent a lightbulb, a tractor or a vacuum cleaner, and you could guarantee that the pigeons would be messing on your home-town statue in perpetuity. But now the market for most practical products is saturated. Manufacturers used to respond to this problem by competing primarily on price, but beyond a certain point that gets too painful. So they began instead to offer more options – creating whole new wants and then supplying things to meet them.

This trend went hyperspace in the 1990s, to the point where today we find ourselves swept up by a carnival of new extras, formulas and packaging. A favourite trick of factories is to jazz up old products as 'new, improved' and 'now with added . . .' by splitting their existing product into different sub-types. Marketing people call additives such as aloe vera and jojoba 'pixie dust': just sprinkle in the absolute minimum to make it a legitimate addition and, ta-daa, sales head north for a while . . . until our excitement at the novel formula becomes dulled by familiarity, and the cycle begins again.

Our minds love novelty. Adolescents' brains, it seems, are particularly excited by new stimuli. New objects and experiences can fire up their whoopee-button dopamine reward systems about as robustly as a hit of cocaine, says R. Andrew Chambers, an Indiana University psychiatrist. As we saw in chapter one, evolution seems to have tuned our mammalian reward system to seek new things, such as new tools or unknown foods: 'This system is so powerful for mammals because it's critical for survival,' says Chambers. 'It is what's going to tell you what the resources and dangers are around you.'

Teen shoppers hooked on novelty may also turn into lifelong new-product addicts. The adolescent brain is highly plastic and trainable (the prefrontal cortex, the region associated with planning and controlling actions, is still developing), so the repetitive thrill and reward of retail novelty-seeking may – just like youthful drug taking – ultimately imprint a wired affinity that lasts for life.

All this may help to explain why there are now nearly a thousand shampoo types on the world's shelves. And if you're thirsty, there are 27 different varieties of Coca-Cola and Pepsi-Cola alone to choose from. That's a lot of ways to sell fizzy syrup. This mass outbreak of differentiation is why the average shopper spends more than 40 seconds weighing their options in the soft-drinks aisle, compared to 25 seconds seven years ago. Confronted by a barrage of confusingly similar products, many buyers now head for the high-priced hills in the hope that spending more will mean getting more. Take designer jeans: no matter that denim was originally produced as tough, cheap workwear, and no matter that the vast majority of jeans come from the same sort of sweatshops, consumers will spend more than £100 on an 'exclusive' pair of the things simply because the fat price tag might somehow guarantee that this trouser among all the thousands of others will be somehow . . . better, and thus make them feel secure in their choice.

While we're doing all this agonising over infinitesimally small options, we may well get seduced into buying something else, either in the shop, or online, where the phenomenon is called Wilfing (short for What Was I Looking For?). One in four British internet users spends nearly a third of their browsing time – equivalent to one working day per fortnight – randomly browsing the net. Shopping websites are the main Wilf-magnet, say researchers, who caution: 'Although people log on with a purpose, they are now being offered so much choice and online distraction that many forget what they are there for, and spend hours aimlessly Wilfing instead.'

With gadget-selling there is another perverse reason for all these options: niche gizmos make the manufacturers' perfectly robust goods seem much less durable. By perpetually creating 'limited editions' with special 'added extras', the marketing people can plant in our famine-conscious Stone Age brains the worrying illusion of scarcity, despite all the abundance so plainly surrounding us. This is the kind of 'First World angst' that gets affluent women tearing off each other's limbs in order to grab a celebrity-endorsed frock on the first day of the sales. By continually adding new options to technology, the makers can ensure that each tranche of frontier-breaking goods is rendered obsolete by the imminent arrival of another next generation. The thrill of acquisition barely lasts beyond the store exit – and all that scientifically advanced use of precious planetary resource soon ends up either in landfill, being recycled via an energy-intensive process, or chucked in the back of a cupboard, lest last year's gadget makes us feel like last year's person.

Our brains add further to the confusion. They tend to amalgamate all the best available options from the different products and lump them together into one imaginary, super-optioned übermodel, which renders whatever item we eventually choose nigglingly less satisfying. So then we have to spend more life-hours striving for the next minutely 'better' bit of kit. And if the manufacturer-supplied options aren't sufficiently satisfying, maybe we might be better off picking them ourselves. In the world of motor cars, Maserati offers four million 'personalisation variations' for its Quattroporte saloon. That's just the extreme end of a widespread motor-selling trend. There are only so many ways to design a car, and they've all been done now – so the makers swerve round the problem by giving buyers the chance to choose the colour of their cup-holders as an expression of their individual freedom and personality. Initially that seems to offer a vast artistic palette for the secret auto-design genius that's always been bursting to get out of you, but it's also four million opportunities to fret about the fact that you didn't choose the right options, ruined your precious Maserati and blew your chance to get the maximum pleasure from it.

Enough options? In the secret megalomaniac fantasy world where I'm in sole charge (come now, we all have one) the old Chairman Mao suit would play a pivotal role. Everyone would have to wear their grey Beatle-jacket uniform all the time. But as part of my retro-despot revival, citizens would also be granted the freedom to exchange their buttons for different colours and different shapes – maybe even switch the positions around a bit. That should give humankind sufficient leeway to exercise personal choice and self-expression without things getting too far out of hand (though the more extreme button-swappers might promptly split into violent factional rivalry).

The Mao suit plan might sound like a blatant affront to our freedom-of-choice culture, but according to investigators at Cornell University, many of the modern options we're offered are in fact no more meaningful than swapping the buttons on a tunic. The Cornell psychologists report that free choice is useful when deciding between things that are wildly different, but it just doesn't work like that in the shopping aisles. When the researchers told a group of volunteers that they were about to receive either chocolate or a bad smell, the volunteers who were given the option to choose between choc and pong were far happier than those who merely got what they were given. But when the choice was between items whose differences were hard to discern, such as two different blends of coffee (as opposed to totally different drinks), the volunteers who were denied choice were just as satisfied with the drink they received as the volunteers who got to choose their own brew. The Cornell researchers conclude that although we can spend ages in stores agonising over different brands, we know subliminally that these options won't make any great difference.

That sounds rather odd. Could it really be that most of the personalised options we face every day are in fact just a conveniently mind-diverting mass fiction – that they aren't real choices at all? There's a free and easy way to test whether you really have such a wealth of freedom to choose, and that's to walk around your local temple of temporal options – the shopping centre. My local mall is called Churchill Square. I could describe it in detail, but I'm sure you pretty much know it already: white walls, shops, piped music, shiny marble-type floors, security guards and lots of people milling around. It's about 200 metres from my home, but usually I only venture there about four times a year to pick up my next batch of contact lenses. This time I went in on a mission to pay rapt, Martian-like attention, lurking around the shops that promise to liberate your true self via the things you opt to drape about your person. By the time I had browsed ten clothes stores, my feet were museum-tired and I felt driven to conclude that if you ignore all the myriad minor points of detail, there's pretty much the same on offer in any shop you enter – T-shirts and jeans and combats and sneakers and crop-tops and baseball caps and this year's shape of skirt. And there ya go.

I'm failing, of course, to acknowledge one crucial element of most modern mall options: the all-important branding proposition. Aside from the fractional differences in price-points and style mutations, all these options have created a new human sensibility: the idea that we *are* what we *choose*: I plump, therefore I am. Brands are painstakingly created to encourage people to identify with them, to believe that their favourite labels have exactly the same kind of human values as they do. It's like having an impressive best pal to be seen hanging with. Our Stone Age brains are designed to relate primarily to other people and animals – and this way of relating tends to get slapped on to inanimate objects, too. We habitually anthropomorphise, which is why so many of us call our cars 'she' and even give them cutesy names. Likewise, we increasingly attribute human-like personality to brands.

Marketing research shows that we can even believe that the brand has an attitude towards us, so we develop tight 'primary' relationships with them that are on a par with marriage, friendship and kinship. So branding introduces an entirely new and bizarre level of false choice when trying to discriminate between different makes of products: subconsciously, we think we're choosing life partners.

Branding power enables one Churchill Square store only to sell shelf upon shelf of the same make of trainer, while the shop next door sells pile upon pile of variously tailored but devoutly one-name jeans. The people who buy from them are convinced that they're opting to express their individuality. But when you stand back and view these mall-shoppers from a few metres' distance, the sum-total of all these time-consuming micro-dilemmas, these high-stakes options for expressing our crucial, ineffable uniqueness, appears remarkably homogeneous. Everyone there basically looks, acts, dresses and speaks much the same.

Then I had a thought: if all the options are pretty much the same – and if the prices aren't really that different, either – why not make the options optional, and just blind-buy in a generic store? It's odds-on that you'll end up in a postmodern pick'n'mix of leisurewear similar to that of your fellow browsers – and surely you'll come out looking no worse than some of them (i.e., badly malled). So I decided to try a kind of Buddhist no-choice style of purchasing. I walked into the next retail outlet down the aisle, and had barely ventured between the clothes racks before a salesman greeted me. 'Need any help there?' he asked (apparently this tactic is not even aimed at selling clothes, it just deters shoplifters). 'Yes please. I'd like some trousers.' My young shop-help smiled and said, 'Sure! What style?' I replied, 'Oh any kind. Which exact trousers would you recommend?' To his credit, the lad's eyes betrayed only the most fleeting expression of 'Holy fuck', before he pointed to a rack of combats, and said, 'Well there's the combats over there. There's some new colours just in. Or we've got a great range of jeans. They're mostly over there by the wall, every style. And the shorts are basically over there . . . and over there. They're all new in for this season.' Then he smiled his winningest smile.

'Excellent,' I replied. 'But what *particular* trousers would you exactly recommend that I buy?' In footballing terms, I was offering the salesguy an open goal. With the goalie comatose. And a tailwind. I'd buy whatever he told me to buy. But he wasn't having it. 'It's all great stuff, mate,' he said. 'Why don't you check out the combats, first? They're all great. Have a look round. I'm sure you'll find something that grabs you. See you in a minute.' Then he ushered himself away.

I slunk from the shop, my strategy a failure. Perhaps the salesguy thought I was propositioning him. Maybe I shouldn't have used the word 'trousers'. To continue the experiment, I picked a more perv-neutral clothing item. Shoes. Surely the only foot fetishists in a shoe shop are the ones flogging the products. 'Looking for any particular shoe?' asked the salesman. 'No style in particular,' I replied. 'What would you recommend?' He looked at me: 'I'm thinking either formal or casual,' he said. 'Fine,' I responded. 'What do you recommend?' . . . 'In formal or casual?' he asked. 'Indeed, which do you recommend?' 'Formal or casual?' . . . 'Indeed, which do you recommend?' Finally he clicked. 'I've never been asked that before. Why don't you have a look round?' he said, nodding at the men's shoes. 'Get an idea of what you like. Then I'll come straight back to you.' So there you go. If you want your own modern no-real-choice Mao suit, you'll probably have to make your own choices. Certainly, no government is going to set up an Options Tsar to prune your possibilities. As Newt Gingrich, the right-wing former speaker of the American House of Representatives, declared: 'If you were to walk into a Wal-Mart and say to people, "Don't you feel really depressed by having 258,000 options? Shouldn't it be their obligation to reduce the choice you must endure?" they would think you were nuts.'

But does any of that matter, beyond the mere fact that this option-crammed world can turn many of us into anxiety-ridden fusspots buying overpriced samey stuff that no sane person truly expects to last? Being practical creatures, we have learnt ways to tackle choice-blizzards, primarily by blanking out information on the options on offer. Unfortunately, we often choose perilous areas for exercising this blindness. Tamar Kasriel of the Henley Centre, the media-forecasting company, has seen this happen with nutrition labels on food. Faced with having to consider yet another variable when choosing between shelves of brightly packaged foods, we tend to ignore all the worthy numbers and letters on the back of the product in favour of the exciting logo, brand and picture on the front. This is despite the fact that often the nutrition label offers the only honest facts that we will ever get about what we are eating. 'When it comes to wellbeing, people only really want to know that the food labelling is there,' Kasriel says. 'They often don't read it. They just feel reassured that it exists.' That's even if the label translates into the message: 'Contains so much salt and fat that your arteries will burst.'

Likewise, we tend to cover our ears and sing 'la-la-la-not-listeninnng' when faced with another of life's big choice-conundrums, picking a pension. The financial services industry habitually creates huge arrays of new products. Shlomo Benartzi, an accounting professor at the University of California, says his study of investors shows that excess choice has odd effects on our decision-making. When we're faced with too many financial options, we tend to stick a pin in the plan that looks most average, instead of doing the maths and picking the best for our circumstances. Our lost profits get creamed off by financial consultants, mortgage brokers and insurance advisers.

That's only the small-screen picture. On a wider scale the promise of infinite choice is more corrosive. It is fostering an entire culture of non-commitment. The consumerist promise of 'always a better option' encourages us to believe that no matter what we are, or do, or own, something far more wonderful is just about to appear. Making a choice and committing to it invokes the dread fear that you have slammed the door on the next options – ones that will really meet your deepest needs. We're back with old *homo expetens* – 'wanting man' – the striving hominid who colonised most of this planet in less than 60,000 years, always seeking better things over the next hill and across the next river. Expectations don't have limits. But at some point the more-more promise of better options ceases to be rewarding. We have reached that point now. We're entering a vicious cycle. Once we attain any of the choices we've been chasing, we soon start to think, 'Hmm, still not happy. In fact, I feel a bit disappointed now. This isn't good enough. Better elevate my expectations again. Pursue better choices.'

This is making our culture increasingly butterfly-minded. As one retail example, the American company Blik now offers a range of wall-coverings billed as 'wall graphics for the commitment-phobic'. Based on the humble sticker, these oversized decorative decals can be stuck on to walls – and when you get tired of the design, you just peel them off. No more 'wedded to the same old wallpaper day in, day out' trauma. The entire interior décor industry, lifestyle magazines and all, now refers to '*this season's* paints and fabrics', as though finding oneself on last season's sofa might induce terminal ennui. Similarly with holidays: why manacle yourself to last month's moth-eaten vacation plans if a fresher option might suddenly arise? The online agent Ebookers.com recently launched a policy that offers financial protection if you suddenly decide that you don't want to travel. Ciaran Lalley, the company's UK managing director, calls it 'disinclination cover' and hails the policy as 'the perfect solution for commitment-phobes'.

If wallpaper, sofa and holiday commitments feel too onerous, what about the rather more potentially burdensome prospect of living with another human being in any kind of long-term sexual relationship? The Office for National Statistics has identified a new social trend with its own acronym: LATs (Living Apart Together relationships). The term describes two people who are in a 'committed' relationship but who feel disinclined to share the same front door. An estimated two million Britons are now LATs – that's one and a half in every ten of us – similar to the proportion of people now cohabiting but unmarried. As for marriage, American brides are increasingly rejecting the vow to love 'till death do us part' in favour of pledges to stay together 'for as long as our marriage shall serve the common good'.

Beyond LAT-ing, another media-friendly acronym has been invented for an emerging epidemic of serial choice-changers, lifestyle-swappers, commitment-dodgers and general dilettantes: they are called the Yeppies – Young Experimenting Perfection Seekers. Confronted by modern life's lengthening list of apparent options they've become like Goldilocks in an endless room of bowls, perpetually moving onwards to sample the next oaty spoonful from the next ursine breakfast. Kate Fox, of the Social Issues Research Centre, is the anthropologist who coined the new tag. She says that Yeppies are unsure how to achieve their ambitions, so they experiment through a shopping-style approach, trying to find the perfect job, the ideal relationship and the most fulfilling lifestyle. Yeppiedom postpones big, life-altering decisions until all the options have been exhausted. It will be increasingly considered quite normal for people to keep life-shopping into their thirties, Fox predicts. 'The "something" that Yeppies are searching for may well be unattainable. But they have high – some would say unrealistic – expectations and they move from job to job, or from career path to career path, desperately seeking perfection.'

The Yeppie ideal is that, by trying on different work-hats, hair-dos and lifestyles, they learn what suits them, what they are good at, and eventually they will discover who they are and what they want. Fox's study suggests that they have the flexibility to change direction and move on when something doesn't work out, rather than settling for an unsatisfactory existence. But Yeppies often fail to find their arrival point: instead they tend to procrastinate in all spheres of life. This trend (along with high property prices) helps to explain why more youngsters live at home for longer. More than 40 per cent of men between 24 to 29, and a quarter of women in the same age group, are still living with their folks. But often it's the only practical way to be the law graduate who yearns to write novels or the junior surveyor planning to chuck it all in and go back-packing in South America. We are, in the words of the old cliché, being spoilt for choice.

You don't have to be that young to get stuck in the life-shopping cycle. Take Paul. I've known him since he was a nipper, but now he's rapidly hitting his late 30s and, like an alarming proportion of his old male schoolmates, still hasn't quite found out what he really wants to do with his life. He's a sometime artist and runs a small marketing business from home, but primarily he works in the insurance industry, although he's half-heartedly been trying to escape it for the past decade. So he hasn't bothered to develop his skills. But what encapsulates Paul's problem more than anything is his relationship with women. He's tall, dark, charming, witty and empathetic, so has little trouble navigating his way into female affections. He's been serially in relationships since his late teens. None has ever stuck, including the one that produced his bright little son. He's entering his teens and would love him to settle. But Paul hasn't even cohabited seriously for the past decade. His son was particularly upset when Paul's last long-term relationship broke up after four years.

Paul was deeply upset, too. And he says it was the same old problem, one that he knows so well: 'I know it's wrong, I know it's stupid. But I always think the next woman will be the one I really, really want. I'll walk into a room and know that I'd like to try relationships with all of them. I don't really do much about it nowadays, but it sorely affects whatever relationship I am in. My head's never fully there. I never feel that I'm landed, either with a woman, or with a job, or with a life. I know I'm getting older and this is starting to look a bit pathetic, but I still just feel that I'm always waiting for this next great opportunity. The real one.'

For the purpose of this book, I had decided to challenge Paul to commit utterly and completely to something, anything, for a long-sounding stretch of time and see what happened. But when I caught up with him to discuss this, he told me that he and his (sort of) girlfriend of the past three months had decided no longer to be (sort of) boyfriend and girlfriend and were now just good friends.

He looked down-but-OK about it, so I decided not to rub it in.

Being a serial switcher in this easy-opt society can get you into some surreal pickles. A prime example is the millionaire Iraqi-born businessman Sam Hashemi, who had a sex-change operation to become the long-haired blonde Samantha Hashemi, and later decided to change back again, to become Charles Kane, a quintessential Englishman. This all began when Sam, a millionaire, lost his vast wealth, followed by his wife and children in 1997. He then became severely depressed and decided that the only way to salvage his life was to become someone else entirely – a woman. A blonde woman at that. He found a surgeon who would sign him up for £35,000 worth of gender-reassignment surgery, but within four years Samantha started to regret the decision. Ever since, he has been working to become a man again. 'To be truthful, I missed my penis,' he says. Now named Charles, he has since endured two painful operations to reconstruct his manhood, had his breast implants taken out and a mastectomy in order to return to masculinity.

What's the alternative to getting swept away by a vast tide of lifestyle options? One response is to try simply refusing to choose (although, ironically, this is another form of exercising choice). This is the tack taken by the 'voluntary simplicity' movement, a small but growing band of people who typically opt to flee the urban rat-race for a quiet country life where the options are pared down to choices that are only local, ethical, sustainable and renewable, and where in turn the pressures are lower and the outlook is simpler. The roots of this stripped-down ideal run deep, right back to ancient Greeks such as Epicurus, who stressed the importance of fulfilling our pleasures in the simple things of life, such as good meals and good friends. More recently, the philosophy was espoused by the American Henry Thoreau's 1854 book, *Walden; or, Life in the Woods*. In this pioneering piece of lifestyle eco-journalism, Thoreau built his own wood cabin by Walden Pond, Massachusetts, a mile from his nearest neighbour, and lived there for more than two years. He spent the time earning a living only by the labour of his hands, while a stream of people came visiting to find out what being a hermit is like.

The simplicity wish also lay at the heart of that gentle TV comedy favourite of the 1970s, *The Good Life*, all about cute and cuddly Tom and Barbara Good's laughable bid for suburban self-sufficiency in Surbiton. But after the giggling had died down, this humble yearning was taken extremely seriously by Duane Elgin in his seminal 1981 book, *Voluntary Simplicity: Toward a way of life that is outwardly simple, inwardly rich*. The title took off, and so did Elgin's downshifted aspiration. Now this lifestyle option has become elevated to a pinnacle of our society's new green ideal. Many of us opt to shop into the aspiration by visiting weekly farmers' markets and joining organic veg-box delivery schemes.

But if you want to do more than just dip your toes into the simplified agrarian idyll, the logistics can be extremely difficult – unless you've spent time chiselling cash from a City career such as banking or broking. Deirdre Shaw, a Glasgow University academic who has studied voluntary simplifiers in depth, says: 'To organise your life to be one of simplicity requires quite a lot of complexity.' The primary problem is

163

the considerable financial boost needed to escape the gravitational pull of standard 21st-century Western life: you can't just knock up your own wooden cabin next to a pond, and it takes a fair wodge to fund a mortgage-free, Home Counties smallholding with ethically sourced local roses round the door. 'In order to decide to simplify radically, to have less, you will have had to have had much in the past,' says Shaw, who is a member of the somewhat paramilitary-sounding International Centre for Anti-Consumption Research. She adds that you need one other thing in order to pursue agrarian anti-choice: the ability to ditch your plainspun ideals every now and then: 'These simplifying professionals have got a lucrative financial skill that they can go back and sell, if needs be. So they can get money if they want it.'

Meanwhile, the rest of us will just have to face the challenge of option-overload from within mainstream society (and even if we could all rush out into simplified rural idylls, the result would be a lot of empty cities and an awfully crowded countryside). There is only one enoughist answer here: to exercise non-choice constructively, by committing ourselves to a limited but genuinely rewarding array of options.

Until this last eyeblink of human history, we were always short of resources and sadly lacking in choice. True wisdom lay in learning to be satisfied with the little that we had. Today, beneath our avalanche of options, we must evolve a new approach – we must wise up to the new world by reducing our palette of possibilities to the ones that truly enhance our lives, and then devoting ourselves to them. So let's declare 'Enough options' and slash and burn the rest. This is, admittedly, a tall order: it requires self-confidence, self-knowledge and resolve. But the alternative is for us all to be left as whining, stressed and angry people amid a world of teeming abundance, burning up our personal and planetary ecologies while locked into a cycle of dissatisfied consumption.

## Choose *enough*

### Heads or tails?
If choosing between two options – be it in life or down at the shops – has got you stuck on the horns of a dilemma, one deceptively simple-sounding answer is to flip a coin. The answer does not lie in whether the coin comes up heads or tails, but in your response to the result. If you feel rather heartsunk or instantly think to yourself, 'OK, best of three', then you really ought to be pursuing the other option. You've discovered your secret preference. It's a form of soul-mining divination, a very stripped-down version of reading your tarot cards or throwing the I-ching.

### Go small
Avoid unnecessary and pointless permutations by shopping only in smaller establishments that lack the floorspace to accommodate ever-expanding options. If the shops are independents, all the better: with luck the proprietors will know their markets and only stock wise choices that take false dilemmas out of your day.

### Try the six-month test
When confronted with life's many choices, we often lose our sense of perspective. Immediate decisions can seem overwhelmingly daunting; their very proximity gives them a soaring importance that may be way out of proportion to their true

import. When we look back on such dilemmas, we wonder why we lost sleep over choices that now seem either straightforward or trivial. One way to get a better view on our crises over life options is to throw in some artificial perspective. Ask yourself, 'In six months' time, will this choice really matter to me?' If it won't, there's little need to agonise over the decision.

## Beware the ethical option con

Retailers want you to confuse true ethical choices with shop-shelf choice. Labels saying eco-this and ethical-that are being adopted *en masse* by manufacturers as another option with which to tempt buyers. Of course, we should try to ensure that the items we buy are as harmless as possible, but if, for example, a clothing label says 'low carbon footprint', the stores often use that to whisper, 'Go on. Look, it doesn't matter if you only ever wear it once or twice . . . it's low carbon footprint.'

## Embrace futility

Our emotional resilience is far stronger than we often imagine. We tend to return to our usual pre-set levels of satisfaction with life, no matter what things happen to us. Modern culture, however, encourages us to become control-freaks, to believe that the options we choose are absolutely vital to determining the way in which our lives turn out. But, in John Lennon's often-quoted words, 'Life is what happens when you're making other plans.' So why angst over choosing between options when your choices probably won't make much difference?

## Leave your ego at the door

Dissociate your ego from your purchasing decisions. We often use retail choice to define who we are. Judith Williamson, the author of *Decoding Advertisements*, puts it this way: 'Shopping gives you a sense of choice and power which is often absent from the rest of your life.' How extremely sad.

## The non-optional option

Instead of being fogged by ephemeral extras, the one non-optional extra we should seek is sustainability – that everything we choose is built to last, repairable and beyond the vagaries of manufactured fashion. We should also aim for sustainable life choices, ones to which we feel we can commit ourselves wholeheartedly, rather than starting off with the life-shopping thought, 'Well if it doesn't work, I can always . . .'

## Practise counter-absurdity

Try dealing with the ridiculous level of consumer choice that confronts you by making equally absurd buying decisions, such as only buying goods with, say, three vowels in their name or labels with the colours red and black in them.

## Satisfice yourself

Satisficing, in the jargon of social scientists, is the sensibly shod alternative to maximising. When you satisfice, you don't let an impossible quest for the perfect option destroy your enjoyment of the merely OK. Maybe it's time to decide that life now is pretty much as good as it will get, and it is well worth warmly appreciating. And maybe (just maybe) a T-shirt is a T-shirt is a T-shirt.

# 6 | ENOUGH Happiness

*She had friends who had taken up the serious practice of yoga, or started on antidepressants or embarked on the sort of wilderness expeditions that required you to collect dew on plastic sheets for your drinking water. She understood their not-enoughness. The fear that they were not happy enough or valued enough or beautiful enough or fill-in-the-blank enough.*

Jean Thompson, *Wide Blue Yonder*

Hopping off my commuter train at London Bridge one recent morning, I saw above the crowds a large poster showing an urban hipster who had been cloned several times. Each clone was dancing for joy. The slogan beneath this ad for the chip-maker Intel declared: 'More Computing Power Means More You'. I imagined the copywriter congratulating themself on this catchphrase, one surely bound to set my soul skipping along platform four, singing, 'Yippee, yippee, more me.' As an egotistical knee-jerk, the prospect of more me must be the single most marvellous possibility in the material universe. As a consumer dream, it's bang on the button. But for the rest of the day, that slogan kept popping into my head, raising odd questions.

Would I really want to be (or have) more me? A glance at my personality spectrum reveals swathes of my selfhood where there's already quite enough, thank you – and some aspects, such as the egotism, suspicion, self-pity, pointless regret and maundering envy, that might do with toning down. Would anyone else want to have more me? I suspect my wife would declare 'Enough husband' with a readiness that bordered on the abrupt. Anyway, what on earth would more me be like? Could it feel internally any different from being just me? In terms of philosophy, semantics and, most important, my soul, I suspect it's not possible. I am only this me – boundless, yet limited. That's how it feels from the inside. That's pretty much how it will always feel. So, for myself at least, this promised land of 'more me' hit the buffers at London Bridge station.

But the poster's ego-multiplying promise, coupled with the chance of owning a newer, cleverer, quicker computer, may well seem to offer an attractive lifestyle solution for the random yearnings of many of my busy fellow passengers. It could even be the mission statement for our times, promising finally to resolve our sense of not-enoughness. We could all wear a corporate human logo: 'Working towards more me'. Intel's snappy slogan would, however, have been condemned as darkly satanic in the fifteenth century, when the spiritually proper approach meant declaring 'Less me'. In one of his more celebrated sermons, the fifteenth-century German monk Thomas a Kempis urged believers to stamp out all vestiges of self-worth or face a trip to damnation: 'If I acknowledge my nothingness, if I cast away all my self-esteem and reduce myself to the dust that I really am, then grace will come to me and its light will enter my heart; thus will the last trace of self-esteem be engulfed in the depth of my own nothingness, and perish for ever.'

Sackcloth, hair shirts and ashes are mercifully out of vogue now (though I'll wager that Kempis got a hefty great ego boost out of being *really, really* humble). Amid the necessary humdrum of modern-day existence, we are allowed the luxury of spending periods feeling guiltlessly good about ourselves. These bursts of inner warmth are so agreeable that it is sorely tempting to try to extend them ever further, into an earthly bliss that stretches way beyond the normal levels of human happiness. Surely modern life, with all its wealth and high tech, can pave the road to infinitely more (happy) us? That's the big hope that keeps us driving technologically ever onwards. And if modern life isn't actually making us any happier yet, then this hope has at least given birth to a whole new lifestyle sector – the fulfilment industry – which thrives on selling the idea that you can quite easily develop much more self-esteem, self-awareness, satisfaction and joy than you already have: it's medicine for the human condition.

The fulfilment industry's promise has become ubiquitous so quickly that if you reject its basic tenets, you tend to look like a miserable old git. Of course, humans have always tried to improve aspects of themselves. It's why we now walk upright and mostly eat with our mouths closed. In the early Victorian era, for example, young ladyfolk were expected to develop improvingly intricate skills in needlework, music, dancing and languages as feminine 'accomplishments' (though evolutionary psychologists today might call them sublimated displays of genetic fitness to reproduce). And personal improvement books have enjoyed a long and profitable history: their pioneer was the marvellously named Samuel Smiles, one of 11 Scottish siblings left fatherless in

1832, who rose to industrial eminence and gave the entire genre its name with his 1859 bestseller, *Self Help: with Illustrations of Character, Conduct and Perseverance*. He followed it up by writing three more backbone-stiffeners; *Character*, *Thrift*, and *Duty*. The white-bearded patriarch's books preached the Victorian gospel of work and featured morale-boosting lines such as: 'It will generally be found that men who are constantly lamenting their ill luck are only reaping the consequences of their own neglect, mismanagement, and improvidence or want of application.' Nevertheless, Smiles also knew the selling power of positive messages, such as this spirit-lifting affirmation: 'I'm as happy a man as any in the world, for the whole world seems to smile upon me!'

Nineteenth-century American readers enthusiastically embraced the self-improving book, primarily as a guide to building their new and infinitely perfectible nation. The old myth has it that every young man heading west carried a copy of Ralph Waldo Emerson's most famous essay, *Self-reliance*, in his pocket and had taken to heart Emerson's exhortation to 'hitch your wagon to a star'. In the twentieth century, Napoleon Hill, who was born in true American Dream-style in a humble mountainside log cabin, began his self-help career by publishing a classic business primer, *The Law of Success*. He then wrote the 1930s popular classic, *Think and Grow Rich*, which offered an avuncular compendium of scattergun advice on life, love and writing an attractive CV. Then, of course, there's *How to Win Friends and Influence People*, written in 1936 by Dale Carnegie, a failed Missouri farmer, failed teacher, failed journalist, failed actor, failed novelist, failed husband and failed investor, who invited us to benefit from the wisdom he'd gained from his blunders, and whose winning advice included the exhortation: 'Force yourself to smile!'

As the years passed the self-help books put steadily more emphasis on happiness. In 1952, Norman Vincent Peale penned the bestseller *The Power of Positive Thinking* and urged everyone to improve their moods – to make it 'a habit to be happy'. In the 1950s happiness was still being sold as a helpful personal habit, but by the 1970s aspiration inflation had set in and we were being told that we were *entitled* to be happy. Since then the target has been lifted even higher, to the point where it increasingly feels that happiness is an obligation: the British Government's official feelgood tsar, Lord Layard, argues in his book, *Happiness: Lessons from a New Science*, that: 'Happiness is that ultimate goal because, unlike all other goals, it is self-evidently good.' So, no arguments, please: happiness is now your ultimate life goal.

An entire literary genre based on the H-word has suddenly sprung up, with titles such as *Authentic Happiness*, *The Art of Happiness*, *The Happiness Hypothesis*, *Stumbling on Happiness*, and *Happiness: a Guide to Developing Life's Most Important Skills*. But does such an imperative really help people to feel better about themselves? Declarations like Layard's reinforce the growing social pressure to believe that you're not adequate enough if you're not yet resolved enough, fulfilled enough or joyful enough. And if you're not striving to make yourself better, happier, more emotionally evolved and generally more you, then something must be wrong. Why are you deliberately lagging behind in the human race?

More than anything else, the happiness industry presses us to reinvent ourselves as people – an endeavour that involves chasing another ever-more, on top of the fantastic career, the perfect possessions, the ideal home, the flawless partner, the trophy holidays and all the other latest best lifestyle options. If all those things haven't left us feeling better, then 'learning how to feel better' surely will. And there's no shortage of products offering to assist you. My desk at *The Times* (where I've edited, among other things, a section called Psyche) is shadowed by towering stacks of self-helpful books and DVDs – coaching manuals, yogic styles, meditation techniques, spiritual paths, astonishing lifestyle revelations, positive psychology, guides by gurus and gallimaufries of celebrity wisdom. Every morning's post adds another inch or two to the teetering piles. I'm in peril of being crushed by an avalanche of advice.

And who knows, any one of the answers on offer might be the one that works. Perhaps it could be the book that promises: *You Can Change Your Life*, or the one entitled, *You Can Be Amazing*, or if being amazing isn't enough, how about *You Can Have Everything You Want*? If that sounds too overbearing (and where would you put it all?), what about *De-stress Your Life In Seven Easy Steps*? Perhaps seven whole steps sounds too time-consuming. You could always whizz into *Shape Shifter: Transform Your Life In 1 Day*. Yes, one day.

These quick fixes get quicker with every fix, and the promises get evermore inflated. Though hey, why waste a whole day on transforming your life? What's wrong with getting it all done and dusted in the morning, leaving you free to spend the afternoon basking in new-found bliss?

I've yet to be posted the *One-minute total life makeover*. Maybe it's rolling off the presses right now.

But we should perhaps expect an obsession with instant change from the fulfilment industry, because the industry itself has only recently gone through a massive instant reinvention. The hard-sell happiness drive we know today only began in earnest at the dying end of the 1960s counter-culture, when America's youth got tired of trying to change the world and started instead trying to change themselves by pushing at the frontiers of good feeling. Suddenly, 'the personal was the political'. It's surely no coincidence that the counter-culture drugs of choice changed at this point, too: from booze and speed – which get you wild, aggressive and out on the dancefloor – to cannabis and heavy LSD, which get you inside your own head, accessing dreams and visions that were previously attained only through years of dedicated meditation.

Interest in esoteric religion and self-healing – the founding creeds of the new church of the self – quickly grew. And academics such as Carl Rogers and Nathaniel Brandon soon caught on to the possibilities of feelgood potential. Brandon wrote the seminal *Psychology of Self-esteem* in 1969. It's still in print. Rogers invented the idea of 'unconditional positive regard', originally as a technique to help children cope with feelings of inadequacy when they failed to meet their goals. By the end of the 1970s, many schools in America were dedicating several hours a week to counselling and self-esteem classes. Curriculum programmes, such as the educational psychologist Michele Borba's *Esteem Builders* inspired more than a thousand off-the-shelf exercises, such as, I Love Me, where students complete sentences such as,

'I am . . .' using words such as 'gifted' or 'beautiful', and then memorise them. This sort of glowing self-affirmation has become a mainstay of the self-help guides.

In only four decades, the mass marketing of self-esteem has grown into a multi-billion-pound global industry with a pantheon of top-sellers such as John Gray, Stephen R. Covey and Deepak Chopra. The collective annual income of these three gurus alone totals tens of millions of pounds. The entire sector's worth is expected to top £6 billion in 2008. Where there is big money, there's also bound to be some big charlatanry – and commentators such as Steve Salerno, the author of *Sham*, have been quick to expose the quackery, fraud and snake-oil salesmanship that have grown up around the happiness movement. Human nature means that these sorts of shenanigans are to be expected in any fast-growing industry. They don't necessarily mean that the whole self-help sector should be condemned. But something else is starting to happen in the happiness movement. Among the many millions of converts and cheer-leaders, a growing legion of disillusioned punters is starting to emerge. They've taken up the self-improvement challenge and worked hard on themselves, but now they are starting to believe that chasing cheerfulness can backfire.

Take David Granirer, a Vancouver-based counsellor who describes himself as a card-carrying neurotic as well as a short, bald geek (the photographs tend to bear this out). Granirer says that he spent 20 years and thousands of dollars on workshops and books that claimed to hold the secrets to obtaining material abundance and self-built joy: 'I worked at self-actualisation. I've said affirmations, visualised abundance, aligned myself with my spirit guides, communed with my power animals, meditated, chanted and danced into the light. And after doing all that, I'm no richer, sexier, healthier or more confident than I was before. I haven't achieved inner peace or found true bliss. I'm still as neurotic as ever,' he says.

Now he has turned his back on the straightforward self-improvement route and is trying a different approach. He has published his own book, *The Happy Neurotic: How Fear and Angst Can Lead to Happiness and Success*. Happy neurotics, Granirer says, learn to manage their negative emotions and work with them in productive ways that build their self-esteem: 'Rather than berating themselves for not achieving these personal growth ideals, happy neurotics use their sense of humour to celebrate their fear-driven and neurotic way of getting things done.'

Then there's Jennifer Louden who, on 15 May 2007, launched the International Freedom from Self-Improvement Day as an event that encourages self-help fans to put down their books, DVDs and podcasts for 24 hours and instead try to practise self-acceptance. She is the author of six books including *The Woman's Comfort Book*, *Comfort Secrets for Busy Women* and the recently released *The Life Organiser: a Woman's Guide to a Mindful Year*, which makes me think that she's rather self-helpy herself. But Louden, an attractive, bob-haired woman who describes herself as 'both a personal coach and social commentator', says she had a Damascene moment that made her realise where the self-improvement movement was going wrong. It took her another step on her 'transformation from a well-read self-help author to a cultural leader and life guide,' she explains: 'Sitting in meditation one day, the idea came to me: what if we all collectively gave up on being any different than we are, just for 24 hours? What a perfect holiday for me to create. Because if self-improvement worked, we'd all be self-levitating, multi-lingual, size-zero billionaires by now. And because we know, deep down inside, that we already have everything we need right now, exactly as we are, and that accepting ourselves moment by moment, over and over again, is the fastest, cheapest and actually only way to ever be truly happy.'

Only one problem here. Rejectionists such as these two are still urging us to pursue new ways to find *happiness*. Different products, but the same goal: more happy me. It seems that once you have jumped aboard the joy-chasing carousel, it's extremely hard to hop off, so seductive are the promised rewards. There's a looming taboo here, too: if you reject the more-happiness promise, you'll be pooping the entire Western cultural party. And we can't have that. But whichever way you choose to smack your head against the brick wall called 'more happiness', it still involves banging your head against a brick wall. From the crystal-clear viewpoint of human evolution, the idea of being able to boost your happiness significantly is founded on a fallacy. If we look at our evolutionary wiring, we have to conclude that we are not designed to have happiness as our natural default state. It is not something that lies like a wall-to-wall carpet under a shoddy jumble of unhappinesses that can be vacuumed away. Nor can our happiness be grown beyond its usual proportions, like some weird-looking specialised insect mandible.

We can't even say that high levels of happiness are a 'self-evident good'. When psychologists followed the lifetimes of

1,216 children whose personalities were assessed in 1922, they found that those who were most happy died earlier in adult life than those who were less cheerful. The researchers found that the markedly happy kids grew up more likely to drink, smoke and take more risks – possibly because having a happy worldview makes the dangers appear smaller. The psychiatrists conclude: 'Although optimism and positive emotions have been shown to have positive effects when people are faced with a short-term crisis, the long-term effects of cheerfulness are more complex and seem not entirely positive.'

When you come down to the dull facts, happiness is an evolutionary adaptation that exists to make us engage in certain behaviours at certain times when they might optimise our chances of surviving and reproducing. Happiness makes us tend to pursue some things and avoid others. But it's the same story with our less compelling emotions: boredom, dissatisfaction, sadness and all the other negatives. They all evolved in our souls to make us behave in certain ways at certain times, in order to optimise our chances of getting laid and getting breakfast. Humans feel happiness. Lower-order creatures, such as sea squirts, don't. Humans feel boredom, dissatisfaction and sadness. Sea squirts don't. As Theodosius Dobzhansky, the geneticist, argued: 'Nothing in biology makes sense except in the light of evolution.' If an emotion is there inside us, it's because it evolved there – because it had a use. Trying to deny our deeply wired nature, or to displace the aspects that we don't like is, in the words of the old Zen joke, like a naked man trying to tear off his shirt.

What use could all the negatives be? Our rush to create

alchemist's gold from positive psychology has made it seriously unfashionable to seek good reasons for the existence of our unsmiley side. But it has long been known that having a moderate dose of pessimism can make us see the world more accurately. Psychologists call this phenomenon 'depressive realism'. It works because, in general, life dishes out more rough deals than good ones, and people with mildly miserablist outlooks are better at predicting the outcomes of real-world situations than cock-eyed optimists who, in tests, tend woefully to overestimate their success, their status and the chances of happy things happening around them. A dose of thermometer-sucking hypochondria is entirely healthy, too: we are built to worry about whether there is something wrong with us, because our Neolithic ancestors needed to stay perpetually alert for infected food and infectious diseases.

The slight evolutionary advantage that depressive, hypochondriacal cave dwellers had over their happy-go-lucky neighbours meant that, over millions of years, the most carefree died young and the anxious ones thrived. If you're permanently happy, you don't want things to change. You don't evolve. Constantly cheerful Stone Agers would have lolled about grinning while their wounds festered, their crops died and bears devoured their children. If you're less than happy, you want to improve yourself and your world.

Randolph Nesse, a psychiatry professor at Michigan University, argues that depression not only has strong evolutionary reasons for existing, it can still help us today. Depression often interjects in life to tell us to stop what we're doing and to reconsider, he explains. This is particularly useful when something genuinely depressing happens in our lives, such as a job loss or relationship break-up, where it is a healthy part of human experience to slow down to take time to grieve, to mull, to reassess the way that we act in this world and make changes. Doctors, however, are increasingly keen to dull this pain with pills and get us off the convalescent couch. When the *Archives of General Psychiatry* published an American study of 8,000 people who had been diagnosed and treated as depressed, it reported that up to a quarter of them were not clinically glum, they had just undergone a normal life event such as family bereavement. Their symptoms, it said, should be left to pass naturally, although that wouldn't help the drug multinationals to sell ever-increasing numbers of sadness-numbing chemicals.

Depression-damping can have strange side-effects, too. If naturally timid, depressive people have their inhibitions Prozac-ed away, this may warp our social structure and even flip our financial markets into resounding booms and busts. Big traders might not be notorious for their timidity, but they do tend to be stressed out, anxious and subject to plunging morale – and thus often get prescribed antidepressants, so they may trade more aggressively if the happy pills remove their natural caution. Prozac-type drugs boost the brain's levels of the hormone serotonin, which can also make us more status-hungry. Research shows that tribe-leading monkeys have twice as much serotonin as the others in the group. If the top monkey loses his position, his serotonin levels plunge. Any one of the other monkeys could be made the boss by just giving it an antidepressant to boost its serotonin levels. Thus, high-pressure workplaces may become even more pushy when the life-challenged Prozac-poppers all start wanting to become top monkey.

If, on the other hand, we don't think we're entitled to be the top monkey, we might be suffering from low-self esteem, the lumbering bogeyman of the positive psychologists. Having anything less than a bounding sense of self is now considered sickly and dangerous. In 1984, Nathaniel Branden wrote that he couldn't think 'of a single psychological problem – from anxiety and depression, to fear of intimacy or of success, to spouse-battery or child molestation – that is not traceable to the problem of low self-esteem'. Branden's creed rapidly won widespread acceptance: we all need to feel better about ourselves. It sounds like another of Lord Layard's 'self-evidently good' things.

And who's to argue? Who is bold enough to stand up for boringly moderate levels of self-worth? Enter Nicholas Emler, a professor of psychology at Surrey University, who has examined the available scientific evidence, which amounts to tens of thousands of psychological studies, and concludes that the self-esteem movement is profoundly mistaken. 'In government papers it's considered that everybody should have more self-esteem,' Emler told an Edinburgh conference. 'It's thought to be the answer to crime, abuse, aggression, risk-taking and almost every problem, even unprofitable bank customers, unproductive employees and farming failures.' From all the studies, however, there is no good evidence to show that low self-esteem causes anti-social behaviour. Quite the reverse: people who rate themselves highly are the ones most prone to do violence and most likely to take risks, believing themselves invulnerable. Exceptionally low self-esteem is indeed damaging, but only to the person who has it, not to anyone else.

On top of that, there's something fundamental in human

nature that rather stymies all the esteem-raising books, courses, initiatives and policies, says Emler: the research shows that it's exceedingly difficult to make any real difference to a grown-up's esteem level. 'It can bobble up and down in response to circumstances, but any individual's self-esteem has a typical level around which it bobbles.' Studies of twins indicate that our genes have the single strongest influence. Even in children, markedly high or low levels of self-esteem are extremely resistant to being shifted by positive or negative experiences. 'High-self-esteem pupils will explain away failure to suit their previous high opinions of themselves: they make excuses that they were unlucky, suffered some bias or that they didn't try,' says Emler. 'Odder still, those with low self-esteem will not be buoyed up by academic success. Sadly, they will regard it as a fluke and continue with their previous low estimation of their abilities.' He concludes that having stratospheric self-opinion is just as big a handicap as having rock-bottom levels. 'People with very high self-esteem ignore all advice, all wise counsel, and that ain't good. Those with very low self-esteem don't even notice that someone is trying to influence them. It's the people in the middle range who are listening and evaluating and, on the whole, reacting sensibly to influence.'

Low self-esteem moments may even provide a life-preservingly glum message: watch out pal, you're being a bit of a loser. When you are confronting someone at work or in a bar, both you and they instantly have a pretty good idea of who is the more powerful, either by the size of your desks or the breadth of your biceps. If you look like you're going to lose, it is often a smart move to back down.

Animals have much the same sense, and biologists call it resource-holding potential, or RHP (though no one seems to have explained this to small dogs in parks). In humans, RHP may have evolved into the sort of low self-esteem that keeps your head down when it's in danger of getting whacked by someone more alpha.

This sounds eminently sensible, especially when working in modern multi-layered corporations where most normally adjusted office workers' self-esteem levels have to yo-yo throughout the day, depending on whom they're sharing space with. This is the only logical explanation why, in my newspaper office, I have never felt a scintilla of concern about performance anxiety when sharing urinal space with the work-experience students, but an incident several years ago remains burned into my memory: the top-honch editor stood himself beside me – and though I tried and tried and tried, I could not go at all. Not a dribble. Such is the power of deference.

Maybe our current problem with low self-esteem isn't simply that it exists and feels unpleasant. Perhaps it's that our culture repeatedly slaps our self-esteem downwards rather than (as the self-help books claim) offering unprecedented opportunities to feel good about ourselves. We have to remember once again that our Pleistocene-era brains tend to believe that what we see on video screens and in magazines is all taking place within the narrow geography of a Stone Age tribe. It wouldn't feel so thrillingly relevant otherwise. Our brains originally evolved to compare our skills, status and beauty against a few hundred locals at most. In ancient hunter-gatherer clans you could expect to find a niche by excelling in some trade or task, but today it is no longer possible; you'll always know of someone else on the planet who is far cleverer and more celebrated.

We are also exposed every day to images of the world's most beautiful women and wealthy men, which makes our Stone Age brains feel pathetically inadequate by comparison, particularly when rabidly competitive media hype means that these people's elevated status keeps looking more elevated. There's no health warning on the pictures saying, 'These people have been airbrushed to infinity, lead vacuous lives parading before phalanxes of clicking paparazzi and only crave publicity because their souls are gnawed raw by hyperneurotic insecurity: do not try to emulate them.' Instead we are repeatedly told that if we worked at it, by working on ourselves, we could keep up with these mythic super-Joneses. In this more-happy-me culture, it's getting increasingly difficult just to feel adequate.

Meanwhile, we're supposed to keep smiling. Oh dear. As an analysis in the *Journal of Clinical Psychology* entitled 'The Tyranny of the Positive Attitude' asked, 'Could it be that the pressure itself to be happy and optimistic contributes to at least some forms of unhappiness?' Part of the problem is that what we often call happiness is in fact a 'flow state' of unselfconsciousness, the sort of thing that happens when you're so engrossed in a hobby, such as macramé or model-railway building, that you just don't notice time passing. You lose yourself as your ego and your preoccupations fall away. You can't force this, but willing it to happen can cause a kind of self-help psychosis – the psychological equivalent of watched kettle syndrome. We become hypervigilant for happiness and turn into emotional hypochondriacs when it doesn't happen: 'Ask yourself if you are happy,' John Stuart Mill famously wrote, 'and you cease to be so.'

A recent study of marriage helps us to understand another reason why chasing happiness so often fails: above a certain level of life-satisfaction, it gets much harder to push your morale any higher. The study of more than 3,000 people found that those who suffered depression got the biggest psychological boost out of getting wed, even if their marriages turned out to be pretty average. Marriage lifts miserable people 7.56 points on the depression scale, while previously happy people get a rise of only 1.87 points. The higher you go up the happy curve, the steeper it gets. Happiness-chasers are bound to reach a paradoxical point, beyond their reasonable level of enoughness, where trying to be happier achieves such frustratingly fractional results that it's going to sap their morale and send them tumbling back down the curve. Sadly, the self-improvers' response to this setback may well be to try harder – which can rapidly become increasingly depressing and expensive.

In fact, the vast majority of psychological research indicates that as adults we seem stuck with ourselves, whatever we are like. Unless we are suffering from a medically fixable pathology, our personalities generally do not change after about the age of 25, when the concrete has set, entombing each of us within a lifetime of general habit, attitude, approach and other brain pre-sets that we come to know as our selves. You can win big on the lottery or you can lose both legs in an accident, but studies show that a year after either incident your morale will most likely have returned to its former level. That's it. That's us. And that is why we need as individuals to develop the habit of being merely content with our own general degree of happiness.

Nevertheless, we're still sorely tempted to keep pushing, to keep singing the 'more happy me' mantra because *homo expetens* nags us to strive ever onwards. We've even reached the ridiculous point of having to invent new high-end psychological needs to fulfil. That's why psychologists have been busy building new attic rooms on to the famous pyramidal structure that is Abraham Harold Maslow's hierarchy of needs. Maslow, a doctor of psychology, invented a triangular theoretical model of what humans desire most. It will be familiar to anyone who has been taught the basics of psychology, sociology or any other ology, and is commonly accepted as a useful model of what humans want. At the bottom, step one covers the absolute basics for survival, while step five, the thinnest, topmost one, involves all the spiritual and intellectual experiences a human can want. Maslow felt that unfulfilled needs lower on the ladder would stop a person climbing to the next step. As he pointed out, someone dying of thirst quickly forgets their thirst when they have no oxygen.

When he devised his pyramid in the 1950s, his levels ran like this:

1. Biological and physiological needs – air, food, drink, shelter, warmth, sex, sleep, etc.

2. Safety needs – protection from elements, security, order, law, limits, stability, etc.

3. Belongingness and love needs – work, group, family, affection, relationships, etc.

4. Esteem needs – self-esteem, achievement, mastery, independence, status, dominance, prestige, managerial responsibility, etc.

5. Self-actualisation needs – realising personal potential, self-fulfilment, seeking personal growth and peak experiences.

But soon the experts decided that this wasn't enough. In the 1970s, shortly after Maslow died, two more layers were added at the top: cognitive needs (the desire for knowledge and meaning) and aesthetic needs (the appreciation and search for beauty, balance, form and so on). But still that wasn't enough. In the 1990s, an eighth stage was stuck on top, called transcendence needs. This apparently means 'helping others to achieve self actualisation', which makes it sound as though the ultimate in human experience involves working as a psychotherapist, life coach, rebirthing guide or parish priest.

I feel confident that we will see even more stages being plonked on to the pyramid. Because today's society and Maslow's hierarchy seem to disagree on one fundamental point: Maslow's pyramid, being pyramid-shaped, tidily stops at the pointy top. This is where people should be completely satisfied and, to Maslow, it would represent enoughness. But in modern culture, as created by *homo expetens*, the lines at the top of the pyramid don't just stop at the pinnacle, they cross over and keep going, creating an hourglass figure, where the higher you go above the point of reasonable and healthy desire, the larger the amount of more-me wants there are.

Perhaps Abe Maslow missed this possibility because he was such an idealistic intellectual. He was born in the early twentieth century, the first of seven children of illiterate but ambitious Russian Jewish parents who pushed him into being an academic success. He turned out, perhaps unsurprisingly, to be a lonely, bookish lad who reluctantly entered the study of law. But then he found his metier and transferred to studying psychology under his first mentor, Professor Harry Harlow, at Wisconsin University, where he began investigating primate dominance and sexuality, which back then was an academic discipline rather than a couple of hours spent watching *Big Brother*. After that he moved to Columbia University to pursue similar studies and found another mentor in Alfred Adler, one of Freud's early followers.

Subsequently he moved to New York's Brooklyn College where he found two more mentors, the anthropologist Ruth Benedict and Gestalt psychologist Max Wertheimer. He was so impressed by them professionally and personally that he began to take notes about the pair's behaviour. These 'wonderful human beings' provided the basis of his research into mental health and human potential, and became his models for 'self-actualised humans' – the epitomes of fully resolved people. Maslow generalised that, among other characteristics, self-actualising people tend to focus on problems outside of themselves, have a clear sense of what is true and what is phoney, are spontaneous and creative, and are not bound too strictly by social conventions. 'What a man can be, he must be. This need we call self-actualisation,' Maslow explained.

Thus Maslow's idea of the pinnacle of human existence was based on his bordering-on-creepy admiration for the sort of scruffy, convention-shunning, non-materialistic liberal intellectuals who had so kindly moulded his fate for the better – rather than the status-obsessed, surface-only, thrill-seeking celebrities and politicians whom our society now holds as the prime exemplars of *homo expetens* potential.

The culture we have constructed clearly does not encourage us to aspire to be quietly resolved upper-pyramid dwellers. Instead we're blitzed with infotainment telling us that up above the pyramid, in the ever-expanding world of new wants, is where all the cool action is at. In the effort to surmount this infinite state of super-grace, we are creating evermore new aspects of our minds and bodies to improve (and thus, conversely, to feel inadequate about). Vaginas, for example. Lih Mei Liao, a consultant clinical psychologist at University College London, recently reported in the *British Medical Journal* how demand for cosmetic genital surgery, called genitoplasty, is growing with astonishing rapidity. The number of labial reductions in the NHS has doubled in the past five years, despite the fact that the operation carries serious risks such as the loss of sexual sensitivity.

To find out why genitoplasty is becoming so popular, she interviewed women who had undergone the operation, and found that more and more Western females are troubled by the shape, size or proportions of their vulvas. The patients consistently wanted their vulvas to be flat, with no protrusion beyond the labia majora, 'even though there is nothing unusual about protrusion of the labia minora or clitoris beyond the labia majora', she says. Some women brought along images to illustrate the appearance they desired, and these were 'usually from adverts or pornography that may have been digitally altered'. Such pictures are prompting an entirely new question for figure-conscious females to fret about: 'Does my front-bottom look big in this?'

Lih and her colleague, Sarah Creighton of the Elizabeth Garrett Anderson Institute for Women's Health, caution that the media-led trend may seriously distort young women's body-image even further in pursuit of some kind of Photoshopped perfection: 'The increased demand may reflect a narrowing social definition of normal, or a confusion of what is normal and what is idealised. Genitoplasty could narrow acceptable ranges further and increase the demand for surgery even more.'

Vaginas are only the leading edge of our endeavours to improve our physical selves far beyond the level of enoughness – a process that so often backfires because picking on innocent bits of our bodies and blaming them for our inbuilt dissatisfaction tends to produce only an enhanced sense of self-disgust. This often happens among the people most dedicated to chasing the ideals of healthy perfection. For example, a study presented to the American College of Sports Medicine reports that women who exercise and read fitness magazines showing images of hyper-trained women report more anxiety and depression than those who read magazines with no idealised images.

But the trend doesn't only affect magazine-reading adults. Our unease with our not-happy-enough selves is spreading through society and down into childhood: a survey of

Australian children aged between 7 and 14 reports that girls' biggest wants nowadays are to be thinner, to be more popular with boys, to have differently coloured hair and clearer skin. As they reach adulthood, this may only get worse, particularly because cosmetics companies have to keep peddling this sort of insecurity to stay competitive, so they keep identifying new potentially ugly bits for us to worry about. No cosmetic company has yet been so gauche as to market an earlobe conditioner, but Marks & Spencer has helped to create another body-related neurosis with its newly launched Anti-Ageing Nail Treatment. It 'helps nails look younger,' claims the packaging blurb. Has anyone on this planet ever thought to themselves: 'Wow, that woman doesn't half look alluringly youthful. Oh, but hang on, she has the fingernails of a muttering crone . . .'?

Professor Anthony Elliott, a leading researcher in the new field of extreme reinvention, believes that many consumers are now so obsessed with boosting their bodies and person-alities that they end up suffering depression and emotional crisis. Some even kill themselves. Elliott, a professor of sociology, is an amiable Aussie who retains a cheerful sense of the absurd about this phenomenon. But when we discuss tackling it, he admits: 'Reinvention has become so main-stream so quickly that it's difficult to talk about it negatively without sounding like a dismal curmudgeon.' He believes that we are entering an unprecedented era where people feel pressured by makeover shows, self-help books, celebrity culture, corporate life and 'want-now' consumerism to create fundamentally new personal identities.

Some of the main persuaders that Elliott fingers seem rather innocuous (or dull at least): television shows such as BBC 2's *Garden Invaders*, a quiz that transforms competitors' lawns into lifestyle icons, and Channel 4's *10 Years Younger*, which offers plastic surgery to wipe a decade's worth of living from women's faces. Nevertheless, he argues, 'The obsession with celebrity and TV makeovers is driving people to really believe that they *have* to improve themselves. There is a rising need for instant change and reinvention.' It adds up to another way to chase that fleeting promise of more happy you.

In some ways, self-transformation has indeed never been easier. Take your own name – it's one of the first things that you ever learn about yourself, and constitutes a foundation stone for your entire sense of identity. Don't like your sense of self? Then change your name – as more than 50,000 people did in Britain in 2007, according to the UK Deed Poll Service. Ten years previously, only 270 Britons altered their name by deed poll. It's so quick and easy now: you can access all the paperwork on the internet, fill it in and, bingo, you're a freshly rebranded you. Don't like your figure? Why endure the emotional struggle of dieting when you can get it all vacuumed out? The number of British women having liposuction operations nearly doubled between 2005 and 2006. Dislike anything else about your face or body? A survey of members of the British Association of Aesthetic Plastic Surgeons found that they had performed 30,000 lifts, snips, implants and reductions in 2006, a rise of around a third over the previous year.

It's this 'more faster' aspect of 'more happy me' that particularly disturbs Elliott, the author of *The New Individualism: the Emotional Costs of Globalization*. 'Our quick-fix society is very different from the days of

Freudianism. People used to commit to a lengthy process of self-reconstruction involving an hour's psychoanalysis, four to five times a week, for five years or more,' he says. 'That's no longer the case. If you instantly change your face or your name as a guarantor of your identity, what will be the results?' Elliott spent six years interviewing radical self-reinventors and says he has seen various levels of emotional damage, ranging from confusion and anxiety through to fairly intense depression and two cases of suicide. This problem helps to explain why women who have breast implants are three times more likely to kill themselves. It's not that the implants cause some kind of silicon psychosis, it's the fact that women who seek implants often have a poor self-image, and the implants sadly fail to keep their promise to transform it.

Radical self-improvement does not just frequently fail to fulfil its promise of a happier self, it can cause real harm in another, deeper way – a process that Douglas Coupland, the author of *Generation X*, has defined as 'de-narration'. He believes that modern consumers can become so obsessed with ditching or improving aspects of their selves that they can ultimately lose hold of their life stories. They become an agglomeration of tacked-on extras with no integrated soul at the middle, no consistent 'I am' narrative, only a fractured identity consisting of imperfectly improved bits and implanted desires. Coupland claims that Marilyn Monroe was our first de-narrated celebrity, a beautifully facaded emptiness. When the former Norma Jeane Mortensen was found dead at her anonymously fashionable home, the only personal items in her bedroom were a pile of handbags and purses.

There's another paradox about chasing personal perfection: we can only judge how well we're doing by how others are doing, and this gets us into another unwinnable arms race. Self-fulfilment, like income and possessions, is largely a 'positional good' – we get a much bigger kick out of it if we think we have got more than the person next door. It's not just 'more happy me' that we are after, it's 'more happy me than happy you' – hence the quote attributed to Oscar Wilde: 'Whenever a friend or colleague of mine has a great achievement, a little part of me dies.' But mathematically, we can't all be above average. In seeking ways to show that we are happier and more resolved than the Joneses, we are piloting another route to being less happy and less resolved. This sort of paradox was even foreseen by Gilbert and Sullivan in their 1889 opera, *The Gondoliers*: 'When everybody is somebody, then no one's anybody.'

Predictably enough, the happiness pushers staunchly deny any link between the rapid growth in clinical depression and the exponential rise of the fulfilment industry. I think it's safe, though, to state that the widespread pursuit of happiness has at least failed to stem the unprecedented growth in people who feel unhappy enough to seek psychological or pharmaceutical help. National Health Service statistics show that in 2006 more than 31 million prescriptions for antidepressant drugs were written in Britain, a record level that was up 6 per cent on the previous year.

And while we don't know how many people are paying to see psychological therapists in Britain (because the vast majority of these therapists are unregulated) we do know that the therapists' numbers are spiralling. Phillip Hodson, of the British Association for Counselling and Psychotherapy, one of the largest of the 30-odd therapists' organisations in the UK, says the association now has nearly 30,000 professionals on its register: 'In the past decade, our numbers have grown by 10 per cent a year. That's an incredible rate, and I reckon it's unsustainable, because if it carries on like this everyone in Britain will soon be working as a psychotherapist.'

If self-help isn't helping, if esteem-raising isn't lifting us up, if therapy isn't curing, if happiness-chasing can make us miserable, then perhaps we should explore an alternative route: the route of *enough* happiness, by putting realistically curt limits on the path to self-fulfilment and waving goodbye to the promise of ever-increasing bliss. Practising this type of anti-ambition may seem extremely ambitious in our world of 'more me', as it requires us to swim against the rip-tide of rampant social expectation. Nevertheless some hopeful signs of resistance are already emerging – at least among the mums. The trend began in 2004, when Muffy Mead-Ferro, an American advertising copywriter, balked at reading the pile of parenting books she had been given to accompany the birth of her first child. The prenatal library, she realised, was effectively a primer for meeting the expectations of alpha-motherhood – a corporately correct twenty-first century regime of maternal excellence that involved the perfect baby, the perfect nursery room, the perfect mother-baby interactions and the perfect yummy-mummy image.

Rather than flagellate herself with unattainable expectations, Muffy rebelled and sat down to write *Confessions of a Slacker Mom*, a humorous homage to the messy baby-sick-down-your-shoulder world of just-OK-parenting. 'One reason we're caught up in hypercompetitive parenting is because of marketing,' she says. 'You feel like a loser if your kid isn't learning to play the violin or reading before kindergarten. But you know what? It's OK to turn the car around. You don't have to play the game.' As it turned out, her daughter, Belle, did fine without having to listen to Mozart while floating in the womb. So did her second child, Joe. Muffy's book sold quietly for several years, while she developed a side-career proselytising her message: 'It is possible to over-perform as a parent,' she told the press. 'Parenting has really changed in the last ten years. It's gotten very competitive and aggressive.'

The world didn't take too much notice, though. Parenting continued to get more aggressively competitive, with enthusiastic help from the marketing people. In December 2006, for example, I received a press release from Asda, the supermarket chain. It declared that the daftly amateur-ish pleasure of cobbling together a shepherd or sheep's costume for the school Christmas play was now done for: 'Competitive parents, eager to make their children look like Hollywood stars in the nativity play, have sent sales of tailor-made costumes soaring,' it trumpeted. 'They're switching from traditional props – tea towels, tin foil and tinsel – to bought-in, ready-made outfits so that their children will look stunning in front of hundreds of friends, family members and rival parents.' I think it was the phrase 'rival parents' that really made me choke on my mince pie.

Asda's nativity clothes had begun to outsell its normal adult range, the press release rejoiced, and the chain had been forced by a stampede of demand by time-starved, status-hungry mums and dads to urge its suppliers to rush through an emergency order for 30,000 more outfits. These included ready-made nativity sheep with 'smart, made-to-measure white wool, and realistic looking ears'. The angels' outfits, 'in diaphanous white lace', were predictably flying off the shelves. 'So intense is the competition,' explained the chain's spokesman, Ed Watson, 'that in some productions the main characters will probably look more like Angelina Jolie and Brad Pitt rather than the Virgin Mary and Joseph.' Nice. There goes the seasonal story of infant innocence and goodwill.

And there goes carefree childhood too, thanks to status-hungry parents' anxiety to make everything perfect for their kids – an anxiety that also drives them to schedule their children's lives with constant educational activities. This flies in the face of all the best study evidence, such as the American Academy of Pediatrics' new guidelines, which urge parents to remember that the best thing for children is low-temperature, no-pressure, unstructured free play, the sort of butterfly-chasing aimlessness that appears devoid of developmental value.

Ruth Coppard, a chartered child psychologist based in Barnsley, South Yorkshire, agrees that childhood should be less pressured: 'Scheduling children is not in fact teaching them very much, if it means they are going from a busy school day to after-school club, to Brownies and then choir before bedtime,' she says. 'The media is full of suggestions for things like toddlers' self-defence that children can excel at, and parents can hand-on-heart say that they think they are doing the best for their kids, but often the best quality time the children get is in the car travelling between activities. The result is that, later on, you get children who are bored. They are not good at inviting friends round, because they have grown up with very little time to do that. They are not used to being rather than doing.' The sum total of all this alpha-parenting may be to create a generation of hothoused achievement-chasers who reach the key, character-fixing age of 25 feeling like lonely, bored neurotics – and that's how they'll stay, no matter how many self-help happiness books and courses they subsequently buy.

But something significant seems to be changing. Muffy has ceased to be a lone voice. In fact, she's in peril of getting stampeded by a rush of 'beta mum' authors. Rene Syler, a former CBS news anchor, has published *Good-Enough Mother: the perfectly imperfect book of parenting*, while Katie Allison Granju, 39, an online TV producer, has just published *Let Them Run with Scissors: how over-parenting hurts children, parents and society*. In Britain, the newspaper columnist Fiona Neill has published *The Secret Life of a Slummy Mummy*. Then there's Trisha Ashworth and Amy Nobile, a pair of advertising execs who co-authored *I Was a Really Good Mom Before I Had Kids*. Add to this a newly launched slacker-lifestyle monthly for mothers, *Hybrid Mom* magazine, which defines its target audience as 'an adult female who has discarded unrealistic conceptions about motherhood'.

This could all, of course, be a mass folly by publishers, but maybe, just maybe, something is in the ether: if mothers are starting to rebel against pressure to infect their children with never-good-enoughness, then perhaps we might be seeing the first rumblings of an enoughist shift, of people swapping the more-happy-me ideal of perfection for the mundane sanity of 'just fine'. Parenthood is the most pressured fault-line in our more-more society. If we're ever to shift towards preserving our personal ecologies, then this may be where it starts. Perhaps the cracks might begin to spread from these beta mums to their beta kids and onwards, even inspiring beta dads to find satisfaction in beta working hours. Such ambitions might still seem optimistic, but what's the alternative? To keep chasing the dream of 'more happy me' ever harder?

We have instead to embrace the fact that happiness is not potential nirvana, but part of an evolutionary trick to drive us on through life. We are built to seek lasting happiness, but not to find it. When we progress healthily through life, we travel from goal to goal, from dissatis-faction to dissatisfaction, propelled by our inextricable tangle of positive and negative emotions. We can find this human quirk neatly dramatised if we blow the dust off an old English book. Although Samuel Johnson wrote *Rasselas, Prince of Abyssinia* in just one week in 1759 (he urgently needed the money), it serves as a fable for our querulous times. We meet the hero, Rasselas, living regally amid the splendour of Happy Valley, where materially he wants for nothing. But the prince's yearning soul tells him that there must be more to life than this. He sets off with his companions 'in pursuit of happiness' (Johnson coined the phrase), travelling through Egypt seeking the most joyful mode of life. They never find it. Each mode of living they study fails.

So far, so us. But the prince at least has his wise personal tutor, Imlac, for company. The old philosopher has a refined sense of enoughness. On seeing the pharaohs' great follies, their funerary pyramids, he calls them monuments to 'that hunger of imagination which preys incessantly upon life'. Imlac also understands the ultimate futility of fulfilment-seeking: 'What is to be expected from our pursuit of happiness, when we find the state of life to be such that happiness itself is the cause of misery?' he asks. 'Why should we endeavour to attain that of which the possession cannot be secured?'

At the novella's end, Johnson returns our travellers to the Happy Valley far wiser, but no happier. Such is the human condition – and Johnson even calls his final chapter, 'The conclusion in which nothing is concluded'. What the prince and his retinue have learnt, declares Imlac, is that people should spend their time modestly enjoying the day, rather than worrying if they're on the path to perfection: 'While you are making the choice of life, you neglect to live.'

It's a lesson that our culture sorely needs to relearn. Ever since the Industrial Revolution we have tried to convince ourselves that science and technology, and then shopping and self-help, would create a magic portal through which we could step, leaving all our negatives behind. It hasn't happened. We're still the naked man trying to tear off his shirt. We're lumbered with our selves, with our griefs, anxieties, quibblings and sniping jealousies – and all the other apparent negatives that make us who we are. Happiness is but one facet, and it remains fleeting and capricious. It's not to be found in McDonald's Happy Meals™ or in reading happiness books or in fun-sized snacks or even by singing, 'If you're happy and you know it' – no matter how much we clap our hands and stamp our feet.

And what would actually happen if joy could be lassoed and tamed? In Will Ferguson's satirical novel *Happiness*, a self-help book is finally published that does the unthinkable: it works. Everyone becomes happy. As a result, the global economy collapses. People stop buying stuff that they previously thought would make them feel better. The book's hero sees it coming: 'Our entire economy is built on human weaknesses,' he cautions. 'Hair salons. Male mid-life crises. Shopping binges. Our entire way of life is built on self-doubt and dissatisfaction. If people were ever really, truly happy, truly satisfied with their lives, it would be cataclysmic.'

To sustain our individual, collective and earthly ecologies, we need precisely that sort of cataclysmic calming of our happiness-chasing busyness. Even if it won't result from an epidemic of joy, we still might make it happen by achieving some measure of mere contentment. The next step in our species' social evolution is to embrace the happiness paradox, to nurture our appreciation for the satisfactions that we have, rather than burning everything up in the all-consuming pursuit of the unattainable. Lasting happiness is not the destination. It's the quest. And it would be easier for everyone if we stopped trying so damn hard.

## Happy *enough*

### Just in case: how to spot you're a therapy addict

★ Do you declare your emotions matter-of-factly and with pride – 'I'm angry and I feel good about that' or 'I'm upset, but that's all right'?

★ Or trumpet your therapy appointments – 'Sorry, I can't do lunch tomorrow, I'm seeing my therapist'?

★ Do you often serve as surrogate therapists for your friends? Therapy addicts don't say, 'I know just how you feel.' They say things like 'Could that have something to do with your mother?'

★ Do you compare yourself favourably with Woody Allen, as in 'I'm not Woody Allen or anything'?

★ Are you scoring yourself on this questionnaire?

# 7 | **ENOUGH** Growth

*Nothing is sufficient for the man to whom the sufficient is too little.*

Epicurus

'**A**re we there yet? Are we there yet?' It's the eternal chorus from the back seat of human evolution. Like impatient car-bound kids, our ancient instincts chime out the same repetitive questions: Are we happy enough yet? Are we informed enough yet? Are we busy enough, fed enough, and so often, are we rich enough yet? If the sage of twentieth-century economics, Lord Maynard Keynes, were in the driving seat, he'd turn round and reply, somewhat testily, 'Bloody hell yes, now get out and start enjoying the view.'

Keynes, who helped to navigate Britain out of the mass unemployment of the 1930s after orthodox economics had failed, would look at the Western world today and declare, 'Fiscal job done. Let's get on with the interesting stuff.' In the depths of the Great Depression, Keynes had predicted that economic growth would pave the way to bright horizons, to a liberating world that he sketched in an essay entitled, 'On the Economic Possibilities for our Grandchildren'. His ambitions were modest but profound: Keynes predicted that in three generations' time (i.e., just about now) the 'economic problem' would be solved. Keynes's idea of the economic problem was simply the challenge of allocating scarce resources so that everyone would have enough to satisfy their needs and basic desires. Once we had passed that historic point, he thought that we would at last be free to explore the greater potentials of humankind. And how we'd flourish, into the arts, into culture, into perfecting the ultimate refinements of beauty and friendship.

For Keynes, economics was a dirty game, and the business of earning and spending was a sordid obligation that humanity should shrug off as soon as possible. Once we'd got ourselves 'out of the tunnel of economic necessity into daylight', he predicted, 'I see us free to return to some of the most sure and certain principles of religion and traditional virtue – that avarice is a vice, that the exaction of usury is a misdemeanour and the love of money is detestable . . . We shall once more value ends above means and prefer the good to the useful. We shall honour those who can teach us how to pluck the hour and the day virtuously and well.'

Keynes seems to have ignored the possibility that, once we'd got the 'economic problem' solved, we would use our newfound liberty to shackle ourselves into chasing ever-more possessions, celebrity, happiness, junk information and all the other ever-mores. But then Keynes was hardly a man of the people. This elitist Old Etonian was a deeply complex character, one of those 'old-type *natural* fouled-up guys' (to hijack Philip Larkin's self-description), and just the sort of creative, convention-snubbing problem-solver that Abraham Maslow would have admired. For starters, Keynes could be meteorically temperamental. He once replied to a Colonial Office official's financial memo by saying: 'I agree with everything in this, if "not" is put in front of every statement.'

On top of his tetchy economic genius, he was a key figure in the Bloomsbury Group, the bohemian circle of artists, critics and writers such as Virginia Woolf and Roger Fry, which sought to pioneer a libertarian world of post-Victorian morals – one where every Bloomsburyite seemed to be hopping a-bed with every other Bloomsburyite. As a young man, Keynes enjoyed a gay relationship with the biographer Lytton Strachey. In turn, the pair vied for the affections of the Bloomsbury artist Duncan Grant. He and Strachey also went in nocturnal pursuit of rough trade in London's less salubrious neighbourhoods. Keynes subsequently married a former Russian ballerina, Lydia Lopokova, and in the 1940s chaired the progenitor of the Arts Council, the Council for the Encouragement of Music and the Arts.

What Keynes predicted in 'On the Economic Possibilities for our Grandchildren' represents a super-idealised vision of enoughness – a virtuous cycle that would run something like this: if we consume less consumerist propaganda, if we feel less hurried and worried, then we should feel that materially we have enough and therefore need to spend less, strive less and earn less. Then we will have time and energy to spend in more fulfilling ways. In time, we will find new balance points that suit our personal ecologies.

At this extremely simple level, the idea works brilliantly – until you try applying the theory to people stuffed with *homo expetens* urges. But then economics generally would be far more accurate if it weren't for pesky complex humans who, like Keynes, just don't seem to add up properly on paper. This problem has long stymied classical economics. In order to depict economic decisions mathematically, its practitioners have had to pretend that we are both rational and predictable. Since the early nineteenth century they have used the imaginary model of *homo economicus*, who has consistent preferences, stable moods, and makes only rational decisions in his best interest. If you've ever met such an epitome, report them to the police. They're bound to be hiding something. This blinkered tack has produced theories that can help us to predict what happens in world markets, but it fails to explain our constant drive for increasingly wasteful possessions.

We have to find a better economic way around the human problem. We have already seen manifold examples of how our ancient brains are overexcited by the neon environment that we've built for them. They develop evermore wants, and we in turn invent evermore must-haves. The American marketing guru Victor Lebow, a former director of Fabergé, described this trend in the *Journal of Retailing* back in 1950, when unprecedented wealth was chinking around in Stateside shoppers' pockets: 'Our enormously productive economy demands that we make consumption a way of life, that we convert the buying and use of goods into rituals, that we seek our spiritual satisfaction, our ego satisfaction, in consumption,' he said. 'We need things consumed, burned up, worn out, replaced, and discarded at an ever-increasing rate.'

The post-war period of rapidly spiralling consumption was great for manufacturers, but it rather quickly became apparent that it wasn't necessarily so beneficial for people or the planet. By the 1970s a welter of new ideas was beginning to emerge about the need to limit our exponential growth. The most famous examples are two books: E.F. Schumacher's *Small Is Beautiful: Economics As If People Mattered*, and the high-powered Club of Rome think-tank's *Limits to Growth*. The latter challenged one of the core assumptions of economic theory – that the Earth's supply of resources is infinite and will provide what's needed for our ever-increasing prosperity. Ever since its publication, we have lived with the growing awareness that our ecosystem is fragile, that perpetual economic growth is impossible and that every time we earn or consume, we may make the world potentially worse for our children. By the late 1980s, even the *Sun* newspaper had appointed its own green correspondent. Today the most bullish Western consumers' consciences are regularly punctured by shards of eco-understanding. So why hasn't anything changed? Why is our culture still continuing to grow, to strive, to produce and consume evermore, when we know that it may very well prove calamitous?

Economic science has long tried to explain the compulsion behind growth. One of the earliest attempts is Say's Law, which basically decrees that supply creates demand. The Frenchman Jean-Baptiste Say formulated it at the start of the nineteenth century, early in the Industrial Revolution when the use of coal for energy dramatically boosted many European coal-mining nations' wealth. In turn, these nations spent more on manufactured iron goods, which meant that more iron goods needed to be manufactured, which meant that more coal was needed. Say's Law helps to explain why we buy many unnecessary things when we get some extra money, and why we light our houses more than necessary when the price of electricity is cheap.

But it only describes visible human behaviour, rather than explaining its deep motivation. Of course, Monsieur Say did not have the benefit of MRI scanning machines to look into our brains as they debate economic decisions. Now, thanks to the scanners, we are beginning to understand how our society both over-stimulates our instinctive Stone Age brains' want-circuits and circumvents our higher brains' more considered and cautious thoughts. We are stuck in two minds, and our higher ones often get brutishly overruled.

A fine example of this cognitive dissonance popped through the letterbox on the day I was writing this section. On page three of our local newspaper, the *Brighton and Hove Leader,* were laid out two stories, one above the other. The uppermost, headlined 'Student's project has a green ring to it,' featured 18-year-old Katie Kuhrt with her end-of-year art college exhibit. 'Windmills made from eggboxes and sweet wrappers aim to make people think about rubbish and the need to recycle,' said the opening paragraph. That's one way to get a picture of a pretty young woman on the page, which always helps to shift papers, but it's also an enthusiastic stab at the current fad for eco-stories. Below this was the main story, headlined 'Designer brands on waiting list to be beside the sea.' The lead paragraph lamented, 'Brighton and Hove is missing out on more than £1.2 billion a year from consumer spending, according to a council study.' Apparently, the city still doesn't have enough shop space, which means 170 more high street retailers can't open up. This is a bad thing, but we could knock down a conference centre and build more stores.

No one at the *Leader* appears to have spotted the ecological oxymoron. But conceptualising all this Earth-saving stuff is extremely hard on human brains that evolved for surviving the lifelong camping trek called Pleistocene life, rather than having to comprehend their role in a planet's system. To confuse things even more, we've thrown in the astonishingly rapid growth of our economic world. In Stone Age culture there were only a few hundred tradeable products and no capital investment beyond tools such as hand-axes. In modern cities there may be ten billion different things to trade. Most of these, along with the system that invents, produces and sells them, appeared in the past 250 years. It's all proving too sudden for our poor old hardware. The way in which our brains try to make sense of all this – and often produce strange, self-defeating and shortsighted answers – is the subject of the young discipline of neuroeconomics.

David Laibson, a Harvard University economics professor, has studied the problem of our higher and lower brains in relation to the difficulties employers have in attracting contributions to company pension schemes. Even though some employers offer to match their workers' investments, their workers remain deeply reluctant to take the offer. Laibson says that people find investing threatening and alien, but there is also a natural tendency to procrastinate, to say, 'I really value the present, and the future not so much,' and to push difficult tasks such as learning about finance – or making deep changes to save our ecology – into the maybe-sometime future. Laibson believes that this is due to the brain's combination of lower and higher operating systems. Our ancient, lower, limbic system is emotional, intuitive and rapid. It cares only about the present. In contrast, the prefrontal cortex, the higher-thinking system that evolution added over time to our brains, enables us to exert self-control and imagine complex plans. We don't yet know precisely how the debate between these two systems plays out, says Laibson, but it seems that where boring old long-term money questions are concerned, the want-it-now lower brain often wins.

Where shopping decisions are concerned, it seems that much of our economic behaviour can also come down to simple pleasure and pain – or in cartoon terms, having an angel and a devil on your shoulders. Carnegie Mellon University researchers discovered this by scanning volunteers' brains while they considered purchasing consumer goodies that flashed up on a video screen. In each round of the task, the volunteers were first shown a product such as a DVD or box of chocolates, and then its price. Then they were given four seconds to make up their minds. To make the test more realistic, two randomly selected sales were real, funded by a £20 credit slip the volunteers had been given – and they were told they could keep any change as well.

The researchers found that different parts of the brain were involved at different stages of the test. The nucleus accumbens, which is involved in processing rewarding stimuli such as food, recreational drugs and monetary gain, was the most active part when a product was being displayed. The more desirable the product, the more this desire centre lit up. When the price appeared, other parts of the brain jumped in. Nastily high prices increased activity in the insular cortex, a brain region linked to expectations of pain, upset and loss. The researchers also found greater activity in this region when the volunteers decided not to purchase an item. Self-control hurts.

Beyond pleasure and pain, Dutch scientists report that our rational attempts to weigh desirability and value get knocked further awry if a consumer object is endorsed by a celebrity expert. Their study found that this lights up the brain's dorsal claudate nucleus, which is involved in fostering trust and learning. Areas linked to longer-term memory storage also light up when a well-known pundit points approvingly at a product. Worse still, we are also significantly more prepared to trust attractive strangers than less attractive ones over economic matters, according to a study that asked volunteers to play a computer-based bargaining game, based solely on mutual trust, with other players whose photographs they could see on-screen. The players whom the psychologists judged to be the most attractive were also trusted much more by their fellow gamers, which meant that the pretty ones could earn significantly more as a consequence. The scientists call this effect the 'beauty premium'.

All this brain-study leads us to a scientific conclusion that we've suspected all along – we are rotten at making long-term practical decisions about crucial economic questions. This helps to explain why we are proving resistant to changing our economic ways to protect our personal and planetary ecologies. A recent BBC poll, for example, found that around half of people in many parts of Britain admit they remain extremely unwilling to alter their behaviour to cut carbon emissions. Countless others choose to believe that filling green boxes with old newspapers every week offsets the damage wrought by their new cars and trophy holidays.

Often, we don't even seem to act wisely when making apparently green economic decisions such as buying 'eco-friendly' cars like the Toyota Prius, with its hybrid petrol/electric engine mix. Toyota's study of the 24,000 people who bought a Prius in America in May 2007 shows that many of them purchased it as a third family car. Yes, a third big lump of world-heating, resource-draining manufactured metal. But it's greeeeeen, innit? So that's OK. This sort of eek-illogical behaviour should come with its own bumper sticker: 'My other, other car is less ecologically ruinous.'

Trying to address our conscious, thinking brain about these matters, it seems, can prove depressingly futile. For democracy's sake, we should doggedly continue to target voters' higher brains with considered arguments about why they should behave in more sustainable ways. But the evidence shows that we must also take the fight to the lower brain, where many of the real economic decisions are made, and where the more-more world of marketing has spent years causing mischief. We need to find something that appeals to our Stone Age circuits, to the stuff that makes us crazy humans rather than Spock-logical Vulcans.

Our best bet may be the human herd instinct. We love to think of ourselves as unique, self-directed individuals, but our behaviour shows otherwise. One of the latest theories about stock-market fluctuations focuses on our urge to flock together in times of uncertainty, with perverse results. Robert Prechter, the director of the Socionomics Institute in Georgia, calls his theory the law of patterned herding. He says that when faced with volatile markets, even the most adventurous investors head for safety in numbers, thanks to their unconscious herding impulses. When a stock's price rises, demand for it tends to increase. But when prices are cheap, few people want to buy. This is the opposite of what happens in the grocer's shop or shoe store. It also contradicts the economic theory of what is supposed to happen in stock-markets, where the best way to make money is to buy low and sell high.

This flocking behaviour also explains why, on every bank holiday, thousands of Londoners feel compelled to drive to Brighton, even though they know that it involves two hours in traffic jams, another hour searching for a parking space, and a couple of hours pushing through crowds of similarly short-tempered, time-pressed daytrippers to get fish and chips. Then it's time to go home. But everyone does it because everyone does it.

More than 150 years ago the Scottish poet and journalist Charles Mackay spotted the herd phenomenon – particularly the way in which human herding can spark collective frenzy over investment crazes. Mackay, a strict rationalist, wrote his seminal work on crowd psychology, *Memoirs of Extraordinary Popular Delusions and the Madness of Crowds*, 'to collect the most remarkable instances of those moral epidemics which have been excited, sometimes by one cause and sometimes by another, and to show how easily the masses have been led astray, and how imitative and gregarious men are, even in their infatuations and crimes'. The book is still in print today.

Mackay's many examples of our sheep-flocking side include the outbreak of tulipomania in 1624, where wild financial speculation over the newly developed horticultural marvel of tulip bulbs sent prices so high that the flowers traded at a higher price than gold. Then came the inevitable crash, bankrupting thousands of normally parsimonious Dutchmen. Mackay also detailed the massively oversold Mississippi Scheme of John Law, an arch manipulator whose shares scam almost ruined the economy of eighteenth-century France. Then there was the South Sea Bubble, the shipping-company speculation that convulsed London in 1720 and led to a disastrous slump.

We mimic each other socially as well as financially, which is why yawning and laughter are so contagious. Yawning is generally thought to be a group activity stemming from a time when we sat in tribes round fires at night. When the leader yawned, it signalled to others that it was time to hit the hay. The use of canned laughter on TV comedy shows is evidence of another evolutionary artifact. Laughter is a synchronous activity, often sparked by hearing others guffaw, that operates as a way of building group consensus. Negative feelings are the most easily spread of all. They can ripple through a crowd in a manner called 'emotional contagion'. Numerous workplace studies show that a single person with a negative attitude can bring down an entire group. This is probably another survival adaptation – we had to be alert to others' anxiety, in case it indicated that something nasty was lurking in the long grass.

The human herd mentality even gets us marching in step. When the Millennium Bridge, the futuristic 320-metre pedestrian span connecting the City of London to trendy Bankside, opened to great fanfare in June 2000, it rapidly had to be shut amid great embarrassment because it had started wobbling violently. The bridge had surpassed standards for withstanding weight and wind, and every non-human element had been tested. But the designers hadn't expected pedestrian bridge-crossers to synchronise their footsteps subconsciously. As the swaying intensified, more and more people got in step – again, possibly as a stick-together defence mechanism. A study of the bridge in the scientific journal *Nature* suggests that humans in crowds synchronise naturally because it is a phenomenon fundamental to the organisation of the universe, and can be seen at work in such disparate objects as neurons and fireflies.

But what could get us walking together in enoughist step? Good old peer-pressuring social envy might do the trick. Lifestyle ideas are just as contagious as yawning, marching and misery. Our brains are acutely attuned to fitting in. We've seen it in the shopping mall where, despite the fact that we are all exhorted to 'express our individuality', we all end up dressing pretty much the same. What we really want to say is not 'I'm different from you' but 'I'm the same as you – only better'. The human herd instinct drives us to find people who think like us, to form single-minded circles, be they football crowds or book clubs, and to consider people outside the circle deeply suspect (the word egregious, meaning conspicuously bad or offensive, derives from the Latin, meaning 'outside the flock'). The vast majority of us physically hate being marginalised or rejected. Neuroscience has recently discovered that social rejection activates the very same zones of the brain that generate the sting of physical pain. The brain's pain centres seem to have developed hypersensitivity to social banishment, probably because in human prehistory tribal exclusion was tantamount to a death sentence.

This dread has led us to treat life as a perpetual catwalk: we have to compete to make good impressions because flirting, friendship and flattery can win us smiles, sustenance and social cachet from our fellow tribespeople. On the other side of the coin, low social status gnaws at our souls: a long-term study of Whitehall civil servants shows that it's not the high-status, stressy business leaders who are heading for an early demise – it's the worried underdog. People at the bottom of entrenched hard-working hierarchies are three times more likely to die early than those at the top, and not because they are poorer or have less apparently healthy lifestyles. Similar patterns are found among wild baboons in the Serengeti in East Africa. Social strain is to blame. 'What really bothers subordinates is not being attacked by a leopard, or even worrying about being attacked by a leopard. It is being yawned at by a higher-ranking male at a distance of three feet,' says professor Robert Evans of British Columbia University, who conducted the research.

The twin tracks of pleasure and fear are what keep us 'well adjusted' and on the prevailing social rails. Being popular and accepted raises our levels of feelgood hormones. But a sharp dose of social anxiety and shame plays a crucial role in making most people change to fit in with what's socially acceptable. The fear of being ostracised and the desire for recognition are so extremely powerful that, depending on the regime in which we live, they get us rushing to donate blood after a disaster – or working as an internment-camp guard.

To foster widespread enoughist change, we need to co-opt this human compulsion. We need to radically change our icons of the good life. All the look-at-me-I'm-a-top-status-monkey stuff is currently focused on possessing more and more material goods, the very things of which we all now have enough. What's the point in competing for more material wealth when everyone's got everything material? We have to find less damaging grounds on which to show who's coolest and who's cleverest. The social competitor who lurks within all of us doesn't just want things – it wants other herd members to also want them and to have difficulty obtaining them. Slickly napped flints, fast red cars, calm satisfaction: we've tried the first two, so now perhaps we should go for the last one. Our emphasis must shift from mere quantity and brand of things, to the quality of our whole experience. This, of course, is the kind of anti-materialistic message that sandal-shod sages have been preaching for centuries. But their appeal has always been addressed exclusively to our higher minds.

Focusing on our personal ecologies is a better way of appealing to our lower brains because it's far more immediately satisfying, easily grasped and self-interested than worrying about the big global eco-thing, where we're told we have to make 'sacrifices' (ouch) that may prove futile if everyone else doesn't join in. There's also a real danger that too much high-minded enviro-preaching from well-meaning politicos and celebs may provoke a far more damaging backlash, which I'll call STP – Sod The Planet – where people pay lip-service to greenness but ultimately reject eco-awareness *en masse* because they're bored with it, because 'being ecological' hasn't provided an instant consumer fix and instead has become just another exhausting extra on our list of aspirational lifestyle ever-mores. Personal eco-cool should offer a quicker hit.

As the advertisers know, it is far more effective to appeal to people's lower-brained basic self-interest. Enoughism may catch on if we brand it as aspirational, if we gift-wrap non-materialistic goods to satisfy the lower-level human need to be admired, to be cool, to be top-monkey. This could work because all the higher-level human commodities that we might increasingly value as status symbols – such as time, space, leisure, balance, energy and autonomy – are now becoming increasingly scarce and precious. And although they can't actually be bought (buying things costs time, space, leisure, balance, energy, autonomy), they can be liberated by practising enoughism. The new swank should be: 'I'm having a better time than you because my personal ecology's cooler – because I know I've got enough.'

This type of conspicuous lifestyle-shifting is already starting to emerge – in the shape of green-box snobbery, where eco-living has rapidly become a social statement, a them-and-us thing. A growing but unspoken belief among the middle classes is that nice, well-educated, *caring* people recycle and go to farmers' markets. Nasty, ignorant, common people don't. This is of course appallingly élitist and we should ultimately strive to remove this spiteful instinct from the human psyche. But in the meantime we've got personal and planetary ecologies to save. Life-sustaining practices such as enoughism have to be made to look hip and aspirational, rather than nerdy-preachy.

As part of this, we also need to make today's more-more symbols of social achievement look increasingly naff, low-rent, selfish, self-defeating and sad. Even a little subversion can help. For example, I loudly offer to help people with lumbering 4x4s to parallel park — whether they want help or not. And they don't. They find it extremely annoying, not least because they fear that everyone else seems to be in on the joke.

There's some hope, too, in the fact that the world of more, more, more is groaning under the weight of its own contradictions. As a culture, we have become increasingly uncomfortable with the reality of the things we are encouraged to crave — which is why many social-achievement symbols are no longer sold on their own dubious merits. Mortgage companies don't advertise their wares using pictures of people working late to pay for the brick boxes in which they sleep. Car-makers don't show drivers fuming in commuter jams. Such items are marketed as offering the rewards of sustainable enoughist lifestyles: time, space, freedom. If you pass a big high-street poster of a beautiful person meditating in the lotus position, it's guaranteed that they won't be selling meditation classes: their image will be used to flog room-fresheners, shower gels or — in the case of the billboard around the corner from my home — a new apartment block. And it's being sold, not for its mod-cons, but for the tranquility that might be attained from living there. Keynes's great economic dream, that we would be materially liberated to explore the higher realms of human experience, has finally come true — but only on the advertising hoardings.

Is there any chance that the world of ever-more will collapse under the weight of its own overblown promises, slump like a giant lifestyle soufflé? From where we stand today, the fall of this monolith, this all-pervading consumerism, seems impossible. But other isms have toppled. Communism fell, as did socialism and fascism. It's tempting to hope that, in a few decades' time, we might inhabit an emotionally sustainable environment where undergrads in university departments of consumerism studies will gaze back at our hedonistically crazed pursuit of ever-more with the same kind of bemusement we feel when watching 1920s newsreel of manic Charleston-dancing flappers.

But meanwhile, what next? What would happen to our exclusively growth-based economy if we suddenly did all start to embrace enoughism? Would the world's finances collapse? This question turns out to be the fiscal elephant in the eco-living-room. As an economics ingénue, I thought it would be a simple task to find some outlines of the kind of model of sustainable economy that we should all be aiming to create. But wherever I looked, in ecological policy papers, in conference reports, on websites, that model was mysteriously absent. I rang a number of environmental economists. None wanted to help much, other than talking in abstract policy terms about intergovernmental strategy forums and position statements. But they all pointed to one man: Tim Jackson, Surrey University's professor of sustainable development, as the ideal guy to ask.

Jackson is an economist who has studied the psychology of green consumption – and he sits on the Sustainable Development Commission, a UK government watchdog that was established in 2000. He seems sceptical about the possibility of large numbers of individuals changing their ways spontaneously. Instead, he feels that politicians have a big role to play in shifting our social emphasis away from consuming and producing evermore. He and I cheerfully agree to disagree on that point. But what if we were to wave a magic wand, so that one morning we woke to find that suddenly everyone in Britain was living a personally and planetarily sustainable existence? Jackson is disarmingly frank. 'This is the hardest question of all. I've just raised this at our commission and was told by a Treasury official that switching to true sustainable development might mean that we have to go back to living in caves,' he says. 'The government has a split personality on this. It keeps telling people to get out of their cars and consume less. But we would be up the creek without a paddle if everyone did. As it currently exists, our economy relies strictly on increases in consumption.'

Jackson says nothing for a moment, sighs and then continues: 'It's extremely hard to find political space to have this discussion. It is closed down very quickly by the interests of economic stability – there's a lot of "We have to protect the economy at all costs". Eastern Europe during the collapse of the Soviet Union shows what can happen to people's levels of happiness in a falling economy. I don't know the answer to this, but I feel that it's the only question worth working to solve. On my own I don't feel that I have got what it takes to come up with the answer. It's astonishingly difficult. It will have to entail a cultural shift with its own momentum.'

Then he begins to brighten a little: 'There is a possibility that this momentum is beginning to accumulate, with initiatives such as Live Earth [the rock concert] and the increasing interest in emotional wellbeing. The Organisation for Economic Co-operation and Development has launched a programme called "Beyond Gross Domestic Product", so all of a sudden they are prepared to ask the question at that high level. If there is change, then maybe things could move quite quickly.'

Speed is indeed what we need. Beyond the complex and somewhat demoralising arguments about economics, there seems one plain looming reality: we are rushing past the point of planetary enoughness. The Earth's natural balance does not seem to be able to support our current levels of activity, let alone sustain continued and infinite economic growth. To make the ecological ledger start to balance again, we need less activity, fewer humans, or both. Or else we hit the buffers. Sir Geoffrey Palmer, the former prime minister of New Zealand, argues that the term sustainable development may be an oxymoron. 'You could either have sustainability, or you could have development, but not both.'

The gun is at our heads. Let's take population numbers. In the year 1000, there were about 270 million people in the world who could expect to live, on average, 24 years of hand-axe-owning under-consumption. They barely had a carbon toenail print. Today our world contains more than six billion people consuming as much as they can, and on average they can each expect to do this for 67 years. The United Nations forecasts that by 2050, the world's human population will have grown by about half as much again, to reach nine billion, about the maximum the planet is thought capable of holding.

When Mathis Wackernagel, the environmentalist who originally developed the concept of the carbon footprint, measured the ecological demands of humanity and compared them to the 'carrying capacity' of the planet, he concluded that we are currently consuming a fifth more of the Earth's resources than it can sustainably provide. Measured this way, humankind was last at the point of enoughness in the 1980s. Since then, we've been whizzing past. A recent report by the ecologist Helmut Haberl of Klagenfurt University, Austria, concludes for example that we now consume a quarter of the world food-chain's foundations. And in some areas of the world, up to 63 per cent of all the energy produced by plants – energy that would normally fuel native ecosystems – has been pressed into service for humankind.

The result is more extinct species and much bigger deserts. If we move to using biofuels instead of fossil fuel to power our cars, homes and holiday flights, Haberl predicts that our crop-harvesting levels could double (biofuels might sound green, but they require vast tracts of land and resources to grow the crops that make them). At some point, humankind will require every last calorie produced on the planet for its own use. One study, in 1986, predicted that we would hit that point in less than 40 years' from now if our consumption rates remained at 1986 levels. But that research was performed before the prospect of biofuel production raised its head. Maybe we've got 30 years left – if the fresh water available for crop irrigation doesn't run out beforehand.

Throw the Chinese and Indian consumer revolutions into the calculations and it looks like we are all on the express train to global exhaustion. By hook or by crook, the growth in human numbers and economic activity will slow, stop and reverse. This will either happen through our own decisions and actions, or through global warming and resource depredation. This is precisely the dilemma predicted back in 1972 by *Limits to Growth*. Three decades later the book's authors, Donella Meadows, Jorgen Randers and Dennis Meadows, revisited their topic to see whether the world had heeded their warnings. Their conclusions are hardly cheering: 'We are much more pessimistic about the global future than we were in 1972,' they say. 'It is a sad fact that humanity has largely squandered the past 30 years in futile debates and well-intentioned, but half-hearted, responses to the global ecological challenge. We do not have another 30 years to dither.'

They believe that unless the world's rich societies turn down their consumption significantly, we are headed for the same kind of planetary boom and bust that our short-sighted, short-termist, ancient brain-wiring currently causes stock-markets to experience. It will be just like the dotcom bubble of the 1990s, only slower and more painful, the three authors say: 'The growth phase will be welcomed and celebrated, even long after it has moved into unsustainable territory (this we know, because it has already happened). The collapse will arrive very suddenly, much to everyone's surprise. And once it has lasted for some years, it will become increasingly obvious that the situation before the collapse was totally unsustainable. After more years of decline, few will believe that it will ever end. Few will believe that there once more will be abundant energy and sufficient wild fish. Hopefully they will be proved wrong.'

Unless we create a culture that turns down our primitive brains' rapacious neediness, rather than constantly amplifying it to ever greater levels, we are going to be in serious trouble. It's an immensely difficult subject to debate, not least because our culture prefers to divert itself from the problem through dummy-sucking existential distractions such as overworking, producing and consuming goods that we don't need and obsessing about lifestyle choices that aren't really choices. All these more-more activities only add to our unsustainability.

Enoughism offers an alternative path, one that's based on self-interest, but which also acts in everyone's interest. There still may perhaps be time to instil an enoughist approach for our society, through example, through herd-level leadership and through cultural change. That's the wild aspiration, the dopily optimistic soft-focus dream. If, on the other hand, the best thing that results from individually practising enoughism is that some of us get to lead much more satisfactory personal lives while, in the immortal words of Jim Morrison, the whole shit-house goes up in flames, then so be it. But we still can hope.

## Economically *enough*

### The true value of friendships

The world of more tells us that the most important things in our lives are the consumer items that we don't yet have in our lives. But in truth, our most valuable possessions can't be bought or sold, according to a survey of 10,000 Britons who were asked to rate their level of happiness and answer questions on their wealth, health and social relations.

According to Nattavudh Powdthavee of the University of London's Institute of Education, these are the things we value most – and this is how much they are worth to us in monetary terms:

Seeing friends and relatives most days is worth the equivalent of a pay rise of £63,833 a year.

Chatting to neighbours frequently makes us as happy as if we had been handed a £37,000 increase.

Getting married is the same as an extra £50,000 in the pay packet (and that's after the cost of the wedding).

Excellent health pips all of them, coming in at £300,000 a year.

## Zero personal growth

When things wear out completely they need replacing. It's easy to accept the idea that, thanks to the inexorable march of progress, the replacements should automatically be bigger, more powerful and equipped with more features. But it is not necessarily true. This expectation-inflation often drags us beyond the point of enoughness and into pointless waste. To prevent this, we need to adopt our own zero-growth buying policy, particularly where more expensive goods are concerned. Here are five questions to ask:

*Do I really need more size or power?*
If it's a fridge-freezer, for example, are you suddenly going to need to consume more food? If it's a car, will a more powerful engine and heftier chassis help to beat traffic congestion?

*Is the new item more efficient than the last one?*
One might automatically expect that new consumer durables are going to consume fewer planetary resources than the previous generation. But many items, particularly electrical ones,

require far more fuel. Plasma screens can use up to four times as much energy as a normal TV. The amount of resources used by consumer electronics is set to double between 2005 and 2010, says the Energy Saving Trust.

*Am I being up-gadgeted?*
Masses of planetary resources get piled into adding features to make our lives easier. But do they really add anything? If they don't, then we are just spending money on landfill. The classic example is the once-humble disposable razor. I find it increasingly difficult to buy razors now with only two blades and no gimmickry such as lubricating strips or swivelling heads. Meanwhile, the razor-makers have been fighting a battle for custom by adding evermore extra everything. I thought the fight had reached the outer extremes of ridiculousness when Gillette launched a six-blade disposable a couple of years ago. But that wasn't enough. Now the six-bladed razor comes with an inbuilt, battery-driven vibro-motor.

*Is it built to last?*
Manufacturers frequently use more-more upgradings and upsizings as a perversely cost-effective way to disguise the fact that the basic item itself is not well made. Rather than being constructed with sturdy, long-lasting components it has been built down to a price. In such cases, spending a little extra on something more boringly sustainable may prove a much wiser investment.

*Can it be repaired?*
If the consumer item goes wrong, can it be fixed by a locally available engineer at an economic price, or will it have to go

on the junkheap because it has been constructed out of sealed components that cost so much to replace that it's cheaper to buy a whole new unfixable item? Older designs are often more amenable to being repaired economically.

### Think in time rather than money
Time is money. But the converse is also true: money is time. Which of the two is more valuable to you, and when?

When most people look back on their lives, they wish that they had done things that cost time, not money. A long-term survey of terminally ill patients conducted by the Royal College of Surgeons in Ireland concludes that: 'It is much more common for people to regret not the things they did, but that there were so many things that they did not have the time to do.'

So one useful way of working out your priorities is to sit down and write your list of potential deathbed regrets (before it's too late) and then to budget ways of achieving them in terms of how much time is needed, versus how much money.

A short-term way of ensuring that you are using your precious time resource economically is to work out what you earn an hour by selling your skills or expertise, and then to budget that against how much you value spending time on life-sustaining, economically inactive pastimes such as being with your family or enjoying a hobby.

### Value cheapness
It can be a useful morale-booster to remind yourself regularly that intelligent enoughist self-confidence tends to be self-effacing or even invisible, while human insecurity is glaringly apparent through costly consumerist display. Nowadays you can be pretty confident that the display of consumer-item wealth

you are witnessing on the streets hasn't been paid for yet. It's a neon-sign display of credit-debt. The person flashing it about in public is probably worse off than you in terms of time and autonomy, as well as cash.

# 8 | NEVER-Enoughs

*The moment we are content, we have enough. The problem is that we habitually think the other way round: we assume we will be content only when we have enough.*

Shen Sh'ian, editor of *The Daily Enlightenment* newsletter

Clare Grant points out of her kitchen window to the trees in the garden and asks, 'What do you see?' Hmm. 'Trees,' I say. Not quite. 'If you were a bird-spotter, you would see the birds as well,' says Clare. 'That's how it works. If you're a gratitude spotter, you see things that make you thankful.' From her airy Victorian apartment in Tunbridge Wells, Kent, the 29-year-old web designer writes a daily thankfulness blog that is read by thousands around the world, has been translated into Chinese and Spanish, and even won her a place in *Saga* magazine's reader poll of the world's 50 wisest people.

There's something marvellously incongruous about this young woman blogger being lauded by Britain's top read for the over-60s. 'I mean, they've listed people like the BBC broadcaster John Humphrys in there,' she says. But Grant is on to something exceedingly wise. She is helping to proof her mind against the world of more by using something that consumer culture derides as sepia-coloured and sappy. I met her the week that her blogsite, called *Three Beautiful Things*, recorded its 100,000th visit. But while her site is a cult hit in cyberspace, Western society has whittled down the spiritual practice of gratitude to a mere act of social grace.

Our world turns us into ingratitude spotters, gazing fixedly at the limitless things in life that we don't already have. It conditions us to pin our sense of purpose on to pursuing more things, getting a brief bang out of their acquisition, then dropping them as 'so yesterday' and rushing after the next hit. When our soul's well of thanks is boarded over like this, we lose our ability to take delight in the abundances that surround us – something that the Roman emperor and Stoic, Marcus Aurelius, cautioned against in his *Meditations*: 'Do not indulge in dreams of having what you have not, but reckon up the chief of the blessings you do possess and thankfully remember how you would crave them if they were not yours.' That, however, won't keep us busy striving.

Psychological research reveals that the practice of gratitude is one of our crucial never-enoughs, one of our immaterial, inexhaustible resources that offer us sustainable pathways to contentment. Thankfulness can enhance our satisfaction with life in ways that the next consumer product never will. Could you ever, in fact, be too grateful for all the good things in your life? Along with other neglected qualities such as commitment, anticipation and mindfulness, gratitude offers a science-backed way of buoying our souls. We might not have evolved an off-switch for our yearning brains, but these more developed states of mind can moderate our neediness. They can also help us to explore our great taboo question – whether there is life beyond shopping, work, acquisition and status.

Grant launched her blog in May 2004, after she had spent a year keeping a gratitude journal. 'I started the journal because I want to become a writer and I'd heard that it's important to keep diaries,' she says. 'Diary-keeping sounds miserable, so I thought I'd do thankfulness instead.' She had first encountered the power of gratitude as a young girl. 'I'd read someone in a newspaper complain about how hurtful it was to receive formulaic thank-you notes. It spurred me to start writing letters of gratitude almost obsessively, to friends' parents after they'd had me round to play, or made tea or taken me out. It made their day and they would tell my Mum how nice I was.'

When she joined a website company two years ago, she found that a colleague was writing three blogs for a hobby. Grant fancied doing one of her own. 'The best blogs get updated daily, so people keep visiting them. I wondered what I could achieve every day, and thought I might manage three sentences about things. But what things? Three blue things? Three animals I'd seen? Then I thought of recording beautiful things that had made me grateful.' Some colleagues dismissed the blog as girly, but she is adamant that thankfulness doesn't mean fluffiness. 'Gratitude is not just for Christmas. It works because it's about noticing what the universe does.'

The blog launched to no great fanfare, but she kept plugging away. 'People seemed to find it by searching the net for "beautiful things", I guess.' In the meantime, Grant developed a sniper's eye for life's evanescent gems. Take her entry for June 5: 'A bent old man in too-short trousers making baby-talk to a puppy tied up outside Morrisons. The puppy ignores him.' Other days her appreciation is proudly prosaic, such as: 'The amazing difference a new loo seat makes to my bathroom.' Now Grant has a global audience. 'People send me their own beautiful things. For example, there's an amazing American woman whose beliefs I frankly consider seriously bigoted, but despite that, and despite her terrible housebound life, she leaves these lists of small mercies that I find extremely touching.' Gratitude hasn't made Grant a plaster saint either: 'I have ungracious days when I sulk in a corner and won't make the effort. The blog makes up for it. Appreciating things makes me more sunny when I need to be.'

Grant's ideas are supported by a large-scale study that divided hundreds of people into three groups and asked them to keep daily diaries. The first group noted only daily events, the second listed nasty experiences, and the third recorded things for which they felt grateful. Over time, the third group showed higher levels of alertness, enthusiasm, determination, optimism and energy. They even felt motivated to exercise more often, which may explain an *American Journal of Cardiology* report which found that thankfulness seems to improve heart function. The benefits were social as well as personal, because the gratitude-writers also entered a beneficent cycle of kindness. The fact that they were on alert for people's good acts made them much more willing to reciprocate the small generosities they spotted.

Well, we all enjoy reading studies like those. Apparently simple stuff like gratitude feels as wholesome as home baking. But everyday life shows that we often don't practise it so much. Just like many other research-backed ways of improving contentment, we applaud warmly but remain programmed by our culture to carry on regardless. In our busy, busy lives, being grateful can seem a particularly thankless task. Keeping a daily gratitude diary, for example, runs beyond the scope of most people's commitment levels and soon becomes a chore. Then it falters, stalls, and gets added to the lifestyle guilt-pile. That doesn't mean it's impossible to practise gratitude, but it is far more personally sustainable if you stitch it through the day by developing habits that dovetail with what you're already doing.

This is why my wife and I take turns to say a plain secular grace at home before meals. It is about pausing briefly to appreciate the cheap food on our plates, to be thankful for the people and things that made it grow, and to be glad at our luck in having it. At least it is shorthand for all that, though it is prone to coming out as a cursory 'Forwhatweareabouttoreceivemaywebetrulygrateful'. But the thought is always in there somewhere. I've become convinced that saying grace also works like a Pavlovian bell that prepares the digestion, perks the tastebuds and encourages you to be aware of each mouthful (as we saw in chapter two, savouring food can prove a powerful defence against weight gain).

With dining guests, we say grace with a mischievous glint. Visitors tend to exchange glances. Have we gone Goddy-fundamentalist on them? Maybe we're about to hand out pamphlets. But pure simple thanks aren't about addressing some bearded sky-Lord or prostrating oneself before a carved effigy. Gratitude and grace share the same Latin root, *gratus*, meaning 'thanks' and 'welcome'. For visitors, it might be better to preface our grace with 'To whom it may concern, or indeed no one, but anyway . . .'

New technology makes gratitude easier than ever. It takes seconds to ping a two-line fan-mail message to people in companies that give good service. Most recently I sent one to my broadband provider, having realised that I had never really noticed them, because they had never goofed on me. A real human being e-mailed back to say thanks for saying thanks (once they had picked themselves off the floor and double-checked my message for irony). In a world where so many things go invisibly right – taps bring clean water, shops serve clean food and electric switches bring electricity – it is ironically much easier to focus on the things that go wrong. Our maximising-machine brains do not care if something works well, but tests show that they pay extremely close attention when matters go awry. Sending thank-you notes also makes me feel far more self-righteous when firing off complaints. At least I'm even-handed.

Gratitude also appears to help to combat the more-more world's tendency to make us feel alienated, envious and over-competitive. Studies performed in Texas show that the higher your levels of gratitude, the lower your levels of materialism. The paybacks go further: people who age positively tend to adopt life-enhancing skills such as gratitude, forgiveness and social generosity, thus fending off the stereotypical old-git traits of chronic worry, regret, rigidity, self-absorption and negativity. I find all of this most reassuring, having never quite been able to believe in the existence of pure, reward-free selflessness. Surely when we perform a generous, grateful or kind act, there must be *something* in it for us? The health evidence indicates that there certainly is.

These benefits are not restricted to people who are already nice guys. Even the most suspicious, selfish and competitive people may change if we can cool down our consumerist culture. New studies indicate that our adult brains can be soothed out of culturally ingrained meanness, to get a kick out of higher-brain functions such as gratitude and generosity. So claim psychologists at Israel's Bar-Ilan University who first gave volunteers subliminal cues to put them in mind of someone who offered unconditional love and protection – a parent, a lover, God. The team aimed to induce a feeling of security that might make people more likely to be morally generous rather than defensively selfish. It worked. Israeli Jews in the test declined the chance to inflict pain in the form of hot chilli sauce on their Israeli Arab counterparts (they weren't so restrained when they didn't feel warmly secure). Volunteers were also far more willing to give blood and, when they saw a young woman distraught at having to handle a tarantula, they offered to take her place.

This idea of being able to train your mind out of its Stone Age selfishness is thousands of years old. The Stoics believed that our response to the world had two stages: the first was a knee-jerk primitive reaction, but this might be followed by intellectual reasoning. Brain-imaging research supports this. It indicates that basic primitive emotions are located in the amygdala, the almond-shaped structure in the forebrain that triggers our response to threats. Our higher reasoning abilities, meanwhile, appear to be sited in the left frontal cortex. The two areas seem to wrestle with each other in the medial frontal cortex, a junction that is essential for transforming basic emotions into evolved ones. Italian research shows that people who have suffered damage in this region lack the ability to make moral decisions.

We all have these selfish, suspicious primate, knee-jerk impulses. It's what we do with them that counts. In one brain-scanning experiment, people who are avowedly not racially prejudiced were shown pictures of people from other races. First their amygdalas lit up with primitive suspicion, then their higher regions inhibited this. In racist people, the higher cortex doesn't kick in effectively. But our more-more world constantly fires our base brain's prejudices with jealousy and fear, leaving us so blitzed that our higher brains often do not get a chance to intervene. Over time, the second stage of the system may atrophy. Exercises such as practising gratitude can reverse this and train the higher response to limber fitness. It is like picking up a musical instrument again in adulthood: the brain can re-learn the skill.

This kind of training can also fortify us against our self-obsessed culture by getting us into wider beneficent cycles. As the journal-keeping study found, gratitude makes us more disposed to repay generosities. And when we are in a generous mood our brains receive warmly rewarding boosts from being altruistic. Scientists who scanned people's heads as they donated to charities report that giving money lights up the brain's reward system in the very same way that receiving money does. Another study watched women's brains as they gave $100 to a food bank and found that two ancient regions – the caudate nucleus and the nucleus accumbens – fired when they saw the charity get the cash. These regions also fire when basic needs such as food and friendship are satisfied. So it seems that, as far as our brains are concerned, what you give is what you get.

The idea that doing good benefits the doer may be as old as philosophy itself. Socrates argued that the virtuous person is a joyful person. His student Plato even calculated that the charitable man is 729 times more joyful than the unvirtuous. More scientifically, a decade-long study of 2,500 men has found that those who did no volunteer work were two and a half times more likely to die prematurely than men who volunteered their services. It seems that the sense of meaning and purpose we reap from helping our fellows can help to promote robust health. There are strong evolutionary reasons for believing that socially generous impulses are wired into our minds. Charles Darwin suggested that we overtook rival species when our higher social brains grew to think beyond survival-of-the-fittest individualism and learnt to act for our tribe's collective advantage.

Darwin labelled this winning form of social connection 'group selection'. Connectedness is another never-enough that constantly gets marginalised nowadays – not least by the way in which our society urges us to 'celebrate our uniqueness' instead of exploring how our lives are inextricably woven into the human ecological whole. But despite our culturally inflated egotism, we still seem configured to benefit greatly from our wider connections. For example, an American survey identified the most satisfied people in a large group of students and found that they were the ones who spent the most time socialising and the least time alone.

As we saw at the end of the last chapter, having warm human contact comes second in economic value only to having good health. And when we sing together (something few of us get the opportunity to do nowadays), group connection even provides a life-enhancing high. Manchester University scientists have found that the sacculus, an organ in the inner ear which responds to musical frequencies, is connected to the brain's pleasure centre. The sacculus is sensitive only to low-frequency, high-intensity sounds of the type produced by communal singing. This harmonious response may explain why a study of 12,000 Swedes found that those who sing together live longer.

The innate human urge for connection with our fellows seems also to lie at the heart of humankind's unique sense of spirituality. Spiritual people of all faiths and none often describe their mystical experiences as a 'union' with something larger than themselves. Some call this the universe or nature, while others call it God. Mystical experiences are not exactly rare, either: think of our sense of awe at seeing a beautiful sunset or the ecstatic sense of ego dislocation that happens when you're in love. Some neurological researchers claim to have found the mechanism for producing this sense of universal oneness. They believe it occurs when the brain's 'orientation area', which creates an egotistical wall between our sense of self and our sense of the rest of the world, is shut down. The process, called deafferentation, lets us glimpse our connectedness with everything. It may be produced by meditation or prayer, and can create anything from warm feelings of fellowship to soaring mystic ecstasies.

But we are rapidly losing our longstanding connection with humankind's rich history of spiritual thought and wonder, because the more-more world derides any kind of religiosity as sad, embarrassing and old. Amputated from our vast history of spiritual ideas and debate, we lose our line of communication with people who were just like us, who happened to live in earlier times, who also wondered about the nature of life and questioned what our purpose could be. Consumer society promises to drown out such perplexing thoughts by holding us secure in the certainties of getting and spending. Perhaps we might take our rocketing levels of depression as indicating a certain lack of success in this area.

Meanwhile, the non-dogmatic tradition of spiritual questing quietly continues, if only as a minority sport. I'm rather drawn to the newly emerging concept of scientific pantheism, an approach that harnesses discoveries from fields such as quantum physics and space exploration to support the idea that the universe and what many religions call God are just the same thing. Scientific pantheism's suggestion that 'the cosmos is divine, the Earth is sacred', seems as good a way as any to emphasise our vital interconnection with our planet.

But instead our civilisation wilfully continues to overburden Earth's fragile ecology. Take international travel as just one example: despite our burgeoning eco-awareness, holiday flights continue to break records every year. More than 15 million passengers passed through Britain's major air terminals in July 2007 alone. Such behaviour flouts the basic rule of a sustainable society – that each generation should meet its needs without jeopardising the prospects of future generations for meeting theirs. It's the low-brained, unspiritual logic of acting purely for me-now, instead of working for a connected world of us-future.

Worse than that, we're not even managing to live for

me-now. We are constantly encouraged to ignore another of our nourishing never-enoughs – the bounty of the infinite present moment. Everyday life is accelerating ever faster. We work more quickly, talk more quickly, walk more quickly, read more quickly, feed more quickly, and now, thanks to rapid rehab, we can sin, repent and reinvent ourselves as born-again consumers more quickly too. We feel compelled to rush ever onwards – but towards what? I've loved motor-bikes ever since I first rode a moped at the age of 16, but I also love this story about my friend Robin's laconic Swedish mother. She was in her car at the traffic lights one morning when a man wearing race leathers squeezed his powerful sportsbike by her side. As the lights changed, he roared off out of sight. Robin's mum ambled along until, a few corners later, she found the motorbike smashed into a traffic island. She stopped, watched the shaken rider get to his feet, and then asked, 'If that was where you were going, why the hurry?'

Why the hurry, indeed. But how else could we pack more into our busy lives? We cram it all in. Then we try to cram more on top. One in five Britons believes that they have now 'run out of time'. And if we don't actually seem to have time to pause to savour all the stuff that we're doing, being and consuming, then we can always look back and savour it some time later, whenever later is. Maybe we'll have time in the non-existent afterlife. It's hardly logical. Once again the explanation lies rooted in the way that our survivalist, Stone Age brains try to cope with the world. As a species, we are deep-wired to press perpetually on towards a better, brighter future. This blindly unquestioning optimism kept us trudging onwards through famine, drought, pestilence, heat, cold, damp, war and plague. How could our forebears have managed otherwise?

Take my ancestors: the surname Naish derives from the Middle English '*atten ash*' and denoted someone who lived near an ash tree somewhere near Bristol. It is testament to my ancestors' lack of illustriousness that they were known not by their skills, trade, looks, intelligence, social elevation or achievements, but by their proximity to a tree. Lucky they didn't live near a cesspit. I can picture a long, line of pre-me's underachieving their way through the centuries, enduring brief, rheumatic lives deep in mire on some feudal West Country field-system. The only way they could survive that benighted existence – and bother to nurture further generations – was to harbour deep in their yeoman skulls the reality-proofed conviction that things were always some-how just about to go great for them. 'Keep pushing,' their brain circuits said. 'It's all just about to get much better.' Those whose minds failed to maintain this illusion would have slumped by the genetic wayside.

In the very long run, of course, my forebears were right. The human genotype has, in the Western world at least, finally reached an era of cosseted abundance. We can put our feet up and enjoy a welcome cuppa. But because of humanity's lack of an instinctive 'enough' switch, our heads continue to resound with the conviction that the future could still be so much better. Research shows how we're all orphan Annies singing, 'The sun will come out tomorrow.' Each year since 1964, the Pew Research Centre, a 'nonpartisan fact tank', has performed a study called the Ladder of Life. The survey asks around 2,000 adults about their lives now, their lives five years ago and their lives in five years' time.

Every year, the survey reveals the same anomaly: the future, once it arrives, never fulfils our soaring expectations.

In 1997, for example, people rated their present quality of life at around 6.9 out of ten, but said they expected to enjoy an 8.2 quality of life in five years' time. Five years later, however, the same people rated their opinion of the present as . . . 6.9. This paradox also applies to how we assess our yesterdays. We rate life as worse in retrospect than how we rated it at the time. Generally we believe we were worse off in the past and will be far better off in the future. Instead of treasuring our arrival in this constantly comfortable now, we feel stuck in life's grim waiting-room with an unsatisfactory yesterday and a so-so today – but a glittering tomorrow.

This delusion is revved into hyperactive impatience by our convenience culture's founding creed that everything is much better if we can get hold of it sooner. We tear about, trying to use technology to nip ahead of this dull moment, to pull the exciting future into our unsatisfactory now. Inevitably we fail, which reinforces our belief that life still isn't good enough yet. So we beat on, boats against the current. We are even trying to relax faster. I recently received a review copy of a book called *The One-Moment Master: Stillness for People on the Go*, which declares: 'What's important in meditation is not how long you can do it, but how short you can do it.'

This perpetual acceleration is now beginning to unleash epidemics of new lifestyle illnesses, such as hurried-woman syndrome (HWS) which, according to one newspaper, afflicts three-quarters of the women in Britain. HWS is said to be caused by our chronic time-stress disturbing the brain's serotonin levels. The reported symptoms include weight gain, low self-esteem and guilt. Another of these new speed-life contagions is called 'hurry sickness'. There is scientific evidence that 'life-rush' can indeed cause physical and social problems. Robert Levine, of California State University, has measured the exponential increase in city-dwellers' walking speeds around the world, and he says his findings show that as people move faster, they become less likely to help others (which is bad news for attitudes and behaviours such as gratitude, social generosity, volunteering and connectedness). The fast walkers also have higher rates of coronary heart disease.

Furthermore, speed-craze robs us of our crucial ability to lose our neurotic questing selves in the midst of the eternal now. It is a process called flow – a mildly euphoric state that occurs when we are so engrossed in a task that our jabbering internal monologue tunes out and our sense of time's passage evaporates. Flow, says Mike Csikszentmihalyi, the Chicago University psychologist who pioneered the study of this brain state, describes 'those times when things seem to go just right, when you feel alive and fully attentive to what you are doing'. This deep absorption results from engaging in slow-burn experiences such as learning to play the piano or reading poetry. It is unfortunate that piano-playing and poetry-reading have largely gone the way of spinning tops and shove ha'penny. Although they help to develop our higher-functioning cerebral cortexes, these activities can't be sped up. Losing oneself in an absorbing activity also involves becoming deeply unselfconscious, but meanwhile society urges us to do the opposite – to keep checking ourselves to ensure that we're cool enough.

We have also invented another new way to divorce ourselves from the eternal now: multitasking. Anyone who thinks of themselves as a bright, ambitious player now multitasks all the time. How else are we going to achieve everything? However, studies show how the human brain isn't quite built for multitasking. It needs time to shift gears between jobs, so the more switching you do – between, say, talking on the phone, reading e-mail, and working on the computer – the less proficiently you tackle any of it. Harvard psychiatrists blame the multitasking trend for a new malaise that they call pseudo-attention deficit disorder. They say that workers can't buckle down to long-term projects because they crave the physical buzz of being distracted by new data (the dopamine kick we saw in chapter one). There is an old Buddhist term for this state: monkey mind. You have monkey mind when your thoughts race around like a monkey scurrying through treetops. Monkey mind skims life's jittery surface, failing to enjoy its minutiae or interconnectedness. It doesn't have time for things such as gratitude or compassion.

So how do we settle our heads into the rich, rewarding, eternal now, while all around are monkey-minding theirs? Emerging scientific evidence shows how the simple mental practice of daily meditation can significantly enhance our perception of the present. And if we really do need to multitask, meditating can also boost our brain's ability to attend to several things at the same time. MRI scans of meditating monks at the Dalai Lama's monastery in Dharamsala, India, offer one reason why the practice leaves people feeling more settled. The scans show that experienced meditators have much higher levels of electrical activity in the left prefrontal lobe of their brains, an area associated with positive emotional states such as resilience, contentment and optimism. This heightened stimulation also swamps activity in the right prefrontal lobe, which is linked with negative emotions such as fear and anxiety.

Brain-scans of non-religious Westerners who meditate for about 20 minutes every day report that they have increased development in regions associated with memory and attention. Another reputable study says that regular meditators perform consistently better at boring tasks during the mid-afternoon, that post-lunch period when most peole's concentration flags. New research by the University of Wisconsin-Madison may explain why – it shows how meditators can successfully overcome a design snag in the brain that causes a phenomenon called 'attentional blink'. This temporary amnesia is caused by the fact that we find it hard to watch for two things at once, because it demands so much mental processing power. If you ask someone to look out for a specific number in a sequence of figures on a screen, they'll spot it, but fail to notice what comes just afterwards. People performed much better in tests, though, once they had been trained in meditation for three months. Scans show how they used less brain capacity than normal to spot the first number. Meditation had honed their brains' skill in paying attention, so they had brainpower spare to spot subsequent numbers.

This kind of mind-maxing research has inspired a wide range of organisations to teach meditation to their workers, including Japan's Sumitomo Heavy Industries and, in the UK, Price Waterhouse Coopers and the Department for Environment, Food and Rural Affairs (Defra). A study of

600 Sumitomo meditators by Japan's National Institute of Industrial Health says that they have improved emotional stability, show less anxiety and neurosis, and have fewer physical complaints.

But there's a snag with meditation – a big snag. It can so easily become just another lifestyle aspiration to add to the guilt pile: 'Oh no, not bloody meditation. I tried that.' From experience, I know that you can teach someone to meditate in ten minutes. But you can't, not in a lifetime, teach them to keep meditating. That comes from within. People often try to bolt the practice on to their life without appreciating that life has to change to accommodate it. With meditation, you have to dedicate a chunk of each day to your own stillness. Our culture might foster the idea that it is liberal, inclusive and laid-back, but if you tell anyone (particularly in business), 'Sorry, not right now, this is my meditation time', you get looks. But if you shift in this direction, over time your broader priorities may change, too.

That requires something else that is undermined by our culture of instant gratification: commitment. Often we try a discipline such as meditation or yoga and find to our delight that it really does have an uplifting effect. At this point we may possibly bore our friends rigid about it. But after a while the new life-enhancer no longer seems to work so well; it gets to feel increasingly like hard, unrewarding work. It is sorely tempting to let it drop. There are so many other answers we could try. So we move on to one of the myriad other paths. The hope is that one day we will find the 'right' one – the one that, as our culture promises, will bring lasting results fast. But truly life-enhancing spiritual practices tend to go far beyond the narrow bounds of convenience: they originate in times and places where they were pretty much the only answer on offer. And they demanded single-minded dedication. There would have been little opportunity in Nepal in the second century BC to say, 'Buddhism? Yeah, I've done that. Really inspirational. Really spiritual. But then I got into Sufi Whirling, and both those classes are on a Wednesday evening, so . . .'

One reason why new practices work so magically at first is called the Hawthorne effect. In the late 1920s, a study of the Western Electric Company's Hawthorne Plant in Illinois found that whenever consultants were hired to implement a new way to improve efficiency, the workers' efficiency improved. But only for a while. So the company brought in other new improvements. Efficiency rose, then waned. The consultants turned the lights up. Productivity went up. For a while. They turned the lights down. Productivity went up. For a while. They changed the heating, the breaks, the group dynamics and so on. Each change brought the same short-term boost. At the end of the five-year study, Harvard Business School researchers concluded that the changes themselves hadn't boosted efficiency. Instead, they had exposed a quirk of human nature: when people believe that things may change for the better, it produces a burst of optimism and attentiveness that improves things.

As with factories, so with lifestyle: when we try a new option, we put more effort in, we monitor for changes, we pile our hopes on to it. When anything beneficial happens we attribute it to our new-found path. But it's not possible to maintain this enthusiasm and vigilance. We'd become manic. Instead, we get habituated to the new regime, our motivation wanes, we start to notice that our new path is as weed-strewn as the last one. And it's starting to go uphill. At this point, it is so easy to hop over to another new exciting pathway, because we live in a world that provides us with evermore options and which actively encourages a cult of dilettante cool.

Our convenience culture indoctrinates us with the belief that there is no real point in pushing on after the novelty, the fun, the Hawthorne kick, has worn off. No one exemplifies this better than the five-minute wonderwoman, Madonna. My search of a newspaper database found that in the past decade she has reportedly taken up all of the following: angling, curling, ballet dancing, ashtanga yoga, knitting, fasting, macrobiotics, clairvoyance, jogging, cycling, karate, meditation, Kabbalah, karma beads (under the headline, 'The hottest hobbies for this year'), cigar appreciation, oxygen therapy, spiritual retreats, spin exercise, self-flagellation for fitness, ice skating, roller-disco, leaping between buildings, lipstick-lesbianism and chess. But no one seems to consider all this scrabbling particularly odd or pointless.

This endemic cultural flightiness is diametrically opposed to the commitment needed to nurture our never-enoughs. It takes persistence to pursue the same plain old hard-work paths to contentment that sages have promoted since antiquity. As soon as the going gets tough, we are encouraged to switch to something more immediately gratifying. But without being committed to commitment, how can we develop our long-term, higher-brained, life-enhancing qualities in the face of all the frustrations, failures, pratfalls, setbacks and myriad other inconveniences that such attempts inevitably entail? There seems little point in waiting for someone to market a consumer durable that cultivates intellectual, moral and spiritual development in a quick'n'easy no-mess manner.

We desperately need deep commitment to practise the kind of nourishing self-denial that Aleksandr Solzhenitsyn urged us to adopt in chapter three – a spiritual sense of selflessness in which we learn to restrain our low-brained, want-more impulses in the wider interest of everyone living on the planet, both today and in the future. It is our only way to progress beyond the onanistic loop of earning and spending, to find our communal sense of purpose, our mission rather than our whims. Commitment requires that we go beyond the bump in the highway where our convenience society sticks a sign saying 'road closed'. That is the inconvenient point where panic, self-doubt and disillusion set in. It is the dark night of the soul, the Slough of Despond, and it is anathema to our culture. But if we don't go through it, then our heads don't shift. And if our heads don't shift, then there will never be any hope for a fundamental change in our culture's behaviour – we will remain jammed in a process of chasing easy options that aren't really options at all.

And we have run out of time for playing kiss-chase with fake alternatives. We have to face a looming, non-optional truth that our world of ever-more finds extremely inconvenient. The truth is that there are limits to our human behaviour. There are limits to our industriousness, there are limits to our capacity to consume food, information and goods. There are limits to the choices that we can have in this world. There are limits to our ability to be happy.

And most important of all, there are limits to our planet's resources.

At the moment, we have a society that disconnects us from our inconvenient realities. We are disconnected from our forebears, the people who got us here through their striving and yearning for just-enough. If we could hear them, they would say to us, 'You lucky gits. I hope you're having a fantastic time standing on our shoulders, on the peak of all that we sacrificed and achieved.' Instead of appreciating this, instead of being grateful, we carry on grumpily chasing more. We ignore the wisdom of our ancestors because the world of more reviles yesterday, disdains today and preaches an obsession with some mythic perfect tomorrow.

We are also disconnected from the people who struggle to live in the poor four-fifths of the world. If we listened to them, they might say, 'You lucky gits, aren't you having a fantastic time on the back of our cheap resources and labour?' Instead of wondering at our own actions or even being grateful, we grumpily continue chasing more. We ignore their voices because the world of more tells us to obsess about ourselves. And in our wealthy developed world, we are disconnected from each other, because our culture emphasises our tiny differences rather than our huge commonalities, in the interests of fostering unlimited material competition.

It is time for us to disconnect ourselves from the world of more. It is time to say 'thanks very much' to it, and to continue onwards with the wider progress of our species. Our more-more culture has done its job fantastically well: it has brought us to the point where we can begin to develop a world based on enoughism. We now have all that we need materially to revisit and explore anew our old, nourishing and truly sustainable natural human resources – qualities such as gratitude, generosity and the urge for human connection. And we have all of the eternal now in which to explore these bounties (unless the planet catches fire first). In the Western world, material life is pretty much as good as it can get. There is no point in chasing more. From here on in, we will just be bringing our own wasps to the picnic. It is time to be grateful – and to say, 'Enough'.

## Mindfully *enough*

The world of more-more keeps us continually distracted from the reality of our lives. So the solution must be (to borrow E.M. Forster's aphorism): only connect.

One strategy is to try mindfulness – a form of everyday living meditation. Creating more mindfulness in your daily routines is rather like laying down traffic-calming measures in your head. It can help to counter society's seductive draw towards more hurry, more stimuli, more blur.

Mindfulness is a way of purposefully paying attention to the moments of the life that you are in, catching yourself when you find yourself getting distracted and calling yourself back by using your capacity to be fully present in your own life. One of the traditions that practises it is Buddhism, and you can also find it in most of the mainstream spiritual disciplines. But of course you don't have to be religious to commit to living more in the here and now.

*Three-minute meditations*
In the middle of a busy day – whether you are at work, at home, or commuting in between – stop and relax into a three-minute meditation. This can be done with your eyes open or closed. It can be done in your office chair, in the park or on a train. The key is to stop what you are doing, relax your body and mind, focus on your breathing and let all your hurriedness wash away. Three-minute meditations, done three times a day, have a way of reminding you to be present, not just while you are meditating, but off and on during the day.

*Walking mindfully*
When you are feeling harried (especially when you are absolutely convinced that you have no time for a walk) take a short stroll. Walk slowly with your body relaxed, not to get to a destination, but just to feel your muscles, notice your breathing, and notice the world around you.

*Five-sense meditation*
When you have a bit more time, go to a favourite place outdoors and do a sitting, or a walking, meditation where you focus for a minute or two on each of your five senses. This can be as simple as saying to yourself, in turn, 'Now I am seeing' ... 'Now I am listening' ... 'Now I am smelling' . . . until you have focused on all the five senses we have developed to experience the world. You can do this in short regular bursts at your desk, too. Once an hour, just stop what you are doing, and ask yourself, 'What am I seeing? What am I hearing? What can I smell? What can I taste? What can I feel?'

## Personal sabbaths

Sunday mornings I used to get up reasonably early, to enjoy walking through the city-centre streets as they lay empty and quiet. Over the past five years, however, the pavements have become evermore crowded with shoppers, doing much the same as they do every other day of the week.

We no longer have a special day dedicated to pause or reflection. Nor do we have periods in our day to think gratefully about our lives (unless we pause, for example, to say grace). But if we want to move beyond the world of wastefully frenzied commerce, we have to reclaim some sacred times in our week to be aware of the greater immaterial dimensions of our existence, and simply to break out of the socially destructive habit of rushing.

When I worked with the Royal College of Nursing about 15 years ago, their first morning meetings started with something called 'prayers', a remnant of the profession's churchly Victorian roots. They didn't do *actual* prayers, but someone might say something thoughtful or reflective. This practice has now been discontinued. But we can all get into the habit of starting our working days with a quiet inner reflection, such as 'May my work be helpful and productive', while the computer is booting itself up.

Sundays still offer a great opportunity to dedicate an inviolable hour to some kind of reflective practice, be it reading poetry, writing something, gazing at the clouds, or sitting in a chair doing absolutely nothing. In a sense, it doesn't matter what quiet practice you engage in, so long as the time is marked out as a sacred space away from the distractions of the more-more world.

And as an antidote to our inbuilt time-trashing tendency to

think yesterday wasn't much good, today is a bit better, but tomorrow (always tomorrow) will be great, here's an ancient Sanskrit poem:

Look to this day
For it is life, the very life of life
For yesterday is already a dream, and tomorrow is only
    a vision
But today, well lived, makes every yesterday
A dream of contentment, and every tomorrow a vision of
    hope

# ENOUGH Book

*Nothing in excess.*

Solon, as quoted by Diogenes Laertus, 3rd century BC

# REFERENCES AND NOTES

## Introduction

**P4 Robert Trivers, an evolutionary biologist . . .**
Quoted in 'Why your "lizard brain" makes you a bad investor',
*The Wall Street Journal*, 25 October 2006.

**P4 The Pleistocene era**
It is generally agreed that our brains fundamentally evolved during
the Pleistocene era, between 130,000 and 200,000 years ago, though
detailed debate continues over precisely why, when and how. In the
10,000 years (or 400 human generations) since the Pleistocene, our
higher civilised hardware seems to have continued to evolve. How
much it has evolved is moot, but the basic instinctive circuits also
remain busily at work.

**P5 Nigel Tufnel . . . up to 11**
On the iconic rock'n'roll guitar amplifiers of the 1950s, made
by Leo Fender in America, the volume dials actually went up to
12. But, in the 1960s, Fender decided that a maximum of 10
would suffice – a rare example of spontaneous industrial
enoughism.

**P8 Studies of drivers in central London**
Between 2005 and 2007 the average speed in the central London
congestion-charge zone fell from 12mph to 6.1mph, reported the
*Evening Standard*, 9 July 2007. Nevertheless, we seem determined
to create more jams. A Department for Transport study predicts
that car ownership will rise to 33.5 million by 2031, up from the
present UK level of around 27.8 million (*Guardian*, 10 September
2007).

## 1: Enough Information

**P15 We are bombarded with up to 3,500 sales shots each day . . .**
Figures from the independent World Advertising Research Centre,
Oxfordshire, from 2004. For e-mail statistics, see: Hair, M., Ramsay,
J. and Renaud, K., 'Ubiquitous connectivity and work-related stress',
in the 2007 *Handbook of Research on Virtual Workplaces and the
New Nature of Business Practices*.

**P15 More new information has been produced within the past 30
years than . . .**
This oft-quoted figure comes from an early warning about
information overload, *The Micro Revolution Revisited*, by Peter
Large, first published in 1984. Nowadays, at a guess, we could
shrink that "past 30" down to the past 20, at least.

**P16 Society's most creative minds are attracted by high salaries and
glam cachet to the advertising and marketing industries . . .**
For a fascinating study on how advertisers have cunningly subverted
and co-opted even the most anti-materialistic movements, such as
the hippy counterculture, as new ways of selling material goods
(viz today's 'green consumerism'), see Thomas Frank's *The
Conquest of Cool*, University of Chicago Press, 1998.

**P16 Fewer than one in five conventional ad campaigns has any effect . . .**
My notes from an interview for a *Times* article, 'Info-besity epidemic', 3 April 2004.

**P16 Media multitasking**
Around two-thirds of twentysomething Americans now watch TV while also being online, according to research by Tom Vierhile, the director of Productscan Online. A study at Rodborough Technology College, Surrey, reported in April 2007 that: 'TV accounts for the biggest chunk of teenagers' total media consumption time (22 per cent) ahead of 18 per cent for the internet. Yet it is clear that they use more than one medium at a time, multitasking as they go.'

**P17 Over-communication can be more deranging than cannabis . . .**
The conclusion of 80 clinical trials on 1,100 Britons performed by Glenn Wilson, a psychiatrist at King's College, London University, commissioned by the IT firm Hewlett Packard for an April 2005 report.

**P19 When we grasp a new concept, the click of comprehension triggers a cascade of brain chemicals . . .**
'Perceptual pleasure and the brain', by Biederman, I. and Vessel, E., *American Scientist*, 1 May 2006.

**P21 When a decision forms, the subconscious brain prepares to act up to 500 milliseconds before its owner consciously decides to act . . .**
One of the research findings of Benjamin Libet, the University of California, San Francisco physiologist whose studies of the brain changed our understanding of consciousness and questioned the concept of free will. Libet summarised his research in the 2004 book, *Mind Time: the Temporal Factor in Consciousness*.

**P21 A DaimlerChrysler study says that images of sports cars activate men's brain reward centres . . .**
'If your brain has a "buy button", what pushes it?' Sandra Blakeslee, *The New York Times*, 19 October 2004.

**P21 Our minds light up faster in response to well-known brands**
Findings presented to the annual meeting of the Radiological Society of North America by Christine Born, a radiologist at Ludwig-Maximilians University in Munich, Germany, on 28 November 2006.

**P27 Some psychologists believe that the effect of TV news is so strong . . .**
For example, Linda Blair, a clinical psychologist at the University of Bath, suggests that we should limit the amount of hard-hitting news we watch to 30 minutes a day, or run the risk of becoming clinically depressed.

**P28 'We are already disappearing up our own brainstems' . . .**
Geoffrey Miller in *What Is Your Dangerous Idea* (ed. John Brockman), Simon & Schuster, 2007.

**P28 Chatting with colleagues face-to-face raises bonding chemicals**
Edward M. Hallowell (of Harvard University Medical School), 'The human moment at work', *Harvard Business Review*, 1 February 1999.

**P33 Mobiles are even being blamed for causing mental illness**
Francisca Lopez Torrecillas, a Granada University psychologist, warns in *Mental Health Weekly Digest*, 12 March 2007, that 'mobile-phone addiction' is 'hard to spot'. He adds: 'Someone can spend eight hours a day at their computer or be permanently hooked to their phones, and not be an addict. In the case of

young people, many parents see their over-use as something normal.'

**P40 Video screens and fast-action children's shows are now being blamed . . .**

For a fully comprehensive and (perhaps) over-egged round-up of the dangers in TV-watching, see Dr Sigman's book, *Remotely Controlled: How Television Is Damaging Our Lives,* Vermilion, 2005.

**P42 It is impossible to assess virtual life's precise effects on children . . .**

Some of TV's effects are quite easily established, though. For example, a study of young children in the *Journal of Nutrition and Education* in 1995 found that the higher the number of hours of television watched, the more children request, purchase, and consume advertised foods. Likewise, the think-tank The Compass Group reported in December 2006 that the average 10-year-old has 'internalised 300 to 400 brands – perhaps 20 times the number of birds in the wild that they could name'.

**P47 Limit interruption**

Figures taken from the US Media Foundation.

## 2: Enough Food

**P54 Obesity figures**

America's National Heart, Lung, and Blood Institute says the majority of Americans will be overweight or obese in the next 20 years. Meanwhile, Barry Popkin, a professor of nutrition at the University of North Carolina, told the International Association of Agricultural Economists, on 16 August 2006, that the number of overweight people had topped 1 billion, compared with 800 million undernourished.

**P58 In the 1990s, scientists discovered why eating is such a compelling pleasure . . .**

In 1995, Adam Drewnowski, the director of the human nutrition program at the University of Michigan, discovered why eating is such addictive fun: sweet snacks such as Oreo biscuits act on the same brain pleasure centres that respond to addictive drugs, he reported in 'Energy intake and sensory properties of food', *American Journal of Clinical Nutrition*, volume 6 (suppl.), pages 1081S–5S. Drewnowski said he got the idea from a line in the 1986 Bob Hoskins film *Mona Lisa*, in which a heroin junkie talks of craving ice cream. The notion that a sweet taste could quench an addict's longing sounded right to him.

**P59 Electronically stimulating the vagus nerves in overweight people . . .**

A 2006 study by G.J. Wang of the Brookhaven National Laboratory, published in the *Proceedings of the National Academy of Sciences of the United States of America* (volume 103, issue 42, pages 15641–5).

**P59 We like food. And our brains don't let us forget it . . .**

James Rosen, a psychology professor at Vermont University, reports in *Women's Sports and Fitness* (1 August 1997) that a large part of the human brain is devoted to food memories, and these form some of our most ingrained recollections.

**P59 There's a physical resistance to weight-loss . . .**

Dr Neil King, of the Queensland University of Technology, studied 230 overweight people trying two different dieting regimes over three months. Both groups started well, but saw their weight loss rates plateau after eight weeks. Dr King told the International Conference on Obesity in Sydney in September 2006 that our energy-balance system is programmed to cope with famine, 'not the current obesogenic environment which enforces inactivity and a plentiful food supply'.

**P60 Dieting makes our metabolisms rebound badly**
Researchers from the University of California, Los Angeles, found that in the short run, dieting works, as people could lose up to 10 per cent of their weight on any number of diets in the first six months of dieting. But after this honeymoon period, the weight comes back, and often more weight is added, says their report (Mann, T. et al, 'Medicare's search for effective obesity treatments: diets are not the answer', *American Psychologist*, April 2007, volume 62, issue 3, pages 220–33).

**P60 Mother Nature seems to have made us perpetual dissatisfaction machines . . .**
Berridge, K, 'Opioid limbic circuit for reward: interaction between hedonic hotspots of nucleus accumbens and ventral pallidum', in the *Journal of Neuroscience*, February 14, 2007 (volume 27, issue 7, pages 1594–1605).

**P60** Dr Nora Volkow, an expert on a wide range of substance dependencies, including food, is currently the director of the US National Institute of Drug Abuse and was listed in *Time* magazine's top 100 scientists and thinkers for 2007. Her junkfood study is published in *Synapse*, 1 June 2002.

**P62 Brian Wansink**
This leading researcher in the field of appetite outlines his theories in *Mindless Eating: Why We Eat More Than We Think*, Bantam, 2007.

## REFERENCES AND NOTES

**P64 Uppsala University scientists**
Lindblom, J. et al, *The European Journal of Neuroscience*, January 2006, volume 23, issue 1, pages 180–6.

**P67 We often feel we don't have time to pause to taste our food**
'Fast-food families cut mealtime by half', *Daily Mail*, 28 February 2007. Report of a 2006 survey by the Great British Chicken (a trade body, rather than a patriotic capon).

**P67 A Japanese study of 4,700 volunteers**
14 August 2006 TAR-TASS World Service, reporting from Japan's *Asahi* newspaper: 'Nagoya University researchers blame quick eating for excessive weight.'

**P67 Dieters tend to eat more when preoccupied or stressed**
Lowe, M. and Kral, T. in *Appetite,* January 2006, volume 46, issue 1, pages 16–21.

**P68 Children eat more when in front of the telly**
Temple, J. et al, in the *American Journal of Clinical Nutrition*, February 2007, volume 85, issue 2, pages 355–61.

**P68 Kathleen Melanson**
The results of Melanson's year-long study were reported in October 2006 by research intern Ana Andrade at the annual meeting of the North American Association for the Study of Obesity.

**P69 It seems that humans may have a primitive group-feasting response . . .**
Lumeng, J. and Hillman, K.H., 'Eating in larger groups increases food consumption', *Archives of Disease in Childhood*, May 2007, volume 92, issue 5, pages 384–7.

**P69 Avoid high-variety meals**

According to Barbara Rolls, who pioneered research in this area, variety in the form of colours makes you eat more, and the greater the contrast in taste between the foods on your plate, the more you will eat. See 'Experimental analyses of the effects of variety in a meal on human feeding' in the *American Journal of Clinical Nutrition*, November 1985, volume 42, pages 932–9.

**P71 Those who regularly eat with their families have healthier weight levels . . .**

Fulkerson, J. et al, 'Family dinner meal frequency and adolescent development: relationships with developmental assets and high-risk behaviors', *Journal of Adolescent Health*, volume 39, Issue 3, September 2006, pages 337–45.

**P71 A comparison by Nottingham University nutritionists . . .**

Pettinger, C., Holdsworth, M. and Gerber, M., 'Meal patterns and cooking practices in Southern France and Central England', *Public Health Nutrition*, December 2006, volume 9, issue 8, pages 1020–6.

**P72 Get more daylight**

Rosenthal, N. et al, 'SAD – A description of the syndrome and preliminary findings with light therapy', *Archives of General Psychiatry*, January 1984, volume 41, pages 72–80.

**P72 Sleep tight, sleep light**

Van Cauter, E. et al, 'Sleep curtailment in healthy young men is associated with decreased leptin levels, elevated ghrelin levels, and increased hunger and appetite', in *The Annals of Internal Medicine*, December 2004, volume 7, issue 141, pages 846–50.

**P73 Those who slept an average five hours or less . . .**

Taheri, S. et al, 'Short sleep duration is associated with reduced leptin, elevated ghrelin, and increased body mass index', in *Public Library of Science/Medicine*, Dec 2004, volume 1, issue 3, page 62.

**P73 An extra 20 minutes of sleep is linked to being slimmer . . .**
Verona, R. et al, 'Overweight and obese patients in a primary care population report less sleep than patients with a normal body mass index', *Archives of Internal Medicine*, January 2005, volume 10, issue 165, pages 25–30.

**P73 Another practical reason why less sleep equals more fat . . .**
Abstract presented at Sleep 2007, the Associated Professional Sleep Societies' annual meeting, by Mindy Engle-Friedman, reported in *Health & Medicine Week*, 25 June 2007. And on top of all this, working too hard may make you overweight, too. A study of 47,000 people in the journal *Sleep* (1 September 2007, volume 30, issue 9, pages 1085–95) by Mathias Basner of Pennsylvania University, says that the more hours a person works, the less sleep they get.

**P74 Quiet little places**
Fast music in restaurants makes people eat more quickly, speeding the establishment's turnover as well as encouraging diners to mindlessly eat more, according to psychologist Dr Adrian North of the University of Leicester.

**P74 The magic glasses trick**
See Wansink, B. and van Ittersum, K., 'Shape of glass and amount of alcohol poured: comparative study of effect of practice and concentration', in the *British Medical Journal*, 24 December 2005, volume 331, issue 7531, pages 1512–4.

## 3: Enough stuff

P80 Miller believes that art in general evolved as a sexual ploy . . .
For more on this subject, see Geoffrey Miller: *The Mating Mind: How Sexual Choice Shaped the Evolution of Human Nature*, Heinemann, 2000.

P81 There's a dark side to the celeb effect, too . . .
See Baumeister, R. et al, 'Effects of social exclusion on cognitive processes: anticipated aloneness reduces intelligent thought', *The Journal of Personality and Social Psychology*, October 2002, volume 83, issue 4, pages 817–27.

P83 Brain scans performed by Emory University
Tara Parker-Pope, 'This is your brain at the mall: why shopping makes you feel so good', *Wall Street Journal*, 6 December 2005.

P83 A survey of 1,000 Britons . . .
Performed by the internet insurer esure.com in September 2005.

P84 One in 20 Americans now suffers from 'buying addiction' . . .
See Koran, L. et al, 'Estimated prevalence of compulsive buying behavior in the United States', *American Journal of Psychiatry*, October 2006, volume 163, pages 1806–12.

P85 One study of college students found that anxiety . . .
Coles, M. et al, 'Hoarding behaviors in a large college sample', *Behavioural Research Therapy*, February 2003, volume 41, issue 2, pages 179–94.

P86 Thomas Pyszcynski
Pyszcynski,T. et al, 'Why do people need self-esteem? Converging evidence that self-esteem serves an anxiety-buffering function',

*Journal of Personality and Social Psychology*, 1992, volume 63, pages 913–22.

**P87** Alexandr Solzhenitsyn made his comments in a speech to the International Association of Philosophy in Liechtenstein. A syndicated translation was published as 'The storm clouds gather as a new century approaches', by *The Age* newspaper, Melbourne, 2 December 1993.

**P89 That first 4x4 poisoned the emotional ecology . . .**
For an in-depth exploration of socially toxic consumption, see Michael Marmot: *Status Syndrome: How Your Social Standing Directly Affects Your Health and Life Expectancy*, Bloomsbury, 2004.

**P91 A third of us feel obliged to keep the things . . .**
A survey by home-furnishings chain Habitat in August 2006. Of the recipients who don't keep the gifts, equal proportions give them to charity, sell them on an internet auction site or pass them on.

**P94 Joseph Quinlan**
Quinlan's quip is cited by *The Wall Street Journal*, 23 June 2005, in David Wessel's article, 'In modern era, self-storage has right stuff'.

**P94 Tony DeMauro**
Quote from 'Psychology by the square foot: what the ongoing boom in self-storage facilities says about human nature, uncertain times and the anxieties of American culture', by Victoria Clayton, *Los Angeles Times*, 10 August 2003.

**P97 Economic and Social Research Council report**
*Consumption: Reducing, Reusing and Recycling*, ESRC, June 2007.

**P98 Paul Tate, Children's Society**
From, 'Don't give us soiled cast-offs and broken sofas, charity shops plead', *The Times*, 8 January 2005.

**P105 Drazen Prelec**
Interview on CTV's *Canada AM* television show, 5 January 2007.

**P106 Wealthy Londoners no longer feel very rich . . .**
See *Poverty, Wealth and Place in Britain, 1968 to 2005*, The Joseph Rowntree Foundation, July 2007. Global poverty figures taken from the World Bank and the United Nations Development Programme, www.undp.org.

**P106 Frugal cool**
*The Making of Economic Society*, 4th edition, by Robert Heilbroner, Prentice-Hall 1972. And in America, another cult of non-buying arose as a result of anti-British sentiment. See Witkowski, T, 'Colonial Consumers in revolt: buyer values and behavior during the non-importation movement, 1764–1776', in *The Journal of Consumer Research*, Sept 16 1989, pages 216–26.

**P107 Look Cheap**
Jennifer Argo's findings are detailed in three separate studies involving hundreds of shoppers, published in *The Journal of Consumer Research*, September 2005.

**P108 Avoid special offers**
Janakiraman, J. et al, 'Spillover effects: how consumers respond to unexpected changes in price and quality', *The Journal of Consumer Research*, December 2006, volume 33, pages 361–9.

**P109 Beware the web**
Schlosser, A., 'Learning through virtual product experience: the role of imagery on true versus false memories', *The Journal*

*of Consumer Research*, December 2006, volume 33, pages 377–83.

## 4: Enough work

**P113 Britons toil for longer at work than any other nation in the European Union . . .**
'Stressed Britons work the longest hours in Europe', the *Independent*, 23 February 2006.

**P113 People who work 41 hours or more a week . . .**
Yang, H., 'Work hours and self-reported hypertension among working people in California', *Hypertension*, October 2006, volume 48, issue 4, pages 744–50.

**P113 A survey presented to the European Parliament . . .**
Kanavos, P., Ostergen, J. and Weber, M., *High blood pressure and health policy: where we are and where we need to go next*, April 2007.

**P113 Millions of days of unpaid overtime . . .**
Research by the workplace consultants Croner in December 2005 indicates that our presentee culture is making many of us forgo our time off: some £14.5bn worth of holiday entitlement goes unclaimed every year. Instead, in 2005 nearly five million employees worked an average of one extra day a week in unpaid overtime. A 2005 survey by *Travel Weekly* found that more than a quarter of workers in the travel agency sector, ironically, do not take their full annual leave, with employees blaming staff shortages and increasing job pressures.

**P113 A fifth of the carbon we produce through work . . .**
Figures from the American organisation Take Back Your Time.

P114 **A study by the Institute for Social and Economic Research** . . .
Gershuny, J., 'Busyness as the badge of honor for the new super-ordinate working class', *Social Research*, 1 July 2005, volume 72, issue 2, page 287.

P121 **Ragnar Beer, of Gottingen University** . . .
'No sex leads to less sex, research shows', *Der Spiegel*, 14 May 2007.

P127 **Super-rich people don't tend to believe that their emotional problems** . . .
Warner, S., 'Psychoanalytic understanding and treatment of the very rich', *Journal of the American Academy of Psychoanalysis*, Winter 1991, volume 19, pages 578–94. And poor mental health is another of the family heirlooms – see Grinker, R., 'The poor rich: the children of the super-rich', in the *American Journal of Psychiatry*, August 1978, volume 135, issue 8, pages 913–16.

P127 **A swathe of recent research indicates** . . .
While most people assume that a higher income will make them happier, a 2006 study by Princeton University researchers found that the link between money and happiness is mostly illusory. The study, in *Science*, 'Would you be happier if you were richer? A focusing illusion', (30 June 2006, volume 312, issue 5782, pages 1908–10) was led by the Nobel laureate Daniel Kahneman, a professor of psychology and public affairs. It reported: 'People with above-average income are relatively satisfied with their lives, but are barely happier than others in moment-to-moment experience, tend to be more tense, and do not spend more time in particularly enjoyable activities. Moreover, the effect of income on life satisfaction seems to be transient.' The study concluded that, 'People exaggerate the contribution of income to happiness because they focus, in part,

on conventional achievements when evaluating their life or the lives of others.'

The study's survey showed that respondents who earned less than £10,000 a year reported only spending 12 per cent more of their time in a bad mood than those who earned more than £50,000. The average American income at the time was £25,000, and people earning this much were only fractionally less happy than super-league earners. And rich people tend to kid themselves about their happiness: 'If people have high income, they think they should be satisfied, and reflect that in their answers,' the study says. 'Income, however, matters very little for moment-to-moment experience.' The report cautions that earning more money brings more life problems: 'In some cases, this focusing illusion may lead to a misallocation of time, from accepting lengthy commutes (which are among the worst moments of the day) to sacrificing time spent socialising (which are among the best moments of the day).'

A report in the *Proceedings of the National Academy of Sciences* (16 September 2003, volume 100, issue 19, pages 11176–83) adds further evidence that many high earners simply have their priorities wrong. Richard Easterlin, an economics professor at the University of Southern California, Los Angeles, says people tend to overestimate the lasting emotional uplift they get from money and material goods, and underestimate the considerably more lasting and beneficial uplift to be had from enjoying one's family and health – two things that get sacrificed in the pursuit of earnings. 'There is a need to devise policies that will yield better-informed individual preferences,' Easterlin concludes.

### P128 Daniel Hamermesh and Jungmin Lee
Hamermesh, D. and Lee, J., 'Stressed out on four continents: time crunch or Yuppie kvetch?,' *The Review of Economics and Statistics*, 2007, volume 89, issue 2, pages 374–83.

P129 A brain-scan study by the National Institute of Mental Health . . .
Paper presented to the Society for Neuroscience meeting in Atlanta, 2006, by Caroline Zink, a postdoctoral fellow at the National Institute of Mental Health.

P129 The number of westerners who describe themselves as 'rich' . . .
*Poverty and inequality in Britain: 2006*, by Mike Brewer, Alissa Goodman, Jonathan Shaw, Luke Sibieta. Commentary No. 101, published by The Institute for Fiscal Studies.

P135 We should look to our American counterparts
'Taking a break from taking holidays – American workers have less time off than Europeans', by Christopher Swann, the *Financial Times*, 22 August 2005.

P137 You've experienced a phenomenon that Dutch investigators confirmed . . .
Dijksterhuis, A. et al, 'On making the right choice: the deliberation-without-attention effect', *Science*, 17 February 2006, volume 311, issue 5763, pages 1005–7.

P141 Keep Leisure Cheap
González-Chapela, J., 'On the price of recreation goods as a determinant of male labor supply', *Journal of Labor Economics*, 2007, volume 25, issue 4, pages 795–824.

P142 1.7 million Brits have to take time off to recover from their holidays . . .
*Counting the cost of holidays*, a survey published in September 2006 by the Benenden Healthcare Society.

P142 Men who don't holiday . . .
Gump, B. and Matthews K., 'Are vacations good for your health?

The nine-year mortality experience after the multiple risk factor intervention trial', *Psychosomatic Medicine* September-October 2000, volume 62, issue 5, pages 608–12.

## 5: Enough options

**P147 We buy – but don't use – the extras . . .**
From a study by The TechGuys, a support service provided by the company behind Dixons and Currys, in September 2006.

**P147 One study of mobile-phone-buying decisions . . .**
Maxwell, S., 'Hyperchoice and high prices: an unfair combination', *Journal of Product & Brand Management*, 2005, volume 14, issue 7.

**P147 Many end up so confused by all the alternatives . . .**
For example, a survey by the online payments specialist PayPal in January 2007 reports that 53 per cent of people feel that modern gadgets have now become too complicated.

**P147** Iyengar, S. and Lepper, M., 'When choice is demotivating: can one desire too much of a good thing?', *Journal of Personality and Social Psychology*, 2000, volume 79, pages 995–1006.

**P148 Even when choosing toilet paper . . .**
'Choice that sends out wrong buying signals: too many offers equals confusion, prompting some firms to get back to basics', Brian Bloch, *Daily Telegraph*, 25 February 2005.

**P149 R Andrew Chambers**
Quoted in 'Who's Minding the Teenage Brain?', by Richard Monastersky, *Chronicle of Higher Education*, 12 January 2007, volume 53, issue 19.

**P149 The average shopper spends 40 seconds . . .**
Figures from the retail researcher, Envirosell, in 'Want a Bud? A Coke? Sorry, you'll have to be more specific; overabundance of line extensions threatens to shoo away consumers', *Advertising Age*, 28 February 2005.

**P150 Wilfing**
A survey of 2,412 adults by the YouGov polling organisation, published 10 April 2007.

**P152 It doesn't work like that in the shopping aisles . . .**
Botti, S. and McGill, A., 'When choosing is not deciding: the effect of perceived responsibility on satisfaction', *Journal of Consumer Research,* September 2006, volume 33, pages 211–19.

**P154 We increasingly attribute human-like personality to brands**
Cary, M., 'Ad strategy and the stone age brain', *Journal of Advertising Research*, 1 January 2000, volume 40, issue 1–2, pages 103–6.

**P157 Shlomo Benartzi**
Benartzi, S. and Thaler, R., 'How much is investor autonomy worth?', *The Journal of Finance*, August 2002, volume 57, issue 4, pages 1593–1616.

**P159 Yeppies**
Fox, K., *Coming of Age in the eBay Generation: Life-Shopping and the New Life Skills in the Age of eBay*, published by the Social Issues Research Centre, 2005.

## 6: Enough happiness

**P175 The entire sector's worth . . .**
Report by the research company Marketdata, September 2005.

**P175 David Granirer**
'Embrace your fears and find success!' by David Granirer, *National Post*, 6 June 2007.

**P178 Happiest children died earlier . . .**
Martin, L. et al, 'A life course perspective on childhood cheerfulness and its relation to mortality risk', *Personality and Social Psychology Bulletin*, Sep 2002, volume 28, issue 9, pages 1155–65.

**P178** Boredom has a biological use, according to Sandi Mann, a senior lecturer at the University of Central Lancashire, in *The Psychologist* (February 2007, pages 90-93). She suggests that boredom's main purpose is to alert us that all is not well, that we ought to get off our backsides, change things and seek new challenges. Being in a bad mood can also have a positive effect, says a report by Adam Anderson at the University of Toronto in the *Proceedings of the National Academy of Sciences* (online release, 18 December 2006). It claims that while happy thoughts can stimulate creativity, being cranky or sad may make you significantly more efficient at mundane work such as ploughing through databases.

**P179 Randolph Nesse**
Dr Nesse made his remarks in a presentation to the annual meeting of the American Association for the Advancement of Science, January 1993.

**P180 Doctors are increasingly keen to dull this pain . . .**
Wakefield, J. et al, 'Extending the bereavement exclusion for major depression to other losses. Evidence from the National Comorbidity Survey', *Archives of General Psychiatry*, April 2007, volume 64, pages 433–40. See also *The Loss of Sadness: How Psychiatry Transformed Normal Sorrow into Depressive Disorder*, by Allan Horwitz and Jerome Wakefield, Oxford University Press, 2007.

**P181 A single psychological problem – from anxiety to depression . . .**

Branden, N., 'In defense of self', *Association for Humanistic Psychology*, August–September 1984, pages 12–13.

**P181 Nicholas Emler**

Professor Emler's quotes are from a recorded presentation made at The Centre for Confidence and Well-being's Vanguard event in Edinburgh, Scotland, on 25 October 2006. (See also his book, *Self-Esteem: the Costs and Causes of Low Self-Worth*, York Publishing Services, 2001.)

**P184 Meanwhile, we're supposed to keep smiling . . .**
Held, B.S., 'The tyranny of the positive attitude in America: observation and speculation', *Journal of Clinical Psychology*, September 2002, volume 58, issue 9, pages 965–91.

**P185 A recent study of marriage . . .**
Adrianne French's research in the *Journal of Health and Social Behavior* was reported in *The Times*, 'I will . . . cheer up,' on 9 June 2007.

**P189 Vaginas, for example . . .**
Liao, L.M., 'Requests for genetic genitoplasty: how should health-care providers respond?' *British Medical Journal*, 24 May 2007, volume 334, pages 1090–4.

In the September 2007 issue of its journal, *Obstetrics & Gynecology*, the American College of Obstetricians and Gynecologists warned women against cosmetic vaginal surgery as it can cause complications such as infection, altered sensation, pain and scarring.

**P190 Chasing the ideals of healthy perfection**
Study presented by Ann Wertz Garvin, an associate professor of kinesiology at the University of Wisconsin-Whitewater, to the 54th Annual Meeting of the American College of Sports Medicine in New Orleans, June 2007.

**P191 A survey of Australian children**
Conducted by the children's pay-TV network, Nickelodeon Australia, in 2005.

**P191** Elliott, A. and Lemert, C.,*The New Individualism: the Emotional Costs of Globalization*, Routledge, 2006.

**P193** Douglas Coupland introduces his idea of de-narration in *Polaroids from the Dead*, Harper Perennial, 1997.

## 7: Enough growth

**P203** *Economic Possibilities for our Grandchildren*, by John Maynard Keynes is currently out of print, but was last published by the wonderfully named Entropy Conservationists Press in April 1987.

**P204 Keynes was hardly a man of the people . . .**
See Robert Skidelsky's three-volume biography of Keynes, published by Macmillan 1992, 1994, 2000.

**P206 Victor Lebow**
Quoted in Alan Thein Durning's *How much is enough? The consumer society and the future of the Earth*, Norton, 1992.

**P207 Say's Law**
J.B. Say, *Traité d'économie politique*, 6th edition, 1803.

**P208** *Brighton and Hove Leader*, 28 June 2007.

**P209 The astonishingly rapid growth of our economic world**
See Eric Beinhocker, *The Origin of Wealth: Evolution, Complexity and the Radical Remaking of Economics*, Random House, 2007.

**P209 David Laibson**
See, for example, 'Part of brain may be resisting financial planning; advisers should appeal to the prefrontal cortex, avoid the limbic system', *Investment News*, 4 June 2007. This leads us on to some rather pessimistic Tokyo University research, which says that the people who are most likely to make short-term, shortsighted and selfish economic decisions – rather than long-term altruistic ones – tend to be men who have a lot of testosterone. A prime example of such males are the heads of industrialised nations who are responsible for agreeing global climate-change treaties (see Takahashi, T. et al, Testosterone levels and discounting delayed monetary gains and losses in male humans', *Neurology and Endocrinology Letters*, August 2006, volume 27, issue 4, pages 439–44).

**P210 An angel and a devil on your shoulders**
Knutson, B. et al, 'Shopping Centers in the brain', *Neuron* 2007, volume 53, pages 147–56.

**P211 Beyond pleasure and pain . . .**
'Brain mechanisms of persuasion', a paper presented by Vasily Klucharev of Erasmus University, Rotterdam, at the 2006 Society for Neuroeconomics Annual Meeting, Texas.

**P211 We are significantly more prepared to trust attractive strangers . . .**
Wilson, R. and Eckel, C., 'Beauty and Expectations in the Trust Game', *Political Research Quarterly*, 1 June 2006.

## REFERENCES AND NOTES

**P212 Toyota Prius**
'Americans guzzle hybrids; Prius sales triple in May', *The Seattle Times*, 2 June 2007.

**P212 Robert Prechter's law of patterned herding . . .**
Prechter, R. and Parker, W., 'The financial/economic dichotomy in social behavioral dynamics: the socionomic perspective', *The Journal of Behavioral Finance*, volume 8, issue 2, pages 84–108.

**P214 Herd mentality gets us marching in step**
Strogatz, S. et al, 'Theoretical mechanics: crowd synchrony on the Millennium Bridge', *Nature*, 3 November 2005, volume 438, issue 43–44.

**P215 Social rejection activates the very zones of the brain that generate the sting of physical pain . . .**
Matthew Lieberman and Naomi Eisenberg in *Social Neuroscience: People Thinking about People*, John Cacioppo, Penny Visser, and Cynthia Pickett (eds), MIT Press, 2005.

**P216 People at the bottom of entrenched hierarchies . . .**
'Civil servants suffer like baboons – British Association', *The Times*, 6 September 1994.

**P216 A sharp dose of social anxiety and shame play a crucial role . . .**
Gilbert, P., 'Evolution and social anxiety. The role of attraction, social competition, and social hierarchies', *The Psychiatric Clinics of North America*, December 2001, volume 24, issue 4, pages 723–51.

**P217 Sod the planet . . .**
This backlash is already gathering momentum – see, for example, 'Why green snitches will make us see red', by Cristina Odone, *Observer*, 18 March 2007.

**P219 Many social-achievement symbols are no longer sold on their own dubious merits . . .**
See, for example, 'How mortgage worries turn us into prisoners at the office', *Daily Mail*, 3 April 2006.

**P222 You could either have sustainability, or you could have development . . .**
'Consumerism criticised at environment forum', *The Press* (Christchurch), 3 March 2007.

**P222 In the year 1000, there were about 270 million people . . .**
Richard Eckersley, 'Meanings and values: their significance for progress and sustainability', speech at the Manning Clark House conference, *Our Population, Our Future*, Canberra, 9 October 2003.

**P222 The world's human population will reach nine billion . . .**
United Nations' 2002 world population forecast.

**P222 Mathis Wackernagel . . .**
Wackernagel, M. et al, 'Tracking the ecological overshoot of the human economy', *Proceedings of the National Academy of Sciences*, volume 99, issue 14, pages 9266–71.

**P223 Helmut Haberl**
Haberl, H. et al, 'Quantifying and mapping the human appropriation of net primary production in Earth's terrestrial ecosystems', *Proceedings of the National Academy of Sciences*, volume 104, issue 31, pages 12942-7.

**P224 This is precisely the dilemma predicted back in 1972 . . .**
Donella Meadows, Jorgen Randers, and Dennis Meadows, *Limits to Growth: the 30-year update*, Chelsea Green, 2004.

P225 The true value of friendships . . .
Nattavudh Powdthavee's research is currently in press with the *Journal of Socio-Economics*.


## 8: Never-enoughs

P231 Marcus Aurelius . . .
*Meditations*, translated with an introduction by Maxwell Staniforth, Penguin Books, 1964.

P233 A large-scale study that divided people into three groups . . .
Emmons, R. and McCullough, M., 'Counting blessings versus burdens: an experimental investigation of gratitude and subjective well-being in daily life', *Journal of Personality and Social Psychology*, 2003, volume 84, issue 2, pages 377–89. See also: Bartlett, M. and DeSteno, D., 'Gratitude and prosocial behavior. Helping when it costs you', *Psychological Science*, volume 17, issue 4, pages 319–25.

P233 They even felt motivated to exercise more often . . .
McCraty, R. et al, 'The effects of emotions on short-term power spectrum analysis of heart rate variability', *American Journal of Cardiology*, volume 76, pages 1089–93.

P235 Our maximising-machine brains do not care . . .
Patrick, V., MacInnis, D. and Whan Park, C., 'Not as happy as I thought I'd be? Affective misforecasting and product evaluations', *Journal of Consumer Research*, March 2007, volume 33, pages 479–89.

P235 The higher your levels of gratitude, the lower your levels of materialism . . .
McCullough, M., Emmons, R. and Tsang, J., 'The grateful

disposition: a conceptual and empirical topography', *Journal of Personality and Social Psychology* 2002, volume 82, issue 1, pages 112–27.

**P235 Fending off the stereotypical old-git traits . . .**
Hill, R., 'In consultation, positive ageing: a new paradigm for growing old', *Psychotherapy Networker*, 1 May 2007.

**P236 Psychologists at Israel's Bar-Ilan University . . .**
'When does your brain stop making new neurons? A. Infant; B. 42 Years Old; C. 53 Years Old?' by Sharon Begley, *Newsweek*, July 2 2007. The Israeli scientists' somewhat uncomfortable (to atheists) conclusion that thoughts of a higher power can make you act more altruistically are backed by British Columbia University research on 125 volunteers in *Psychological Science* (September 2007, volume 18, issue 9, pages 803–9), which reports that notions of a higher power make people more co-operative and more generous to strangers.

**P236 Brain-imaging research supports this . . .**
Öhman, A., 'Making sense of emotion: evolution, reason and the brain', *Daedalus*, 1 July 2006.

**P236 Our higher reasoning abilities . . .**
Ochsner, K. et al, 'Rethinking feelings: an fMRI study of the cognitive regulation of emotion', *Journal of Cognitive Neuroscience*, volume 14, pages 1215–29.

**P236 People who have suffered damage in this region . . .**
Ciaramelli, E. et al, 'Selective deficit in personal moral judgment following damage to ventromedial prefrontal cortex', *Social Cognitive and Affective Neuroscience*, 2007 volume 2, issue 2, pages 84–92.

**P237 People who are not racially prejudiced were shown pictures of people from other races . . .**
Cunningham, W. et al, 'Separable neural components in the processing of black and white faces', *Psychological Science* 2004, volume 15, pages 806–13.

**P237 Giving money lights up the brain's reward system . . .**
Moll, J. et al, 'Human fronto-mesolimbic networks guide decisions about charitable donation', *Proceedings of the National Academy of Sciences,* 2006, volume 103, issue 42, pages 15623–8.

**P237 Another study watched women's brains . . .**
Harbaugh, W., Mayr, U. and Burghart, D., 'Neural responses to taxation and voluntary giving reveal motives for charitable donations', *Science*, volume 316, issue 5831, pages 1622–5.

**P238 Doing good benefits the doer . . .**
'Local heroes', by John Naish, *The Times,* 27 December 2003.

**P238 Charles Darwin . . .**
In *The Descent of Man* (1871), Darwin touches on group selection when he considers the development of moral faculties in man: 'It must not be forgotten that although a high standard of morality gives but a slight or no advantage to each individual man and his children over the other men of the same tribe, yet that an advancement in the standard of morality and an increase in the number of well-endowed men will certainly give an immense advantage to one tribe over another. There can be no doubt that a tribe including many members who, from possessing in a high degree the spirit of patriotism, fidelity, obedience, courage, and sympathy, were always ready to give aid to each other and to sacrifice themselves for the common good, would be victorious over other tribes; and this would be natural selection.'

**P239 Singing Swedes**
Dr Lars Olov Bygren, of Umea University in Sweden, found from
a study of 12,675 people reported in the *British Medical Journal*
(volume 313, pages 1577–80) that people who sing together are
likely to live longer than those who don't, when all other life
variables are accounted for.

**P239 The mechanism for producing this sense of universal oneness
. . .**
Newberg, A. and d'Aquili, E., 'The neuropsychology of aesthetic,
spiritual and mystic states', *Zygon*, volume 35, issue 1, pages 39–
51.

**P240 Scientific pantheism**
For a detailed description of scientific pantheism, see http://www.
pantheism.net/paul/index.htm.

**P240 More than 15 million passengers passed through Britain's
major air terminals**
'15 million use UK airports', *Guardian*, 9 August 2007.

**P242 We're all orphan Annies . . .**
We are also more likely to remember bad things than good things,
according to the psychologist Elizabeth Kensinger. This explains
why everyone who was around at the time of the deaths of J.F.
Kennedy and John Lennon and of the 9/11 attacks remembers what
they were doing when they heard the news. 'It makes sense within
an evolutionary framework. It is logical that attention would be
focused on potentially threatening information,' Kensinger reports
in *Current Directions in Psychological Science*, August 2007, volume
16, issue 4, pages 213–8.

**P243 Epidemics of new lifestyle illnesses**
'Could curse of the hurried woman be your downfall?' *Lincolnshire Echo*, 14 January 2005.

**P244 As people move faster, they become less likely to help others . . .**
Levine, R., 'A geography of busyness', *Social Research*, July 2005, volume 72, issue 2, page 355.

**P245 Pseudo-attention deficit disorder**
'The lure of data: is it addictive?', Matt Richtel, *New York Times*, 6 July 2003.

**P245 Meditating monks**
Lutz, A. et al, 'Long-term meditators self-induce high-amplitude gamma synchrony during mental practice', *Proceedings of the National Academy of Sciences*, November 2004, volume 101, issue 46, page 16373.

**P246 Brain-scans of non-religious Westerners . . .**
Jones, R., 'Learning to pay attention', *PLoS Biology*, volume 5, no. 6, page 166.

**P247 Sumitomo meditators . . .**
'Meditation can help boost profits', *Independent on Sunday* 30 June 1991.

**P249 Our world encourages a cult of dilettante cool . . .**
Sadly this erodes our appreciation of the ability to defer gratification, a practice that can bolster long-term mental and physical health. A 40-year study by the Columbia University psychology professor Walter Mischel bears this out. In Mischel's 'marshmallow tests' of the 1960s and 1970s, he offered pre-school children the choice of having one reward immediately – a marshmallow – or

getting two rewards if they agreed to wait for anything up to 15 minutes. Mischel has tracked the children into adulthood. 'We're still in touch, they're now in their mid-40s,' he says. The people who were able to wait longer for the reward as youngsters have done significantly better academically and socially as teens and adults. The children who took the treat immediately were far more likely to have had drug problems by their 30s.

*Quantum sufficit*
As much as suffices (used in medical prescriptions)